Business Environment in India

Business Environment in India

Mohinder Kumar Sharma

Commonwealth Publishers
NEW DELHI-110002
(INDIA)

© **Mohinder Kumar Sharma**

Published by :
Commonwealth Publishers
4378/4B, Ansari Road, Gali Murari Lal
New Delhi-110002

1st Edition : 1989

ISBN 81-7169-007-6

Printed at :
Stylish Composing Agency
Bhajanpura, Delhi-110053

PREFACE

Development of a local design of management presumes a detailed discussion on the local business realities. Transplantation of American or Japanese management, under the mistaken notion of universality of management principles is counter productive. It is this realisation which has prompted introduction of foundational course on Business Environments in all the management development programmes.

Business periodicals often from the basis of classroom discussions on the business realities of India. These periodicals, however, offer only a journalistic account of the environmental changes which lack the needed depth in their analyses. Rather than presenting a balanced view of the opportunities and threats inherent in Indian business environment, they tend to paint a rather wishful or sensational picture. The books available on the topics which form the course curriculum of the various diploma and degree programmes are also inadequate. Most of these tend to reduce business into an economic entity with casual references to the technological, historical, politico-legal and social dimensions of a business organisation.

It is, in order to overcome this gap in existing literature on business in India that the present book has been planned. After stressing the need for environmental awareness, the book provides a historical backgrounder on Indian business. The stress is of course on various institutional developments in managing business.

Technological environment forms the subject matter of the third chapter. The subsequent two chapters deal with social and political system as the supra system of which business is a subsystem. A brief introduction to the legal framework in which business operates follows in the sixth chapter.

The industrial regulation and control machinery devised by Indian government is discussed in the seventh chapter. The industrial support systems are detailed in the eight chapter, the role of government in meeting capital needs of a business receives adequate attention in this chapter.

To review the competition and cooperation among different sub-sectors in Indian industrial economy, the public sector, private corporate sector and small scale sector have been discussed in the chapters nine, ten and eleven, respectively. Finally, the recent trends and a futuristic outlook on Indian economic environment have been outlined.

All the chapters retain a business entity as the focal point around which the environmental forces have been scanned, to highlight the interaction of business subsystems with the suprasystems. Every chapter is followed by a most typical case from the Indian business world which lends empirical support to the discussions in the chapter. The format of instruction for Business Environment courses has to be class discussions on subject matter to be followed by the case discussions. It is hoped that the book will become a satisfactory aid to learning business realities in India.

In the preparation of this book, my main acknowledgements are due to hundreds of M.B.A. and M. Phil programme participants in Faculty of Commerce and Business Administration. It is the participants' feedback during the programme duration as well as after getting into executive assignments which have gone a long way in shaping this work.

I also think my wife and colleague Dr. (Mrs.) Usha Sharma in providing valuable support in writing the present book. My sons Kunal, Kush and niece Nirupma have also seen me through the ordeal of working long hours. The colleagues, Dr. Deepak Sud, Dr. Bal Krishna, Dr. Kulwant Rana, Mr. Chaman Chand, Dr. Ramesh Kondle, Dr. Y.S. Verma, Dr. Suresh and Dr. Dogra have also helped me in numerous ways. I also think my counterparts like Prof. M.A. Zahir,

P.A.U., Ludhiana, Dr. (Mrs.) Preeti Singh of Delhi University and Prof. Sagar Sharma of Psychology department, H.P. University for discussing the book plans with me. Jai Ram Thakur, my long trusted stenographer friend has left no effort spared in expediting the preparation of the typescript. Ultimately, I thank M/s. Verma Brothers of Commonwealth Publishers in printing and publicising the present book.

Mohinder Kumar Sharma

CONTENTS

Preface	(v)

Chapter		Pages
1.	**Environmental Pressures and Managerial Action**	1
	Open System Approach	1
	The Need for Environmental Awareness	2
	Scientific-Technological Revolution	4
	Economic Environment	5
	Political and Legal System	8
	Social Trends	10
	An Integrated Systems View	12
	Environmental Scanning For Strategy Formulation	13
	Case I—The Success Story of Reliance	15
2.	**Indian Business—A Historical Perspective**	19
	Developments in Pre-British Era	19
	Development of Manufacturing in India	21
	War-Time Developments	23
	The Consolidation of Native Business 1937-47	25
	Institutions of Modern Industry	29
	Emergence of Big Business on National Scence	32
	Case II—Indian Industrialists and Mahatma Gandhi	36
3.	**Technological Environment in India**	38
	Organisations for Science and Technology in India	39
	Inhouse R & D in Indian Industry	42
	Policy and Legal Framework for R & D	46
	Transfer of Technology	49

Chapter	Pages
Framework for Technological Collaborations	51
Summing Up	53
Case III—Bhel Siemens Technological Agreements	55
4. Social System in India	61
Demographic Characteristics	61
Caste and Communalism in India	63
Occupational Structure in India	66
Joint Family System	68
Emergence of Middle Class	71
Socio-Cultural Trends	72
Cultural Ethos and Work Culture	75
Case IV—Management Culture of Birlas	78
5. Business and Political System in India	81
Fundamental Rights and Business Management	81
Directive Principles of State Policy	83
Centre-State Relations	84
Chambers of Commerce and Industry	86
Election Process and Indian Business	89
Money Power and Economic Liberalisation	91
Political Realities and Opportunities for Business	94
Case V—Businessmen in Politics	96
6. Corporate Legal Environment in India	99
Regulatory Laws	100
Company Laws	103
Mercantile Laws	109
Labour Laws	112
Case VI—Legal Wrangles of Corporate Wars	117
7. Regulation and Control of Business	120
Industrial Policy of Indian Government	122
Industrial Licensing Policy and Process	125

Chapter	Pages
Agencies of Regulation	128
Price and International Trade Controls	129
The Regulatory Mechanism of the Government	133
Summing Up	135
Case VII—Expansion of Capacity for Soda Ash	137
8. Industrial Support System in India	**140**
Incentive Schemes for New Ventures	141
Institutional Framework for Developing Small Industry	146
Other Promotional Agencies at Central Level	148
State Level Organisations	149
Public Financing Institutions	150
Financial Assistance by Public Financing Institutions	154
Norm and Conditions of Financing	156
Role of Commercial Banks in Financing	157
Indian Capital Market	159
Case VIII—The Guardians of Business	160
9. Public Sector in India	**163**
Rationale of Public Sector	163
Types of Public Enterprises	164
Central Public Enterprises—A Profile	165
Contributions of Public Sector	167
Problems of Public Enterprises	173
Public Accountability *vs.* Autonomy	176
Memorandum of Understanding	178
Findings and Recommendations of Various Committees	180
Limits to Privatisation	185
Case IX—Industrial Relations in Public Sector	188
10. Private Corporate Sector	**191**
Hazari's Study of Private Corporate Sector	191

Chapter	Pages
Private Corporate Sector During Third and Annual Plans	193
Monopolies Inquiry Commission Report	193
Industrial Licensing Policy Inquiry Committee Report	195
Private Corporate Sector 1971-85	196
Internal Stratification of Private Corporate Sector	200
Foreign Investments in India	203
Financing Pattern	205
Profitability Performance	207
Case X—Reorganisation of Unilever Subsidiaries	208
11. **Small, Village and Cottage Industry**	211
Objectives and Strategies for Development	311
Plan Outlays	212
Growth of Unregistered Sector	214
Contributions of Village and Small Scale Industry	215
Financial Sources	218
Commercial Operations of Small Units	220
Capacity Utilization and Economic Sickness	221
Problems of Small Entrepreneurs	226
Case XI—Small Industry : Reality and Myth	230
12. **Changing Economic Environment**	234
Developmental Perspective—A Planning Commission View	235
The Fiscal Crisis in India	239
New Economic Policy	241
International Integration	245
Implication of NEP for Industry and Business	247
Case XII—Chhabrias—The Creation of New Economic Policy	249
Index	252

1
Environmental Pressures and Managerial Action

Management is an information function. Workers on factory floors handle materials and transform these, knowledge workers on the other hand collect, store, process and report data or information. The fag end of the Second millenium has opened up exciting possibilities of using information for transforming human societies. The world is getting far more integrated and even the planets as well as stars are subject matter of social analysis (as evidenced by concern against Star Wars) rather than being subjects of science fiction.

Open Systems Approach

It is in this context that the open systems approach is gaining increasing acceptability in management. Even for miromanagement analysis of an economic or social unit, management of the boundary conditions of an enterprise is becoming the primary task of managers. The survival and growth of any business enterprise depends upon the active exchange between the enterprise and its environment. Environment and management mutually influence each other. The management's success or failure is determined by adjustment to favourable/adverse currents of the environment.

Right since defining goals or purposes of any business activity, the managerial activity focusses attention on adapting the business sub-systems to their environmental suprasystems. The task of maintaining a match of the potentialities of an organisation with that of the opportunities in environment precedes all business planning and organisation. The existing match between the enterprise and environment—the degree of integration with the environment and the relative autonomy of the system has to be cognised. Though the perfect equilibrium eludes managers but they constantly encounter and contain conflict between the requirements of the wider systems and the managed system. Keeping the degree of this mismatch or conflict at a satisfactory level requires organisational development activity and effective managerial action.

In simple terms, an effective manager must have a sense of the setting in which the act of management takes place. The basic changes in environment call for modifications in the way the managers plan, organise, lead and control. Environment outlines the uncontrollables, constraints or the boundaries within which a manager has to manipulate/change the controllables of the business under his control. All the management processes of planning, direction, organisation, control, co-ordination and staffing as well as the levels of specialised staff functions are influenced by the business environment.

The environment of business is dynamic and as such the equilibrium between the business system and suprasystem has also to be dynamic. Organisations must learn to adapt to the threats emerging in the environments and should be able to avail the new opportunities thrown open to them. Bureaucracy as a rigid form of organisation is yielding to new approaches of organisational development due to the immense pressures that contemporary social realities exert. Environmental scanning, in the form of SWOT analysis is a continuing process in corporate planning. Corporate managers monitor strengths (S), weaknesses (W) of their organisations and match these with opportunities (O) and threats (T) arising in the evolving social reality.

The Need for Environmental Awareness

The recent stress on entrepreneurship and intrapreneurship

owes its origin to the fast movements and swift changes in the society, polity and economy. Apart from the drive towards increasing degrees of specialisation in professional management, the wide acceptance of systems approach to management suggests that functioning in the narrow grooves, managers have to avoid becoming the proverbial "frogs of the well". To stress environmental awareness, it is suggested that managers at all levels (not only at the top) have not only to understand their place and activities within the organisation but have to be perceptive to the opportunities opened and threats posed by the wider systems to their business activities. Top, middle or supervisory management are all concerned with critical elements of environment in varying degrees.

While keeping in tune with the environmental pressures, information flows and feedback have to be the key concerns of managers. The so-called 'externalities' of a business when utilised to the best advantage of a business can improve the managerial performance. In managing the external networks which the business has to build beyond its closed system boundaries, information flows provide the bridge. With the advent of large computer memories and efficient communication systems ; storing, processing and communicating information has become easier. Apart from the centralised information pool of environmental movements, the personal computers of the managers even at junior levels should have handy information available about the social, political, economic and technological suprasystems of which their organisation is a part.

Gone are the times were environmental scanning used to be the exclusive concern of the staff of boards of directors. Not only goals and strategic decisions have to be decided in an organisation to accommodate the dictates of the wider systems, every administrative or operating decision can also not afford to be ignorant of the trends in business environments. The organisations at all levels have to network with the suprasystems. Environment linkages may be the primary responsibility of strategicians or planners in the business, execution of the plans has also to be sensitive to the sudden changes/shocks which environments pose to the survival and growth of a business organisation. However, the needed receptivity at all levels of the organisation shall be dependent upon the efficiency of information system in transmitting danger signals or rays of hope apart from routine information to all the concerned executives promptly and clearly.

To further highlight the importance of environmental awareness and monitoring information about suprasystems, we turn to the varied interactions which a business system has with the environment. Let us state at the outset that no single aspect or dictate of environmental pressures can determine the management action of strategically adapting the functioning of business organisations to the changes. The eventualities which the managements have to guard against are that their vision is not blinkered by their narrow specialisations and they don't face the predicament of becoming wiser after the event. The latter is termed as exploitative adaptation of organisations and endangers the very survival of these subsystems.

Scientific-Technological Revolution

Dramatic technological innovations like electronic computers, manipulative biology and new sources of energy have changed the human civilisations so drastically that the phenomenon can only be described as a scientific-technological revolution. Technology is not revolving, it is progressing in sudden leaps and jumps.

In fact, a school of thinkers maintains that technologies determine the social, economic and political systems in the modern times. Information revolution, knowledge industry and the growth of service/tertiary sectors in various economies even at the cost of 'conventional productive sectors' are all creations of the technological leaps. It is suggested that the proverbial ivory towers, *i.e.*, laboratories have the capacity to transform human nature and interactions. Vision computers, test-tube babies, new organisms and monstrous sources of energy are fast approaching us. While these developments of science create opportunities for material advance, they also pose dangers to our ecology and even threaten the very human survival.

No responsible citizen of the world, leave aside the managers, can afford to ignore the rapid advances of science and technology. For example, satellite communications have invaded our homes and we cannot ignore this invasion and its unavoidable consequences. Managers or entrepreneurs shall be called upon to perform increasing responsibilities of innovation in the present context. They will have to create physical and human systems to manufacture increasing number of new products using new processes and to turn scientific ideas socially useful and commercially successful. The fast progress in science shall speed up the rate of obsolescence of existing products and the new technologies may also dictate changed social organisation of work. In fact, authors like Harry Braverman maintain that the new technologies are deskilling vast masses of human population and the distinction between the managers and workers and is disappearing.

Managing new technologies calls for a great deal of mobility, training and development of human resources. Additional personnel with new skills are required, old skills turn redundant. Frequent restructuring of jobs is called and control systems in organisations have to be remoulded as the skill levels of workers grow.

The technological revolution also has resulted in the great divide among the developed and developing societies. The pace of change accelerates that rate of economic growth commensurately in the countries which are ahead in scientific-technological race. The developing world which has lagged behind tries to catch up but starting as it is with narrower base, it is not always successful in overcoming the historical technology lag. Mutual interaction of the various societies becomes vital in order to overcome this divide but technological superiority may also prompt unequal exchange between the industrialised and underdeveloped countries inhibiting the needed interaction.

All these developments have lessons for the business systems and their controllers. In fact the biggest threats in the environments to the existing business arises from new entries in their product lines and late comers, obviously, start with more uptodate technologies. For the new business the opportunities of technological innovation are multiplying very fast. The methods of managing also face a challenge from the new facilities being created for increasing the productivity of human resources. The electronic revolution has created numerous opportunities for a more effective managerial action.

Economic Environment

The production, exchange, distribution and consumption of material products in societies forms the economic environment. The governments in the various countries interfere with the economic domain in regulating all the above said functions. The business enterprises on their own facilitate the production, distribution, exchange as well as consumption of products at microlevels. The number of these institutions proliferates in the economies as they progress.

Number of firms in same product lines, diversity and types of products and financial instruments to facilitate exchange increases exponentially with the passage of time. Factors of production are rewarded in different forms and the producers of one set of commodities consume another set of commodities as raw materials. Gross national product, manpower available and its utilization, monetary units in circulation, price levels of different commodities, wage levels of workers of varying skills, interest rates, etc., are the various economic indicators which keep on changing with the times. All these have important bearing on the functioning of different types of business. Business is an economic unit engaged in economic activities and business decision-making is an economic process.

There are no closed economies in the present era of international economic cooperation. However, different degrees of protection are available to native business in different countries. International economic integration not only poses problems of competition to the native business, it also opens technological opportunities and markets abroad. There are different models of export—led to self-sufficient economic growth and the managers have to learn the advantages/vulnerabilities of their international competitors. In large countries with high population, however, business managers may turn their attention to domestic markets rather than the international ones. However, no economy in the world can be construed as a closed system. Iron walls and Bamboo curtains have crumbled.

Another facet of economic environment which shouldn't be lost sight of is the stage of development of the national economy within which the managers function. Apart from the general level of economic development, the level of industrial development and the state of the industries in which a firm operates are important economic variables. Different types of management techniques shall be needed for managing business in underdeveloped economies as compared with the ones employed in economies where industry has matured. Universality of management principles is not so universal as is assumed by certain theoreticians.

The sectors of economy in which the managers function have their own implications. Management in fast expanding service sector in most of the modern day economies poses a new set of problems as compared to the traditional management methods perfected in the manufacturing sector. An awareness of sectoral movements within a national economy and the problems arising therefrom shall also help in working out the appropriate strategies for growth of the business and required managerial action.

Last but not the least, government-business interaction

should receive the proper attention of managers. In developing economies, the state not only regulates, supports or guides business, it also competes with private business. Working out proper relationships with the governmental infra/superstructures leads us to discuss the implications of political and legal pressures on functioning of business.

Political and Legal System

Governments in various nation-states are involved with the economic systems in varying degrees. Free enterprise is a myth because rules of a business game are set by the governments in the contemporary world. Private property may be a constitutional or legal right in some societies whereas most of the enterprises are state-owned in the others. The constitutions of newly liberated nations also lay down directive principles for conducting the economic affairs. The state even in liberal democracies discharges certain welfare functions. In the underdeveloped economies in order to accelerate the pace of economic development, the governments themselves develop the necessary infrastructural facilities.

Governments at various levels of administration mobilise resources by levying taxes or through public borrowings. Taxation is one of the major determinants of the decisions made by financial managers. Incomes are taxed directly as well as indirect taxes are levied on the volume of business activities. The fiscal policy of the state is not stable or static, it keeps on changing in annual budget-making or longer range economic planning exercises.

Monetary policy, normally, operated through a central bank mobilises savings in politically preferred channels. A network of financial institutions to take up investment is either under the direct control of the government or functions under the guidance of the state machinery through public policy pronouncements. Ideologies of the ruling political parties in Parliamentary systems determine the contours of devolution of taxation powers to different levels of administration, tax rates and the interest rates. The volume of credit to different sectors of an economy is an important tool of public policy.

The federal of unitary character of the liberal democracy is provided in the constitution but the grassroots and the apex share powers in a dynamic equilibrium situation. Not only this, the general attitude of the government to the business community is determined by the pressures which the business interests or groups are able to exercise on public policy making. The business, in turn, finances not only the governments through tax payments but provides a more informal direct support to contending political parties in the electoral politics. Company donations to election funds are used by the businessmen to bring the favoured political party in power so that concessions can be extracted in getting industrial licenses, quotas or permits from the state controlled regulation mechanism.

It is normally assumed by the interventionist State that managers only serve active shareholders/managers and are negligent of the expectations of other masters in a socially responsible model of business. Laws seek to impose obligations on the business to consumers, workers, suppliers, passive shareholders, government and public at large. There are multiple legal acts, sometimes with overlapping provisions to regulate government business interaction. Concern for scientific exploitation of natural wealth of nations, preference for native business and ecological considerations have resulted in yet another set of legal provisions which every manager is supposed to know and respect.

Thus the managers in so-called mixed economies or welfare states have to be aware of the complex politicolegal system. This system determines the functioning of business to the extent that there are a number of constraints within which the commercial objective of profit maximisation has to be achieved. But then laws are the creations of elected legislatures and can be amended from time to time if these become counterproductive. Moreover, executives, sometimes, help the business in bypassing these laws for ulterior considerations.

Business and politics are inseparable allies and so are legislators and managers. A rapport has also to be built with the bureaucrats comprising the "steel-frame" of Parliamentary democracies. This assumes further significance in the recent times because the governments in Third World have emerged to be the biggest institutional buyers of industrial produce. Besides keeping a close watch on the domestic political scene, the successful manager has also to keep track of the international political configuration and the place of the country where he manages in emerging scenerio of international relations. The international relations between nation states determine the volume of international trade and technology transfers.

Social Trends

Politico-economic system conditions the society, so does technology. But the society also provides the context for technological, economic or political experiments and innovations. In countries with ancient civilizations, the societies have emerged through torturous non-linear paths. Social divisions of labour valid at some point in history have persisted even in the present age of detailed division of labour. Religion, language and ethnicity have played a role in establishing prides and prejudices among the people of different regions. Demographic changes have been witnessed and reduction in inequality of sexes or generational gaps have created problems as well as offered opportunities. Rising educational levels all over the world and uneven regional growth of education and scientific thinking shapes the human resources.

Human resources are the most important part of business systems as workers and consumers. They are the products of their social set up. No manager can manage the human side of enterprise without being socially aware and perceptive. There are social norms which may seem to be irrational but are routed in historical evolution of civilizations. There is a resistance to change the established ways of living, dominant beliefs and preferences. While managing personnel or marketing the produce, a manager has to confront the irrational side of human behaviour.

Apart from the much discussed individual differences, the psyche of any population is determined by family, as the predominant social institution alongwith caste and kinship networks. There are customs, traditions and norms of social behaviour which have life-long influences for any child reared up in these environments. The caste, family, community and kinship networks have also acted as support systems for human beings and to analyse the motivations of human behaviour, a manager has to fall back on interpretations based on these systems.

The role of women in productive labour, the attitude of people to dignity of labour, the preferences for particular types of wear, food and shelter all can be discerned from the prevailing social practices and trends. The use of group incentives for inculcating team spirit at the work places, the formation of informal groups among workers have to be studied on the basis of community living experience of the sections of society from which workers are drawn.

The value systems inculcated by the social living experience determine whether material incentives or job satisfaction based on meeting higher needs of human beings shall be needed. Self-centred or sacrificing human beings loyal to the institutions or perpetually anti establishment or diligent human beings are all products of their social circumstances. The traditionally deprived sections of the society behave differently from the traditional haves of the society. Nationality feelings may determine the work behaviour of human beings. Certain products/processes may not be acceptable or may be preferred depending upon religious taboos, dogmas and practices.

In nutshell, social norms determine the human behaviour in business organisations. To increase organisational effectiveness the manager, should lay emphasis on certain incentives/disincentives depending upon the values of the social segment from the society to which the human characters in organisational drama belong. While business and industry have a secularising influence and are a vehicle of modernisation, the process of change in social fabric is a long drawn out affair and lack of this realisation can cost very dearly to any business decision-maker.

An Integrated Systems View

Our discussion of the environment as suprasystem was fragmentary in the preceding text. The classification attempted in terms of technological, economic, political, legal and social was to enumerate the components of the suprasystem of which the firm is a subsystem. Our conception of a firm also assumes the same multiple dimensions of its behaviour as an economic entity. Let us be sure first that as individuals constitute the society, they individualise within the network of social relations. Various institutions also influence the micro level units and taken together the institutional framework constitute the environment.

Systems approach underlines the interactions of various subsystems/components. Different aspects of suprasystem discussed here are interacting and interdependent as hinted in the section on social trends. The social or economic or politico-legal or technological in the environmental analysis are interlocked. The acceptance of business as a healthy economic pursuit needs social sanction. The extent of politicalisation of trade union movement depends on the party system and the democratic nature of a polity. Vocationalisation of education is needed for supplying skilled personnel to industry. Political stability or distability may be due to evenness or imbalances in economic development. This will determine the climate for functioning of business.

We have only emphasised physical environment to the extent, the existing technical knowhow is able to appropriate the natural wealth. Geographical factors like water systems, forests and mineral available in particular regions may become the basis of their agricultural or industrial development. Thus environment includes nature and the human systems like economy, society, polity or technology. In fact, for accommodating the environmental influences, the system objectives of a firm have to be outlined. The boundaries of the firm as a system are extended to include the relevant trends in the different fields like social or technological. Once the problem of business under study is defined, fresh systems boundaries are demarcated and the conventional understanding of the system boundaries has to be revised. For example in case of a selling problem, the consumers who are situated in the economy/ society otherwise construed as externalities of business become a part of the business system. Similarly, the government machinery regulating industrial relations becomes participant in the industrial relations scene.

The currents in business environments have to be singled out depending on the intensity of their pressure on the business situation. A product mix or type decision cannot be taken in isolation from general state of technology and the social need for the product. After the subsystems of suprasystem surrounding the business system are included in the systems analysis, the interaction of the business firm with the cognised subsystems has to undergo a detailed scrutiny. The operations analyses assume different sets of values for the various variables under the control of management within the constraints of environmental or uncontrollable variables. It studies their effect on the value of criterion function selected for evaluating the performance of system. The set of values of controllable variables which gives optimum value of the efficiency criteria is chosen and the solution is implemented.

Environmental Scanning for Strategy Formulation

The management science perspective relying on systems approach does view organisations as multi-dimensional and multifunctional entities. But the flaw with structural-functional analysis is that it is essentially an historical study overemphasising the appearances at the cost of realities. The quantitative information collected about the internal functioning as well as environment indicates only symptoms or trends. In the name of scanning, managers are apt to underplay the information which could yield deeper understanding of the causation of the present reality. The economics, politics and societies develop historically in zig-zag patterns rather than following a linear or even a curvilinear path. There are discontinuities, abrupt changes or revolutions. These could be examined if a historical perspective aimed at outlining laws of societal evolutions was followed.

If social norms have come to the present stage or state intervention has increased to the extent that is visible in various economies, it is not so sudden or unexpected a development. Futurology which should be treated as the mother science of environmental analysis for strategic management has a historical underpinning. But any exercise in plotting future only through Delphi exercises or time series analysis of quantitative data shell be inadequate. Any business in order to succeed has to anticipate future challenges, be these of competitive threats or demand constraints. Strategy formulation or the outlining of "the pattern of major objectives, purposes or goals and essential policies and plans for achieving those goals stated in such a way as to define what business the company is in or is to be in and the kind of company it is or it is to be",[1] is partly an exercise in visualising future. It requires a historical perspective not only on the internal developments of the company but the environmental factors too. In fact, strategy aims at building a linkage with the external environment and the means of preserving it despite future developments which are outside the control of the management. The survival or growth of business depends upon a coherent, consistent and explicit understanding of its strategy.

---

1. Kenneth Andrews as quoted in Bhattacharyya, S.K. and N. Venkatraman, "Managing Business Enterprises : Strategies, Structures and Systems", New Delhi, Vikas, 1983.

In order to make a strategy work in a business, the environmental scanning activity has to be carried out an ongoing basis. This scanning activity in order to be meaningful has to percolate the *understanding* of the environment to all levels of management. The information about the environment is by its very nature not amenable to quantification, it is overwhelmingly by unstructured or semi-structured but has to be future oriented in nature. The relevance of information has to be judged in consultation with outside professionals and the external information needs have to be worked. Since most of the business organisations in India are not able to maintain their own information systems for environmental scanning, they have to rely on secondary sources of environment. That is why the present work on environmental analyses is being taken up.

CASE I

THE SUCCESS STORY OF RELIANCE

When in order to improve the foreign exchange reserves, the Indian government introduced the high unit value scheme which would hopefully promote exports, the government permitted the import of polyester filament yarn against export of raw silks (mainly nylon fabrics) in 1971. Everyone in the textile industry cried that the scheme was a creation of Ambani, by Ambani and for Ambani. More recently in 1987-88 when permission was granted for the new series of Reliance debentures, the response was the same. The fact is *Vimal* fabrics produced by Reliance are as much a draw with upper middle class Indians as Reliance convertible debentures are with discrete investors.

Dhirubhai Ambani, the promoter of Reliance Textiles, is no descendent of the Tatas or Birlas, the legendary Indian business families. This son of a school teacher is a creation of changing Indian business environment. When in 1966, Reliance made a beginning, industrial stagnation had already set up in India. The whole policy framework of licensing was coming under fire for helping the big business to grow further. Faced by foreign exchange crisis, import substitution strategy was being abondoned and export promotion schemes were being devised. Import-export trading was the most lucrative business. Dhirubhai cashed on these changes and made his initial millions in import-export trading.

On the social level, changes in life styles of middle and even lower middle class Indians had forced them to big a goodbye to cotton textiles. Nylon which had gone popular with this section of our society in 60's were being discarded in favour of polyesters. The salaried classes of Indian people were faced with another predicament. The meagre savings which they managed for tax reasons couldn't be invested in real estate or trading due to their primary concerns with their jobs. Government securities were giving very meagre returns by the late Seventies. The middle class in India had not only switched to polyester fibres, they were also trying to look for remunerative investment avenues.

Reliance which went public in 1977 showed the discerning investors that industrial securities could be a worthwhile investment. Later, they sought clearance for a number of new financial instruments initiating the new class of investors into capital market. Convertible debentures owe their popularity to the beginning made in marketing of these securities by Reliance textiles. The public financing institutions also had emerged as an important force in the capital market by this time and Reliance made full use of finances and underwriting facilities provided by them.

The liberalisation of Indian economy had started in 1978. Technology transfers were being permitted for modernisation of textile industry. Reliance made full use of this opening up of the economy and clinched the technology transfer deals with Dupont, American Chemical giant, for import of DMT and TPA based technology for manufacture of Polyester Fibre Yarn. A fete in project management was achieved in putting up the plant at Patalganga in a record of 18 months. By the turn of 80's, when the takeover wave started, Reliance was one of the first few to avail of the tax concessions and financial facilities announced for takeover of sick textile mills. Similarly, when a scheme for NRI investments was announced in 1982, Reliance managed to get Rs. 22 crores non-resident equity invested in its expansion.

The current *Indian Express* compaign against Reliance Textiles gives an impression that Reliance has an enormous influence on public policy making by the Indian government. The business-politics nexus thus has been used to its best advantage by the Reliance Textiles, which currently is the number two corporate giant in India and apart from vertical downstream integration of its business, has created a stir recently by smoothly taking over a prestigious engineering company, Larsen and Toubro. Thus Reliance is a case of designing its strategies according to opportunities offered by changing business environment.

POINTS FOR DISCUSSION

(1) It is alleged that backdoor operations rather than business acumen is the cause of Reliance's success, do you agree with this assessment ?

(2) Do you feel that it is not only business which is affected by environment, successful corporate management requires that business should create an environment which is conducive for their business growth ?

FOR FURTHER READINGS

1. Afanasyev, V.G., *The Scientific and Technological Revolution —Its Impact on Management and Education*, Moscow, Progress Publishers, 1975.

2. Bhattacharyya, S.K. and Venkatraman, N., *Managing Business Enterprises : Strategies, Structures and Systems*. New Delhi, Vikas, 1983.

3. Bhattacharyya, S., *Corporate Planning*, New Delhi, Oxford and IBH, 1981.
4. Blauberg, I.V., *et. al.*, *Systems Theory : Philosophical and Methodological Problems*, Moscow, Progress Publishers, 1977.
5. Braverman, Harry, *Labour and Monopoly Capital—The Degradation of Work in the Twentieth Century*, Trivandrum, Social Scientist Press, 1979.
6. Drucker, Peter, F., *Managing in Turbulent Times*, New York, Harper and Row, 1980.
7. Mohinder Kumar, *Managerialism and Working Class in India*, New Delhi, Sterling, 1982.
8. Newman, William. H., *et. al.*, *The Process of Management : Strategy Action, Results*, New Delhi, Prentice Hall of India, 1987.

2

Indian Business—A Historical Perspective

Entrepreneurial or business history in India stresses the role of certain individuals and families in introducing modern industry in India. Their decisions and strategies to initiate, organise or aggrandise profit oriented business is becoming a subject matter of many studies. In contrast to the approaches of history from below or historical materialism, these studies describe the likes and creations of these crown princes of Schumpeter—Cole Schema of entrepreneurship. In fact, the differences among industrial development of Japan, China and India are sought to be explained in terms of the behavioural differences of various business houses operating in these countries. But even the adherents of this school of history accept that the economic or political environment prevailing in the countries determined the behaviour of these enterprising strata in different societies operating in different historical epochs.

Developments in Pre-British Era

In Indian context, the history of industrial development starts with potentialities of development of manufacturing in medieval India. It is stressed by the votaries of Asiatic mode of production that in India, there were insulated self sufficient village communities with social division of labour. There was limited socio-economic interaction of these communities with each other and on account of this the powers that ruled India in medieval times didn't feel the necessity of investment in public irrigation works or developmental infrastructure. The production prevalent in these communities led to harmonious relations without any substantial internal classifications/contradictions among the labouring classes which could result in any major conflicts in production. The king/chieftan ruling these communities also made little attempts for improving the agrarian economy of these villages. This lack of state initiative in public works delayed the monetisation, commercialisation and consequent urbanisation of Indian economy. Thus, according to some historians the British who invaded India had aided breaking the stagnation of this socio-economic formation by introducing public works like railways and by organising armed forces at national level in India while draining away the wealth of Indian economy to their parent country.

Historians led by Irfan Habib have disputed these formulations and have mustered evidence that there was stratification of peasantry, commercialisation, monetisation and urbanisation of economy in medieval India, on account of production of goods of novelty, war equipments and palatial buildings. Armies of Mughal Chieftans were drawn from villages and were paid in precious metals or coins which resulted in the development of commodity production.

A class of artisans was coming up which did not limit itself to needs of a village community but engaged in production for purposes other than self consumption. The mining, metallurgical and weaving technologies had been developed. In agriculture also innovations like Persian Wheel for Irrigation had been taken up. Commodity production had started but they agree that the socio economic formation existing in Mughal India cannot be equated with classical feudalism with its contradictions which led to the first industrial revolution in England. Thus, though Britishers introduced modern factories, there are ample evidences of existence of guilds of craftsmen, putting out systems and even manufactories of indigenous type in pre-British period. This imposition of British/Western mode of capitalistic economy and land rights in India is believed to have distorted the natural development of technology, polity and economy in India.

Development of Manufacturing in India

Picking up this thesis of imposed development, coupled with a discrimination which the Raj practised in favour of British capital, economic historians of modern India blame Britishers for stunted industrial growth in India. Amiya Bagchi argues that there has been a constant and conscious deskilling of Indian masses by the Britishers to build their technological hegemony. He quotes the examples of the pre-British technical developments undertaken by Parsee ship-builders and the famous handloom weavers of Bengal. In order to build a market for cotton piece-goods of Manchester industry, the East India Company and subsequent British administration coerced the craftsmen to abondon their original occupations and migrate to villages. This process of migration was just the reverse of the process observed in British industrial revolution. It is also argued that the advent of British Raj and the introduction of British property rights further strengthened the semi-feudal relation like *Zamindari* system. The bondage of labour to land was a common practice. Thus, the non-availability of a labour force committed to industrial production in Ahmedabad and Bombay textile units, when this industry was launched for the first time, was due to inability of labour in breaking their rural nexus. It is a semi-feudal system of labour contractors or jobbers which had to be utilized to recruit and operate industrial labour force in early stages of industrialisation in India.

The development of industry in India was initiated in a manner which is quite dissimilar to the Western developments. Initially, the European traders concentrated their activities in coastal cities of Surat, Bombay, Madras and Calcutta. The Indian trading/merchant classes first came into contact with these traders and became their agents for factory-made goods from the West. It is later, that British started their agencies in India in order to drain mineral and agricultural resources of

India to meet the British needs. Indigo, tea, coffee and sugarcane plantations were developed as enclaves of industry type development to export their produce to the European markets.

Jute trading agencies also came up in Calcutta. Cotton textile factories in the Ahmedabad-Bombay belt were started after the introduction of railways and the first Indian War of Independence in 1857. In fact, the first few native entrepreneurs came from the communities of Parsees and Gujaratis who had accumulated capital through their *compradore* role in European trade, moneylending, opium trade and a few of them were landlords.

The fact that Parsees saw themselves as the agents of Britishers is evident from the famous statement of Jamsetji Tata made in 1874. This pioneer of Indian industry stressed that "our small community is to my thinking, peculiarly suited as interpreters and intermediaries between the rulers and the ruled in this country. Through their peculiar position, they have benefitted more than any other class by English Rule, and I am sure that their gratitude to this rule is, as it ought to be, in due proportion to the advantage derived from it……". It is by combining a policy of collaboration and occasional opposition, to extract protective advantages in an era of free trade, that these communities were able to launch manufacturing enterprises.

The logic of modern manufacturing was first popularised by some British agency houses as well as Indian industrialists in cotton textile industry which was first to change over to factory production from earlier putting-out system. But this industry had a cost disadvantage due to discrimination in tariff rates levied by the British rulers, in the interest of the Lancashire and Manchester industry. This led to the launching of *Swadeshi* movement in the first decade of the Twentieth Century, when drain of Indian wealth theories were first popularised. The native cotton textile manufactures actively aided this movement.

It is partly due to inspiration of *Swadeshi* spirit that

Jamshetji Tata could venture to float the first basic goods industry, *i.e.*, Tata Iron and Steel Co. in India. It is interesting to note here that Jamshetji, who considered himself close to the Britishers, had to face stiff resistance of British authorities and investors in this venture. It is only with aid of Indian princes and merchants that he was able to launch his ambitious project. The contributions of Maharaja of Gwalior and Maharaja Mayubhanj to this project brought into being the first major alliance of the privileged of agricultural economy with the industrialists. TISCO was launched as the first Indian basic goods industry in the beginning of the Twentieth Century.

War Time Developments

First World War and the War-time organisation of industry gave a major fillip to Indian industries and groups like that of Shrirams and later Marwaris, a community of traders, made their entry into manufacturing industry in a big way. Biographer of Lala Shri Ram, Arun Joshi points out that it was a War-time order for tents which really launched the Delhi Cloth Mills as a modern industrial enterprise. Tata Iron and Steel Company also got their major orders during the First World War. The *Swadeshi* movement of the Twenties brought some concessions and ensured market for produce of Indian textile industries and the houses like Ranchhod Lal, Kasturbhai, Shrirams, Khataus, etc., fortified their positions. The depression of the Thirties in West provided textile industry in India an opportunity to modernise the units by importing machinery at very cheap rates as is evidenced by modernisation programmes taken up by Shrirams and Kasturbhais.

The Thirties was the period of emergence of Marwaris, the most influential present day enterprising communities. Birlas of Calcutta, who had gained knowledge of industry while acting as agents of foreign houses like Andrew Yule and had a massed huge wealth in opium trade as well as speculative business, made their debut in textiles with the break of the First World War. Birlas led by G.D. Birla were the most forceful native business behind the first pressure group of native business, Federation of Indian Chambers of Commerce and Industry (referred to as FICCI, hereafter) which inspired the *Swadeshi* movement to a large extent. As an aftermath of expansion of textile industry, Birlas apart from diversifying their interests in Jute, Paper and Sugar industry had also started a textile machinery manufacturing unit in 1936-37. Shrirams of North India also launched their Jay-Engineering, Walchands launched the first automobile unit in India, *i.e.*, Premier Automobiles before the Second World War. Kirloskar in West India had started manufacturing agricultural implements and machine tools. Marugapas had made their debut in South Indian industry by this time. Whereas Mafatlals, Khataus, etc., basically limited themselves to textiles during this period, Kasturbhais had started planning diversification into dyes and chemicals. Dalmias had interests in cement. But even among the native big business houses, the houses like that of Ranchhod Lal, the pioneers of textiles in Ahmedabad had been declared bankrupt by 1934. Many smaller industrialists who couldn't internalise the business ethos of unity and struggle with British government also could not survive.

In his classical attempt at studying private investment 1900-1939, A.K. Bagchi refutes the hypothesis of lack of entrepreneurial skills in India. According to him, there was a large number of Indian entrepreneurs who were willing to commit capital to risky ventures. Though small-scale industries also came up yet these ventures failed due to an open door policy and racial discrimination pursued by the British Raj. Apart from merchants and landlords, people practising liberal professions also tried to enter manufacturing industries. But either due to the factors cited above or wrong choice of the industries, these small capitalists did not start an industrial revolution in India.

It may be worthwhile pointing out here that Bombay business community led by Dorab Tata had tried to assert itself as a separate group than the mainstream native business by late 1930's. Tatas were the main motive force behind the organisation of Associated Chambers of Commerce (ASSOCHAM) which lagged behind FICCI in its support to the national movement. The socialistic rhetoric of Jawaharlal had driven them away from the mainstream of Indian national movement. Indian national congress which represented the interests of many privileged groups in India could not always accept the strategy suggested by big business in India. However, 1935 Act and the subsequent 1937-39 period of Congress rule had convinced the native business communities that their interests were safe in the hands of Congress leadership. By 1939, Tatas who were not very favourably disposed to Congress leadership had already made huge investments in their 17 industrial units. This included TISCO, three hydel power generation units and one chemicals plant. But the welcome vision of Tatas to make India technologically self-reliant had not been translated into reality. Bagchi quotes U.N. Calculations for the year 1936 which maintain that, "67 per cent of total volume of employment in factories in India was in consumer goods industries, 18 per cent in industries producing intermediate materials (wood, paper, chemical, etc.), and 15 per cent in other finished goods (mostly capital goods)". It is on account of this industrial structure that the subsidiary companies of multinationals like UNILIVER, ICI, DUNLOP, GENERAL MOTORS, etc., had already made an entry in India.

The Consolidation of Native Business 1937-47

In 1937, the paid up capital of various Indian mixed and European business houses was in proportion of 3, 2 and 3, respectively. The British agency houses like Martin Bird, Andrew Yule and Binny alongwith multinationals were dominating the industrial scene. Whereas business in Calcutta was largely controlled by the European business houses, in Bombay bulk of investments had been made either by the Parsees or Gujaratis or there were mixed investments. In Northern India, groups like that of Shri Rams and Thapars had already emerged and were controlling the industrial investments made in this part of the country. The period of 1937-39 was utilised by the Indian business houses to stabilize their investments. Wartime organisation of production after 1939 and supernormal profits earned by the business families during the War helped them in further consolidating their position. The number of factories established prior to the War was around 2824, during the War period this number increased to 10,000, though the latter also include number of investment, trading and banking companies.

Prior to War, there were no major technical improvements pioneered in India as applied to the solution of production problems in industry. Thus, in 1939, the economy of India remained poor, basically agricultural and colonial. Even the War time organisation of production by the Britishers had allocated only consumer goods to India. Except for "Tatanagar Armoured Cars" manufactured by TISCO which accounted for major part of their 20 per cent increase in steel production during War, no major capital goods or War equipment industries were launched in Indian private corporate sector. Walchands' pioneering effort in starting manufacture of Aircrafts in Hindustan Aircrafts had to face many obstructions from the state. It was argued that since India had a narrow technological base, it is futile to start industries based on sophisticated automobile or armament technology. Hindustan Aircrafts was also launched by borrowing technical knowhow from Allies. In 1942, this company too was nationalised, seeing the political climate generated by Quit India Movement. But, during the War time, industrial investment increased by 8 per cent per annum and the industrial production in the period of 1940-45 was $7\frac{1}{2}$ times that of industrial production in 1935-40. The profits increased at a much higher pace. Due to the rampant speculation and black market operations during the War, the established business houses made huge capital accumulations which they later used to acquire the British interests in Indian industrial economy.

The houses like Shrirams and Kasturbhais who had modernised their textile manufacturing units benefitted a lot from War-time orders. Delhi Cloth Mills, after the War, emerged as a large national textile company with assets of Rs. 4 crores. The company had diversified in sugar and chemicals. Textile manufactures recorded an overall growth of 25 per cent per annum during the War period. Paper and textile industries doubled their production during the War. By 1945, 60 per cent of the total manufactures available in India were already being manufactured in local plants. This speaks volumes for the rapid industrial progress during this period. The Indian business houses had accumulated huge sterling balances. It is on this strength that G.D. Birla, the main spirit behind native chamber of commerce, FICCI in his pamphlet *India's War Prosperity : The Myth Exploded*, made a passionate plea for allowing import of machinery in exchange for the sterling accumulations.

After the War, British agency houses had already started disposing of their major firms in India. Dalmia bought over Govan Brothers and Bennet Coleman ; Bangur acquired Kettlewell Bullen, Surajmal Nagarmal acquired Davenpart and McLeods, B. D. Goenka gained the control of Octavius Steel and Duncan Brothers, Birlas came to control Sirpur Papers and Sir Silks. Kasturbhais and Walchands in West India had gone for major diversifications. Thapars from Northern India had acquired Greaves Cotton. A sea change occurred in Indo-British relations, Indian houses had started making more technological arrangements with US based multinationals. America had emerged as the strongest capitalist power as an aftermath of Second World War, so American interests had also started increasing in Indian economy. Through various technological agreements Indian houses had started diversifying into automobiles, chemicals, engineering and other high technology industries.

Tatas launched their TELCO in collaboration with Nuffield Diamler Benz and Harnischfeger Corporation ; National Electronics Corporation in collaboration with American Power Company ; Tata Finlay a tea packing unit in collaboration with James Finlay and Tata Chemicals in collaboration with ICI. Kasturbhai entered chemicals industry with the help of American Cynamide and Kirloskar started manufacturing oil engines in collaboration with British Electricals and British Oil Engines. Walchands and Birlas launched their automobile manufacturing units in collaboration with multinationals. This paved way for understanding which Indian business houses (due to their technological dependence) were compelled to reach with multinationals, besides striking agreements with local feudal elements like Princes/Zamindars. But overall complexion of industry had changed in India, the Indian investments were more than half of the total investments in India's private sector at the time of independence.

However, the history outlined above suggests that the industrialisation of India in pre-independence period was largely a prerogative of a few big business families. Tata had built up assets of around Rs. 50 crores and were controlling 26 companies. Birlas had assets of Rs. 24 crores and they controlled 29 companies. Similarly, the house of Dalmias controlled as many as 38 companies, Singhanias controlled 42, Thapars 32 and Goenkas 14 companies, respectively. Walchands in Western India had paid up capital of Rs. 7 crores and Shrirams in Northern India had equally dominating position. Mafatlal, Kirloskar, Bangur, Kasturbhais were the other major houses.

Mehta in his study on concentration in Indian industry showed that by 1947, 36 managing houses controlled the largest 600 industrial companies in India. In all 100 persons were holding 1700 directorships in these companies. Why did this degree of concentration arise only in initial stages of industrialisation ? Why stage of free competition bypassed Indian economy ? How traders and speculators came to occupy pivotal positions in Indian industry ? Partly, the replies to these queries are obvious from the historical sketch drawn in preceding paragraphs. For further comprehension of this phenomenon, we study the institutions of Joint Stock Company, managing agency system and use of jobbers for industrial administration. These institutions, though a result of the socio-economic reality of India in early half of this Century, helped the process of concentration.

Institutions of Modern Industry

The early firms in the period under study were either proprietory concerns or extended family concerns. Due to unlimited liability clause in the British partnership laws, Indian joint families found it hard to start business in partnerships. Joint stock companies which had their predecessors in guilds of craftsmen became very popular with Indian entrepreneurs when their capital needs couldn't be supplied by the family accumulations. Joint Stock Companies are an institution of modern industry. Capital is raised from large number of individuals by the promoters. The ownership being so dispersed, the production system in the units floated under corporate system could no longer rely on personal, informal relationships or family ties for its smooth functioning. Management structures had to be evolved to supervise the labour process.

Administration of the work-force which used to be owner's direct responsibility in Small Scale manufactories, had to be entrusted to intermediaries hired specially to perform this function. In keeping with the conditions of labour market which was imperfect, the institution of jobbers, labour contractors, *Sirdars*, etc., performed this function. The enactment of labour laws after a number of enquiries into the labour conditions in the Bombay-Ahmedabad Cotton Textile Industries complicated labour administration. Unionisation of work-force further created problems of labour administration.

However, the mercantile and money-lending background of the Indian entrepreneurs made them more conscious of financial management. In the latter half the Nineteenth industry when cotton mills were being set up, the institution of managing agency which was evolved in banking and insurance companies had extended itself to industrial investments also. In this phase, managing agents, who though belonging to established firms in industry, didn't have enough stakes in the managed companies. But ultimately, managing agency system became a form of industrial organisation where promotion, finance and administration of a vast conglomeration of independent legal entities created for carrying on unrelated activities were controlled by a single family.

First a firm was floated by the family as proprietory, partnership or private limited company. This firm, usually closely held, gained management control over many firms; firstly, in the same industry and later, in unrelated industries like mining, plantations, manufacturing, public utilities, shipping, selling and investing. After gaining management control, conditions were created by the agents in which a sizeable chunk of shareholdings of the managed company were cornered by them. Through this process, the British agencies and the early enterprising Indian families created their business empires or groups. In fact, very few companies of Indian industry were outside the umbrella of the agency houses by the second half of the Twentieth Century.

Due to their early entry into manufacturing the managing agents claimed proven worth in entrepreneurial and managerial skills which made large number of merchants/civil servants stationed in India or abroad entrust their investments to the care of these agents. It is maintained that joint stock companies, the leading institution of industries in India, was just a superstructure on managing agency houses. Managing agency houses virtually played the same role in the field of industrial management as was played by *Zamindari* System in land management. In keeping with the overall socio-economic formation in India at that time, the system synchronized capitalist and pre-capitalist relationships.

The advantages of managing agency system were: centralisation of promotion and management functions, easy transferability of personnel and finances from one unit to another, common purchase and sales policy. Merchants, who in their *compradore* role had attempted primitive or primary accumulation of capital, were reluctant in entering manufacturing activities, so they left the affairs of their companies to be looked after by some entrepreneurs of repute. The earlier thrust of providing managerial services by the agents shifted to arranging finances for the managed firms. In fact, by drawing huge sums as commissions and with sole sales rights, the agents deliberately damaged the financial health of the managed companies. Even in the initial phase of managing agency, the agents charged commissions to the tune of Rs. 30,000 to Rs 40,000 per annum from each of the managed companies. Their earnings from the managed companies helped them in attempting huge accumulations at the cost of promoters and shareholders of the managed companies.

The malpractices of managing agents, started receiving the attention of investing public in the early years of the Twentieth Century. While calling for amendments in Managing Agency System, the following suggestions were made in 1913-14 :

1. The rights of shareholders to renew or terminate contracts of agents should be safeguarded by necessary statutory amendments ;

2. The board of directors, the legal top management bodies in joint stock companies should be empowered to exercise full control over the functioning of agents ;

3. The practice of using managed company's funds for owner's own firms' needs should be stopped ;

4. Profit rather than sales should be made the basis of managing agents' remuneration. The remuneration should be either a fixed salary per month/annum or a percentage of net profits ; and

5. All contracts between the agents and the managed companies to drain the latter's resources should be banned.

Industrial Commission (1916-18), Tariff Board (1926) and Loknathan (1935) brought out the evils of managing agency system in more details. But due to the political clout of the British and Indian agency houses with British Raj, the suggestions made to overcome these evils cut very little ice with the policy framers.

Vertical, horizontal and conglomerate growth of agency houses continued and mergers/takeovers were a common phenomenon of the period 1900-1947. The share of small enterprises in the total manufacturing in the period 1900-1905 was thrice that of the large enterprises. But for 1942-47 the share of large enterprises' production had increased to 1.6 times that of small enterprises. Managing agency system played a major role in these combinations of small enterprises into large ones. Apart from multinationals and British agency houses which controlled half of the Indian investment by 1947, a few families of Indian origin controlled rest of the investment. Managing agency system, apart from increasing the control of individual houses, also brought together the big business groups in cartels. The foundation of Associated Cement Company and the participation of Khatau's in other business ventures are striking examples of this understanding among the big business. The Federation of Indian Chambers of Commerce (FICCI) and Associated Chambers of Commerce (ASSOCHAM), the two organisations of industrialists in India, were making their presence felt not only in economic matters but even in the social and political life of the country.

To sum up discussion on the role on managing agency system in the consolidation of business empires, the system ushered in an era in which financial maneouvres were more important than technological innovations. Even the houses like Tata couldn't break the stranglehold of managing agency system, in spite of their claims to be the legitimate heirs of professional management in India. They were also using their financial power to bring in more and more firms under the umbrella of Tata Sons. Similar was the case of Birla Brothers. In the wonderland of Indian System of Jagirdari had come to play, "the sun of entrepreneur was setting and sum of the rentier was rising". While preserving their feudal hold over their empires, the representatives of Indian big business were trying to assert their class interests in the Indian economy by influencing public policy.

Emergence of Big Business on National Scene

The emergence of native industrialists on national scene was reflected in their close association with the mainstream of national movement. Stanley Kochaneck tells us that the movement led by Indian National Congress was solidly backed by Marwari and Gujrati Capital. The perfect rapport between Gandhiji, Sardar Patel and G.D. Birla, the driving spirit behind FICCI is now very well documented. The liberal democrat Nehru was a little withdrawn from obscurantist Marwaris like R.K. Dalmia and J.K. Birla but he was very friendly with Shri Ram, Singhania and Tata. Scared by the emergence of left in Indian politics, ASSOCHAM leadership led by JRD Tata gave up the idea of floating a capitalist political organisation at the time of independence and veered around the idea of mixed economy proposed by Nehru and mediated by G.D. Birla, R.M. Lala recounts that Nehru had called Jamshetji Tata and as *one man planning commission of India*. F.E. Dinshaw, Sir Purshotam Das Thakur Das, Kasturbhai Lalbhai and Ambalal Sarabhai were the main spokesmen of Bombay industry.

In this context the most important documentary evidence of big business planning the economic strategy of Indian National Congress is Bombay Plan. After Nehru was jailed the work for National Planning Commission was taken up by a group of eight 'economists' in 1944. Four of these belonged to Tata house—JRD Tata, Sir Ardeshar Dalal, A.D. Shroff and Dr. John Mathai. The others being Sir Purshotam Das Thakur das, G.D. Birla, Sir Shri Ram and Kasturbhai Lalbhai. Before we take up a discussion on the details of blueprint of Indian plans after independence, we may mention that the scientific and technological planning was also taken up for independent India by big business, through their trusts like Dorab Tata Trust. Bombay Plan as the document is commonly known was ready a year before India's independence.

The Indian big business had realised that on their own, they cannot accelerate the tempo of capital accumulation so they called for State help by advocating the concept of development state. In keeping with their nationalist stance, the authors of Bombay Plan called for a national government, vested with full freedom in economic matters. They wanted strong protective tariffs. In order to expand the domestic market for industrial goods, they proposed a plan for doubling the national income in 15 years. For the development of infrastructure, heavy and basis industries they called for huge state investments. Deficit financing—the Keynesian prescription was supposed to finance this state effort. About ownership and control of industries, it was maintained that 'state control' appears to be more important than ownership or management.

For mobilisation of all the available means of production and their direction towards socially desirable ends..."over a wide field, it is not necessary for the State to secure ownership or management of economic activity for this purpose. Well directed and effective state control should be fully adequate". A temporary eclipse in the freedom of private enterprise was accepted, provided it helped the subsequent growth of private business by making available cheap inputs initially at reasonable terms. However, the selective state ownership in industries and public welfare activities was welcome in short-run but in long-run "if...private finance is prepared to takeover these industries, state ownership may be replaced by private ownership". The plan stressed that the state owned industries should also be managed with the help of private industrialists.

State regulation of industries should be enforced in such a manner that it doesn't hamper the initiative of management. Thus for modernisation of economy, state had to play the role of the supporter and the promoter of private enterprise. Starting with a mixed economy, an increasing privatisation of public sector was called for.

But the weak position of Indian businessmen was not limited to accepting the role of state a compromise with princes and feudal elements, their technological parasitism also drove them into a compromise with multinationals. The bargain, that freedom was, dictated that the major Indian party to transfer of power didn't call for complete breach of connections with U.K. and U.S.A. multinationals. It has already been pointed out that American and European multinationals had reached a peak investment by the mid-Forties, the time when Bombay Plan was being drafted. So weak was the technological base of Indian capital that it not only required the help of a developmental state for taking up massive investments in capital goods industry but also that of multinationals. In fact, this technological parasitism perpetuated itself, undermining the self-suffcient growth of industry in later years.

In spite of the fact that large scale manufacturing enterprises had made an advent in India by 1947, Indian economy was primarily an agrarian economy. A sectoral analysis of economy suggests that half of the national income was generated in agriculture, one third in service sector and it was only remaining one sixth of income which came from Industry. Out of 17 per cent share of industry, modern organised manufacturing alongwith mining accounted for only 7 per cent, rest being the product of small scale or informal sector. The industrial economy grew at a meagre 4.8 per cent during 1947-51. Industrial policy resolution of 1948 had come forth but the policy was in fact an *ad hoc* arrangement. But the resolution itself reflected the thinking of authors of Bombay Plan. As already stated, Indian enterprises in sugar, cotton textiles, jute, paper had already been established but the need was to build a capital goods industry which could sustain the planned rapid growth of industry.

The partition in 1947, resulted in serious dislocations in raw material supplies to jute and cotton industries. On an average, India retained more than 90 per cent of industrial units, mineral production and industrial work-force. But about 80 per cent of raw jute producing area went to East Pakistan and a significant area cultivating along staple cottons went over to West Pakistan. Government promoted diversion of food producing areas of producing this raw material which resulted in food crisis. Since the food crisis were averted by import of food, foreign exchange difficulties arose. The migration of populations on the two sides of boundary line had an adverse effect, initially, but latter it resulted in commercialisation of the economy.

CASE II

INDIAN INDUSTRIALISTS AND MAHATMA GANDHI

In a secret and personal communication to all Provincial Governors on November 2, 1942, the then Viceroy of India Lord Linlithgow wrote: "I am anxious that every possible step should be taken to trace and bring home to those concerned, the part played by 'Big Business' in the recent disturbances. It has always been known that Congress has depended for financial assistance on a number of wealthy capitalists...". The Viceroy had ordered an enquiry into the matter.

Now it is well known that Gandhiji, the undisputed leader of our National Movement had cultivated businessmen like Ghanshyam Das (GD) Birla. As early as 1924, Gandhiji wrote to Birla: 'God had given me mentors, and I regard you as one of them'. Similarly, on death of Jamnalal Bajaj, Gandhiji wrote a letter to former's friends: "You are aware how intimate was the relationship between Jamnalal and myself. There was no work of mine in which I did not receive his fullest cooperation in body, mind and wealth...". The relations of Gandhiji with Sarabhais and his expounding trusteeship principle while organising workers in Ahmedabad are also well known. It was alleged by the Britishers that Gandhi's Swadeshi Movements were financed by Indian big business. However, industrialists like Kirolskar and Walchand, who stood for speedy modernisation of India's industrial economy resisted the insistence of Gandhi on Khadi, Spinning Wheel and such devices to be retained as the mainstay of Indian economy.

POINTS FOR CONSIDERATION

(1) Do you think that Birlas were acting in "enlightened self interest" by financing Gandhi's political campaigns?

(2) Do you feel that Gandhian emphasis on small and cottage industry could have discouraged the modernisation of Indian industry?

FOR FURTHER READINGS

1. Bagchi, Amiya Kumar, *Private Investment in India, 1900-1939*, New Delhi, Orient Longman, 1980.
2. Basu, S.K., *The Managing Agency System—In Prospect and Retrospect*, Calcutta, 1958.
3. Guha, Amlendu, "Comprodore Role of Parsi Seths", Occasional Paper, Calcutta, Indian Centre for Social Sciences, 1980.
4. Herdeck, M. and Piramal, Gita, *India's Industrialists*, Vol. I, Washington D.C.. Three Continents, 1985.
5. Joshi, Arun, *Lala Shri Ram—A Study of Entrepreneurship and Industrial Management*, New Delhi, Orient Longman, 1975.
6. Kochanek, Stanley, A., *Business and Politics in India*, London, University of California, 1974.
7. Lala, R.M., *Creation of Wealth—The Tata Story*, Bombay, IBH Publishing, 1981.
8. Moris, Moris D., *The Emergence of An Industrial Labour Force In India—A Study of Bombay Cotton Mills, 1854-1947*, Bombay, Oxford University Press, 1965.
9. Rungta, Radhey Shyam, *The Rise of Business Corporation In India*, London, Cambridge, 1970.
10. Sengupta, N.K., *Changing Patterns of Corporate Management in India*, New Delhi, Vikas, 1980.
11. Timberg, Thomas, A., *The Marwaris—From Traders to Industrialists*, New Delhi, Vikas, 1978.

3
Technological Environment in India

Technology has come to play a vital role in economic and social life of various countries. In fact scientific and technological innovation is the pivotal question of Indian industrialisation according to supply side economists. Technological change comprises search for new products/processes to satisfy social needs. The change may have to rely on basic research in natural sciences. However, in the context of developing countries like India, technological development activity is construed to be the acquisition, assimilation and development of imported technology and the adaptation of products and processes to local conditions.

In colonial India, technical manpower was not allowed to develop in natural course and the traditional technical skills in various handicrafts were systematically destroyed. It is contended that the deskilling of vast masses of traditional craftsmen was a conscious strategy of the colonial rulers in reinforcing the dependence of India on Britain. With freedom in sight in 1939, a National Planning Committee was set up by the Indian National Congress. To close the gaps in technology, a study group made suggestions about scientific research and technical education. A close coordination in different sectors of research and laboratory-factory interaction were suggested by the group.

The private industry in India was built during the pre-Independence period on technologies borrowed from the Multinational Corporations (MNC's). Some factory systems established by the British entrepreneurs and MNC's were also taken over by the Indian businessmen. Even the first basic goods unit, TISCO, set up way back in the beginning of the Twentieth Century, had to rely on technology and technocrats from Europe.

It is the unwillingness of private business houses to take up major research and development (R & D) efforts which brought the government in picture for scientific and technological development after independence. The Government of India initiated steps to set up educational, scientific and technological (EST) institutions. In order to co-ordinate the researches of all these EST's apex organisations were set up. A Science Policy was enunciated during the Second Five Year Plan in 1958. It may be pointed out that this was the period when an industrial base was sought to be created to break the technological-dependence syndrome characteristic of Indian industry.

Organisations for Science and Technology in India

In India, science and technology research is mainly carried on by the government resources and institutions. There are about a dozen government agencies to support and finance R & D. These include Department of Science and Technology (DST), Department of Atomic Energy (DAE), Council of Scientific and Industrial Research (CSIR), Indian Council of Agricultural Research (ICAR), Indian Council of Medical Research (ICMR) and University Grants Commission. There are three dozen national laboratories, besides more than hundred research laboratories in the universities and deemed universities. About 90 per cent of the top scientists and engineers are engaged in research in the above said institutions and defence laboratories. There are, of course, a few research establishment like Tata Institute of Fundamental Research (TIFR) which are financed by private industry. All major public sector units and a few private companies have their inhouse R & D establishments.

Planning Commission in India formulates research plans for all the major laboratories and apex organisations but the effort doesn't go beyond allocating funds. Of late, however, more funds are being made available to different scientific agencies for research and training of S & T manpower. The stock of S & T personnel has increased from barely 2 lakhs in the fifties to 3 million in 1985. Numberwise, we have the second or third largest trained force of technocrats, however, as a percentage of population, S & T manpower in India is way behind the developed world. Moreover, our training institutions are geared more to create personnel for manning R & D establishments of MNC's and their training is of little use to the production needs in India.

Ministries of Central government also set up study groups and finance research in specific areas. Ministries of agriculture, irrigation, power have taken up such exercises. In fact planning of research takes place at different levels. National requirements are spelt down in different sectors of research, funds to project teams and research projects are approved. Later research is taken up by these groups in different fields. Most of the Science Policy measures in India were intended to foster indigenous research for the import substitution model which had been at the heart of our industrial policy during the first three plans. Later, the government of India abondoned its Plan priorities because the EST's are not able serve the purpose for which these were created. The government has adopted a model of more open economy and liberal import of technologies.

If allocations for R & D are an indicator, our government has invested increasing amounts for attaining technological self reliance. The expenditure on R & D increased from meagre sum of around Rs. 1 crore in 1948-49 to Rs. 2,865.57 crores in 1986-87. The expenditure has not only increased in absolute terms but also as a percentage of Gross Domestic Product. It was 0.18 per cent in 1948-49 and was 1.10 per cent in 1986-87. Whereas at the time of independence less than ten thousand S & T personnel were working in state sponsored EST's, their number has touched the two lakhs mark forty years after independence.

Table 3.1 gives the break-up statistics of total R and D expenditure.

TABLE 3.1
R and D Expenditure Statistics

(Rs. Crores)

	1980-81	1986-87
1. Central Government	533.18	2,052.02
2. State Government	73.40	258.21
3. Total Government	606.58	2,310.23
4. Public Sector-Industrial	85.36	237.06
5. Private Sector-Industrial	120.69	291.09
6. Total Industrial R & D	206.05	538.15
7. Total R & D	812.63	2,848.38
8. Industrial R & D GS Percentage of Total R & D	25.36	18.61
9. R & D in Private Sector as Percentage of Total R & D	14.85	10.26
10. R & D in Public Sector as Percentage of Total R & D	10.51	8.35

Source : Department of Science and Technology, Government of India.

From the statistics presented in Table 3.1 as Plan expenditure on R & D has increased twentyfolds during the last four plans. It was around Rs. 3,000 crores in the Seventh Plan. Provincial level S & T councils were allotted Rs. 162 crores during the Seventh Plan. Plan allocations for different agencies during the last three plans are depicted in Table 3 2.

From the statistics presented in Table 3.1 and 3.2, it is clear that governmental sector of R & D is not only overwhelmingly important but its relative share has increased over 1980-81 to 1986-87. In 1986-87, it accounts for 81.4 per cent of total R & D expenditure. Defence R & D organisation, department of Space and Atomic Energy account for more than half of this R & D expenditure. Council of Scientific and Industrial Research (CSIR) accounts for only 12 per cent of plan expenditure. Industrial R & D expenditure which was one fourth of the total in 1980-81 has come down to 18.6 per cent in 1986-87.

But whether these investments have yielded the desired results is a moot point. In fact, the Fourth Review Committee on CSIR, the premier research body in India, indicated the council for inefficient operations. To adapt to the new strategy of export led growth, it was suggested that CSIR should change the objectives, charter, structure policies, programmes and activities. National Research Development Corporation (NRDC), the body entrusted with the job of patenting researches of different research laboratories was also a mixed success. While analysing the experiences of Central Mechanical Engineering Research Institute (CMERI), an organisation similar in objectives to NRDC it was observed that the links between the local factories and research laboratories are extremely etnous. Science and Technology Policies are based on false assumptions. The argument that our Science and Technology Policies are often divorced from our socio-economic need, unfortunately holds good. NRDC's performance in its owed aim of transforming research ideas into commercial projects has also been dismal. Inhouse R & D is being stressed by various studies due to failure in bridging the gap between laboratories and factories.

Inhouse R & D in Indian Industry

Most of the inhouse R & D in India is aimed at adapting imported technologies. R & D expenditures bear no significant relationship with the improvement of productivity. Expenditures on modernisation resulted in improvement of

TABLE 3.2

Plan Allocation for Major Scientific Agencies

	Plan Allocation (Rs. Crores)		
	Fifth Plan	Sixth Plan	Seventh Plan
Department of Atomic Energy	167.13 (26.5)	234.59 (15.1)	315.00 (10.7)
Department of Space	128.27 (20.4)	304.56 (19.5)	700.00 (23.8)
Department of Science and Technology	58.96 (9.4)	269.95** (17.3)	543.09 (18.4)
Council of Scientific and Industrial Research	81.77 (13.0)	221.71 (14.2)	355.09 (12.1)
Indian Council of Agricultural Research	153.56 (24.4)	287.10 (18.4)	425.00 (14.4)
Indian Council of Medical Research	31.32 (3.3)	48.08 (3.1)	150.00 (5.1)
Department of Environment	—	40.05 (2.6)	187.91* (6.4)
Department of Ocean Development	—	87.04 (5.6)	100.00 (3.4)
Development of Conventional Energy Sources	—	44.00 (2.8)	130.35 (4.4)
Department of Electronics	18.73 (3.0)	21.05 (1.4)	38.00 (1.3)
Total	629.74 (100.0)	1,558.11 (100.0)	2,944.35 (100.0)

*In addition there is a provision of Rs. 240 crores for Ganga Action Plan.

**Including Rs. 35.07 crores under States/U.T.

Note : Figures in brackets indicate percentages.

Source : DST, Government of India, Research and Development Statistics 1984-85, p. 41.

productivity to some extent in medium and large public limited companies but these expenditures proved to be a drain on small private limited companies. Expenditures on R & D have resulted in increase of profits (may be on account of tax incentives, which the government provides on R & D expenditure). However, some studies point out that some improvements in product design and quality have also been noted on account of inhouse R & D.

With the announcement of tax concessions in Income Tax Act 1961 for R & D and facilities for import of raw materials, equipments, components for inhouse R & D units in 1973, the number of R & D units has increased. The number of R & D units has almost doubled from 1976-77 to 1985-86 and was 896 in the year 1984-85.

The current expenditure on R & D is to the tune of 555 crores on inhouse R & D and has nearly quadrapled during the least decade at constant prices. The number of R & D units in public sector has increased from 52 to 95 but the expenditure at constant price has grown fourfolds. In fact, 865 units in private sector incur R & D expenditure equivalent to the 95 units in private sector. Thus expenditure R & D unit of a public sector on an average undertaking is 10 times the corresponding unit in private sector. Only 8 units in public sector and one in private sector had a R & D budget of over Rs. 5 crores. In 1986-87 investment on R & D by 865 units of private sector was 318.11 crores with an average expenditure per unit of Rs. 36.8 lakhs as compared to Rs. 294.5 lakhs per unit expenditure of 95 public sector units.

Owing to the incentives given by public policy, R & D awareness is increasing and expenditures at current prices are increasing at a satisfactory rate. However, as far as major R & D expenditures on plant and machinery are concerned, Indian industry prefers import of these capital goods rather than rely on inhouse R & D.

Whereas around 5 per cent of sales turnover of Indian industry goes on investment on plant/machinery, inhouse

R & D accounts only for one per cent of the turnover. There are around 25,000 S & T personnel employed in inhouse R & D units and private sector units account for 15,000 of these. Obviously, unitwise employment of R & D personnel works out to an average of 20 to 25. Only 4 per cent of private sector units were employing 100 or more R & D personnel whereas one quarter public sector units had R & D establishments employing 100 or more persons.

The thrust areas for R & D investments in industrial units include metallurgical industry, electronics and electric equipment, telecommunications, fertilizers and defence industries. In almost all these industries public sector units were incurring higher percentage of their sales turnover on R & D as compared to private sector.

Commenting on R & D system in India, G. Balaji in a contribution to the Economic Times (December 23, 1988) observes that the three levels of decision making in R & D constitute the government, the managers of inhouse R & D units, and the scientists/researchers. The functional dependence in these three levels of R & D manifests itself in decision making process at each level. The goals, objectives and missions of each of the levels are interdependent but need to be spelt out clearly in light of societal needs as reflected by the market or the plans. Top management in both public and private sectors can play a pivotal role in promoting R & D, if the recommendations of Seminar on R & D in Public Sector are adhered to. The recommendations are as follows :

(a) Management should ensure the use of modern techniques in the selection, planning, monitoring and control of R & D projects and investment decisions ;

(b) Suitable criteria for evaluation of R & D personnel, projects and organisations should be developed ;

(c) Management of R & D activity should receive equal importance in training besides the normal scientific training ; and

(d) Laboratory-factory interaction should be greater.

Policy and Legal Framework for R & D

Indian government has devised a number of policy instruments and concessions to promote inhouse R & D. We summarise the major incentives as follows :

1. Recognition to R & D units implies liberalised imports of equipment, components and raw materials with lesser duties. The recognition can be sought from the Department of Scientific and Industrial Research (DSIR, hereafter). Laboratories as well as inhouse R & D units can avail of this exemption from custom duty :

2. DSIR has played an active role in laboratory-industry interaction, publicising results of inhouse R & D units to facilitate quick retrieval and analysis of inhouse R & D ;

3. Apart from equipments for R & D even consumable items for public funded research institutions have been exempted from custom duty ;

4. Except for MRTP & FERA units, all units carrying on expansion on new production based on indigenously developed process are exempted from seeking licenses from the government ;

5. Under the Income Tax Act, revenue as well as capital investments on R & D are allowed hundred per cent deduction. Any payments made to scientific research institutions outside the industrial unit also qualify for similar deductions under the income Tax Act ;

6. Organisations like NRDC and CMERI help the flow of researches from laboratories to factories ; and

7. A technology data bank, technology development fund, schemes of public financing institutions to promote R & D alongwith the Technology Absorption and Adaptation Scheme are other measures to promote indigenous research.

The technology policy enunciated in 1983 reiterates commitment to technological competence and self-reliance. Provision of gainful employment by adopting appropriate and mass technologies relying on the traditional skills, less capital intensive methods and environmental awareness is another goal stated in the policy. However, need for rehabilitation and modernisation of machinery is stressed and this doesn't rule out import of technology. A new scheme of Science and Technology Entrepreneurship Parks (STEP) is proposed to facilitate university-industry interactions. In 1970, India had refused to carry on with the Patents Laws of Paris Convention. An Indian Patents Act was enacted. In Section 83 of the Act, it was stated :

"(a) that patents are granted to encourage inventions and to secure that inventions are worked in India on a commercial scale and to the fullest extent that is reasonably practicable without undue delay ; and

(b) that they are not granted merely to enable patentees to enjoy a monopoly for the importation of the patented article."

By being a member of Paris convention, India was obliged to protect foreign manufactures, foreign trade marks and thus the local manufactures relying on imported technologies were discriminated against. The Indian Act came into force on April 20, 1972. In the subsequent year, *i.e.*, 1973, a Foreign Exchange Regulation Act (FERA) monitoring foreign investments in Indian industry was brought forth. The understanding prompting these measures is that Foreign Direct Investments are a very costly method of import of technology. Since the Indian technological environment is not conducive to the required degree of innovations, we have to borrow technologies from the developed world. It is in this context, that pleas are being made now to rejoin Paris Convention to ensure free and unfettered transfer of technology.

Off late, an attempt is being made to promote a sustained effort towards well defined, time bound and mission oriented programmes in different areas of science and technology. The main aim of this approach is to co-ordinate indigenous R & D efforts with the end objectives to facilitate the involvement of various organisations in achieving the stated missions. The five national technology missions being taken up under the guidance of Sam Pitroda are : Drinking Water, Oil Seeds, Vaccination and Immunisation, Telecommunication and Eradication of Literacy. The sixth and seventh time bound missions, *viz.*, Ganga Action Plan and White Revolution have been added to these.

Besides a Technology Information, Forecasting and Assessment Council (TIFAC) has been created. The council shall monitor and communicate international developments in technology, in light of national needs in India. The council shall also assess the imported and indigenously developed technologies on the criteria of their impacts on energy, environment, employment, efficiency and economies. The Seventh Plan, while making these policy pronouncements also aims at more than doubling the resources of S & T to take these Rs. 7,535 crores as contrasted Rs. 3,367 crores of the Sixth Plan. Increase in resource availability during different plans is shown in Table 3.3.

TABLE 3.3
Total Resource Availability for R & D Over Plans

(Rs. Crores)

	Rs.
First Plan (1951-56)	20
Second Plan (1956-61)	67
Third Plan (1961-67)	144
Fourth Plan (1969-74)	374
Fifth Plan (1974-79)	1,380
Sixth Plan (1980-85)	3,367
Seventh Plan (1985-90)	7,535

Source : Jain, Ashok and V.K. Gupta, "Management of R & D—A Overview", *Indian Management*, November, 1988.

Transfer of Technology

Scientific and technological revolution has been uneven over the countries. It was in fact, technological superiority of the West which made them turn countries like India into their countries. During the colonial period, traditional skills in India were systematically destroyed and a dependence on the factory system type production methods was created. The word modernisation and consequent developments are synonymous with the adoption of the Western technologies. Industrialisation relies on these technological innovations in sources of energy and methods of production.

It is obvious that colonies like India had lagged behind in the technological race. Thus transfer of technology from the West was a necessity which we could ignore only by chosing to stay underdeveloped without promoting indigenous research in a big way. Our planners did make an effort to widen the industrial base, promote R & D and skills of our population. As is obvious from a historical sketch of India's industrialisation, the dependence of our native entrepreneurs on imported technologies was too deep rooted to be overcome in four decades. As a consequence industrial R & D in private sector continued to be neglected. Poor assimilation, adoption and development of imported technology is also a characteristic feature of Indian industry.

The principal instrument of technology transfer throughout the world have been multinationals (MNC's). At one state they dominated Indian scene but the import substitution and self-reliance drive has made us take resource to other ways of acquiring international technologies.

Among the various methods of technology transfer in India are : inviting foreign investments, technological collaborations, purchase of equipments and assignment of contracts for turn-key projects. Another indirect method of technology transfer relies on development of human resources. Education, training, participation in international seminars and consultancy services are various methods of the latter type. While multinationals transfer technologies to the individual manufacturing units or corporate entities, government to government transfer of technologies has also become popular in India due to economic co-operation with the Socialist world.

India has relied heavily on foreign sources of getting technology. From 1970 to 1986 87, India must have entered into more than 10,000 collaboration arrangements. In fact, during the late eighties foreign collaboration are touching the peak number of 1,000 per annum. The Reserve Bank of India has been conducting period surveys of foreign collaborations in the corporate sector. In fact, during the first phase of Indian industrial develpment till 1965, free imports were allowed in technology. 1965 to 1977 is a period of restrictive imports and at the end of the Seventies technology imports have been again liberalised.

The characteristic Indian perception governing its technology import policy has been viewed by various authorities in different manners. However, a realistic statement about the need to regulate technology import emerges from the realisation that supply of industrial technology is dominated by large MNC's. Transfer of technology is their global strategy of expansion and their transfer of technology entails purchases of intermediate or capital goods from these corporations. They charge unduly heavy prices for these purchases whereas the cost of transferring these technologies for the suppliers is much lower. As buyers of technology are less experienced than the bargainers of MNC's, they unwittingly accept many restrictive clauses in technology transfer arrangements. In the process, sometimes, obsolete technologies are transferred by MNC's to the third world and even if the Indian firms improvise the products/processes, they are not allowed to compete freely with the original suppliers of technology in the international markets.

However, the spokesmen of MNC's vehemently contest this viewpoint and maintain that their transfer of technologies to poor countries like India don't yield even a fraction percentage of their incomes. On the other hand, it is contended that imported technologies can increase productivity in the countries like India. Cases of low productivity in basic goods industries in comparison to the international standards are cited as example.

Public sector units in fertilizers, heavy electricals and computers have discarded the existing technologies and gone for repetitive and multiple transfers of technology for the similar products and processes. The case with private sector units is no different. It is interesting to note that two recently appointed high powered committees, *viz.*, Abid Hussain and Narasimhan Committees concurred on desirability of repetitive transfers of technology. Horizontal transfers of technologies didn't find favour with them. The Narasimhan committee argued that repetitive import of technology helps in prevention of monopolies or oligopolies and is thus justified. Hussain made a case on similar lines for repetitive transfer of technology and argued against over-regulating it. This free import of technology instead of preventing oligopolies has restricted new entries because small business are not favoured due to lack of resources and small share in market, by the suppliers of technology.

In fact, the product life cycles of products of electronic revolution are so short that international comparisons of productivity are meaningless. The dependence built by such industries on foreign sources of technologies will result in huge repatriation of fees, royalities or dividends to the suppliers of technology through multiple and repetitive foreign collaboration arguments. This is why, government of India promotes R & D in these industries on priority basis and regulates the import of technology.

Framework for Technical Collaborations

The Indian government has restricted imports of technology of certain items in different industries. Annexure I lists the products for which imports are banned. However, the imports of technology for these items can be allowed :

—if the technology is not freely available to enterpreneurs.

—if the technology aims at updating existing technologies or meet increased demand for goods.

—if the collaboration is aimed at boosting exports especially on buy back arrangements.

The normal conditions which a collaboration agreement has to meet include :

1. Freedom for Indian party to sub-license the knowhow/product design/engineering design.
2. Royality shouldn't normally exceed 5 per cent per annum of the actual production.
3. Guaranteed royalty agreements are not allowed.
4. Maximum period of agreement including the project stage of the foreign technology based manufacturing units is 10 years.
5. Procurement of capital goods, pricing policy, or any other restrictive clauses in transfer of technology are disallowed.
6. Free exports of technology should be allowed by the agreement.
7. Foreign brand names cannot be used in the domestic market.
8. Training arrangements, R & D arrangements engineering designs and other measures of absorption, adaptation and development are mandatory.
9. Indian consultancy firms should be preferred for consultancy services in the imported technology based project.
10. Lumpsum royality payment exceeding Rs. 5 millions is not allowed.

The approval of Government of India and Reserve Bank under FERA, 1973 is mandatory for all technological agreements. The import of capital goods and raw materials are subject to Export-Import Policy of the Government of India.

Summing Up

India has a fairly well developed governmental technological infrastructure to assist the industry. Number of schemes like STEP, Small Industry Service Institutions, TRYSEM and various modernisation schemes of Financial Institutions help technology upgradation. In keeping with Gandhian traditions, efforts are also on to popularise and elevate mass and intermediate technologies. The climate for import of technology is also turning favourable as the industrial base expands. The products and process developed in India keep on getting special protection. The S & T personnel trained in the best traditions of modern technology are available at reasonable salaries. The skilled manpower is expanding. India has a natural wealth which provides enormous raw materials. Mining and transportation are fairly well developed in India. With the commissioning of more and more power projects, the energy needs of the industry will also be matched by the end of the century. Non-conventional sources of energy including nuclear energy are also on the agenda of our plans. Right now, laboratory industry interaction is unsatisfactory but it is not due to the lack of initiative of scientific community but the mercantile background of our entrepreneurs and the craze for everything 'phoren' among our bureaucrats.

There are of course certain social taboos like cow-worship, caste divisions which inhibit the spread of scientific tember in our society and create hurdles in the ways of scientific and technological revolution. Our rulers, however, are fascinated by the possibilities of technology and in case, they are able to overcome the populist politics and a greed for making money in overseas deals, there is no reason why India should not be able to industrialise using the most modern as well as appropriate technologies. India is one of those underdeveloped countries which have a very diversified industrial economy and in fact, has started transferring technologies to the underdeveloped world. India has a lever in bargaining with the MNC's because due to its friendly relations with socialist world, it has an laternate source of supply for technology. USA, West Germany, USSR, U.K. and Japan remain the major technology suppliers to India but of late, the balance among the suppliers is shifting in favour of oriental countries like Japan. Hopefully, China will also emerge as a collaborator of significant proportion by the turn of the Century. It is well argued that technology arrangements between manpower surplus countries will be more meaningful. There are a large number of votaries in this country of technological cooperation among the developing countries.

Instead of inviting foreign investments the indigenous research in R & D units of locally controlled units needs to be encouraged. In this context, it is worthwhile to note that a recent UNCTAD study has pointed out that in 36 industries making significant investments in R & D, locally controlled firms spent a higher proportion for this purpose as compared to the foreign controlled firms. Technology imports through foreign investments, in fact, has a substitution effect on indigenous R & D. The rising tide of technology imports can only be means and not the end for achieving and sustaining technological competence in the long run. The governmental policy has to be geared to this premises and the imports of technology have to be regulated by allowing only purely technological collaboration which may become the basis of indigenous R & D on assimilation, adaptation and development of the imported technologies. Expansion of R & D sector shall generate more employment for our S & T manpower which will put brakes on the reverse transfer of technologies in the form of brain drain. Management of R & D personnel requires more flexible control methods because research is strongly individual oriented. The researcher is supposed to inject imagination, nurture creativity and innovation and thus requires freedom to act. Rational legal structures designed in business organisations on the pattern of bureaucracy deter creativity and limit the contribution of creative individuals. Mahajan and Sudarshan are right in maintaining, "The modern Indian science-technology student...is a pushy, ambitions, aggressive youngman". They further contend that "an average scientist in India is rather eager, even desperate, to come to the United States—and so give(s) credence to the charge that science is not done properly or done at all in India". They recommend proper working conditions to scientists in national laboratories and recommend a "leapfrog" rather than "follow the leader" approach for Indian science.

CASE III

BHEL-SIEMENS TECHNOLOGICAL AGREEMENT

BHEL is a public sector company, manufacturing power equipments, set up 25 years ago. It had entered into 64 technological collaborations, some times, involving repetitive technology transfers with various countries and five out of the seven top power generating equipment companies--in the world. But no other agreement, apart from the BHEL-SIEMENS agreement about manufacture of boilers for 500 MW thermal power generation sets raised a controversy in Parliament. The committee on Public Undertakings set up by the Sixth Lok Sabha brought the following features of agreement with the West German firm.

Whereas, the need was for an agreement for 500 MW sets, the agreement offered technologies for a package of products like the Transformers, Switchgears, Motors, Hydro Generator Sets of 200 MW condensers, Porcelain, etc., and systems engineering for power and industrial feeds.

The agreement was made for a period of 15 years and envisaged a payment of around Rs. 40 crores in Deustche Marks, a lumpsum payment in 10 years and a royalty of 1.8 per cent on the turnover, covered by the technical scope of the agreement.

The transfer of technology was to be mainly through documentation consisting of 7,50,000 pages and training of

BHEL personnel upto 1,800 man-months. Additional documentation or training that was required was to be paid for extra, subject to an escalation, the formula for which was not specified. Clarification of the documentation supplied by SIEMENS could be obtained only to the extent that the suppliers considered reasonable. The adoption of technology was the responsibility of BHEL and SIEMENS was not obliged to train BHEL personnel on this aspect of the technology. There was no penalty clause for the supplier in case the documentation/training was found inadequate in commissioning production based on the technology.

In addition, it was demanded by SIEMENS that BHEL should allow former a free access to all the technical knowhow developed by latter's R & D units and also the imported knowhow being used by the latter. In case BHEL was to enter into an agreement with a third party, such an agreement would have to take into account the objectives and interests of SIEMEN and its subsidiaries in India. BHEL was not allowed to compete with SIEMENS subsidiaries in India.

Sub-licensing based on the technology by BHEL was not allowed without extra payments to SIEMENS. The export rights of BHEL were also restricted.

BHEL went ahead with the agreement arguing that 500 MW sets were in great demand. But there was under-utilization of the already installed capacity and it is estimated that even if all the orders of the Seventh and Eighth Plans, *i.e.*, period 1985-95 in India were given to BHEL, is still couldn't mean more than 50 per cent utilization of capacity by BHEL. But the recent amendments in open General License List have included power generation equipment and BHEL is obliged to face global competition from foreign companies including that of the subsidiaries of SIEMENS.

POINT FOR CONSIDERATION

Was it wise on the part of BHEL to have gone for a technological tie up with SIEMENS ? Was it not sufficient for

BHEL to concentrate on production based on its acquired competence without any such unfair agreement?

ANNEXURE 1

ILLUSTRATIVE LIST OF INDUSTRIES WHERE NO FOREIGN COLLABORATION, FINANCIAL OR TECHNICAL, IS CONSIDERED NECESSARY

Source : (See Press Note No. : 9(19)/80-FC-I dated 25.5.1981 issued by Deptt. of Industrial Development, Ministry of Industry, Government of India).

1. Metallurgical Industries:

   Ferrous : Ordinary Castings, Bright Bars, Structural, Welded CI Steel Pipes and Tubes.

   Non-Ferrous : Antimony, Sodium Metal, Electrical Resistance Heating (nickel free alloy), Alluminium Litho plates.

2. Electrical Equipment :

   Electric fans, Common domestic appliances, Common types of winding wires and stripes, Iron clad switches, AC motors, Cables and Distribution transformers.

3. Electronic Components and Equipments :

   General purpose Transistors and Diodes, Paper, Mica and Variable Capacitors, T.V. Receivers, Tape Recorders, Teleprinters, P.A. Systems, Record Players/Changers.

4. Scientific and Industrial Instruments :

   Non-specialised types of valves, meters, weighing machinery and mathematical, surveying and drawing instruments.

5. Transportation :

   Railway wagons, bicycles.

6. Industrial Machinery :

   Building and constructional machinery, oil mill machinery,

conventional rice mill machinery, sugar machinery, tea processing machinery, general purpose machinery.

7. **Agricultural Machinery :**

   Tractor drawn implements, power tillers, foodgrain drivers, agricultural implements.

8. **Machine Tools :**

   Forged hand tools, general purpose machine tools.

9. **Miscellaneous Mechanical Engineering Industries.**

10. **Commercial, Office and Household Equipments of Common Use.**

11. **Medical and Surgical Appliances.**

12. **Fertilizers :**

    Single super phosphate, granulated fertilizers.

13. **Chemicals (other than Fertilizers) :**

    Acetic acid, acetanilide, ethylchloride, viscose filament yarn/staple fibre, melathion technical, sulphate of alumina, potassium chlorate, fatty acid and glycerine, butyl titanate, warfarin, silicagel, lindane, endosulfan, phanthoate, nitrofen, ethyl ether, plastipeel.

14. **Dyestuffs :**

    Benzidine, toludine, carbozole dioxazine violet pigment, cadmium sulphide orange.

15. **Drugs and Pharmaceuticals :**

    Caffeine (natural) ; phenyl butazone, tol butamide, para acetamel, phenacetin, senna extract, diasogenin, clofibrate, 4-hydrozy cumarin, xenthopotozin, calcium gluconate, choline chloride, glyceryl gualacolate, phenylethyl biguanide hydrochloride, scopolamine hydrobromide, niacinamide, ortholelyl biguanide, colchicine, diazepam, sorbitol from dextrose monothydrate, berberine hydrochloride, balladonna, acriflavin calcium hypophosphite, chlordiazepoxide.

16. Paper and Pump Including Paper Products.
17. Consumer Goods.
18. Vegetable Oils and Vanaspati.
19. Rubber Industries :

    Viscose tyre yarn, metal bonded rubber, latex foam, rubberised fabrics, bicycle tyres and tubes.

20. Leather, Leather Goods and Pickers :

    Belting-leather, cotton and hair finished leather, pickers, picking bands, vegetable tanning extracts, fat liquors other than synthetic.

21. Glass and Ceramics.
22. Cement and Gypsum Products.

Note : List is illustrative and not exhaustive. Clarification of details within the broad headings is the responsibility of Administrative Ministries.

FURTHER READINGS

1. Balaji, G., "Between Seylla and Charybids—Decision-making in Indian R & D", *The Economic Times*, December 29, 1988.

2. Beri, G.C., "Research and Development in Indian Industry", *The Economic Times*, December 29, 1988.

3. Chaturvedi, T.N., *Transfer of Technology Among Developing Countries*, New Delhi, Gitanjali Publishing House, 1982.

4. Department of Science and Technology, Government of India, *Research and Development Statistics*, New Delhi (Periodical).

5. Jain, Ashok and V.K. Gupta, "Management of R & D in India—An Overview", *Indian Management*, November, 1988.

6. Hienman, S.A., *Scientific and Technological Revolution, Economic Aspects*, Moscow, Progress Publishers, 1981.
7. Mahajan, S.M. and E.C.G. Sudarshan, "The Indian Scientist—Some Reflections", Chapter Three, Roach, James R. (Ed.), *India-2000*, New Delhi, Allied Publishers, 1987.
8. Rahman, A., and P.K. Chowdhari, *Science and Society*, New Delhi, Centre of R & D Management, CSIR, 1980.
9. Rohtagi, P.K., *et al.*, *Technological Forecasting*, New Delhi, Tata McGraw-Hill, 1979.

4

Social System in India

India is an ancient civilization. The social structure in the country is very complex. It has already been stressed that certain problems/situations in business organisations are only understandable in the light of social context. The process of industrialisation has a two way relationship with the society. The emergence of entrepreneurial class, workers behaviour in industrial organisations, industrial relations and consumer preferences all are dependent on the socio-cultural milieu obtaining in particular countries and particular periods of history. Industrialisation ushers in social changes but the impact of change may be delayed due to the deep-rooted traditions. Any manager has to understand the Indian psyche, social system and the institutions operating in our society.

Demographic Characteristics

India supports her 800 millions on a total land area of 2.4 per cent of this world. 3,000 Indians are born every hour despite family planning measures and add to the one sixth of the world population Population in India is growing at the rate of 2.13 per cent per year adding 16 millions people every year and by the end of millemium population may cross one billion mark. Thus India is richer in manpower rather than other natural resources. Birth rate per thousand is 33 at present and family planning measures aim to bring it down to 21 by the end of the Century. The death rate is about one third of the birth rate at present and is planned to slide down to 6.88

by the end of the Century. Density of population was 211 in 1981, Kerala having the highest of 654 and Sikkim the lowest of 44.

The size of labour force can be gauged from the age distribution. About 54.1 per cent were in the age group 15-60 in 1981 census. Female population constituted about 94 per cent of the male population. Thus in a labour force of around 43.5 crores, 21 crores are females. The literacy rate is 36.15 per cent about 47 per cent among males and 25 per cent among females. But the literacy rate among 39.5 per cent children is much higher as compared to the older people. On an average, only one out of four people in working population may be literate. Life expectancy of a child born in India is 54 years.

5.6 crore adults enter our labour market every year. Factory sector in India absorbs only 3 lakhs of these entrants annually. Rest have to seek jobs in service sector or agriculture. One third of our existing labour force in agriculture is already underemployed. The number of unemployeds registered in employment exchanges is around 35 millions but the actual unemployeds may be thrice the number. As such the level of consumption of daily calories is around 2,000 as compared to biological minimum of around 3,000. Government claims that the people below poverty line who were half the population by mid-Seventies have gone to 37 per cent by mid-Eighties and shall be reduced to one fourth by 1990.

All India Dept and Investment Survey of 1971-72 concluded that 70 per cent of rural households owned assets which were 1 per cent of rural assets. 4 per cent of rich households in rural India own 30 per cent of the total assets. The income statistics also reveal a similar picture. 90 per cent of the population in rural India has shared only one third of the total incremental income in the last forty years.

There are around 4,000 towns and around 6 lakhs villages in India. The urban population is about one/fourth of the total population. The rate of urbanisation may appear to be satisfactory because the urban population has increased from 15 per cent to 25 per cent during the last forty years. But the phenomenon of urbanisation is not directly related with development in India due to what is characterised as 'overurbanisation'. There is a shortage of housing in urban areas and about one fifth of the population lives in urban slums and is closely related with rural nexus they have. Thus there have been pauperisation rather than proletarianisation of potential industrial labour force after release from bondage of landlordism in rural areas. Overall, there is a shortage of 2.5 crore housing units in rural India and the shortage in urban areas is touching 0.4 crore mark. There are about 12 cities having a population above one million but most of these are having large slums.

Caste and Communalism in India

The sociologists have widely discussed the ethnic, communal and caste divide in Indian society. There are dominant castes and communities on the one hand and the lower castes, the backward classes and the dalits on the other. There is also a divide on religious, regional and language lines. Hinduism is the dominant religion of Indians, according for more than 80 per cent of the population. The next important religion is Islam with around 7.5 crores of adherents of this faith in the country. Besides, there are Christians, Sikhs, Buddhists, Jains and others. Hindus practise four rank Varna system based on the ancient social division of labour. *Brahmins* were teachers, religious guides and preachers. *Kshatriyas* were the rulers and warriors. *Vaishyas* were traders, businessmen and moneylenders and *Sudras* were assigned the menial jobs of producing material wealth as manual labour.

Alongwith caste divisions, an arrangement had been worked out in village communities to reward the artisan/service rendering segments of the community. This system was known as *Jajmani* in Northern India and *Baluta* system in Maharashtra. The system even extended to cultivation and there used to be *Jajman* cultivators, who sometimes, by tilling large areas emerged to be very powerful. Due to protection of hereditary occupation, this system resulted in confining certain skills only to artisan, priestly or service rendering castes. Though monetisation of economy has wrecked this social division of labour, rural industrialisation programmes have to reckon with *Jajmani* based distribution of skills among rural folk. Commodity production has brought into being a contractual relationship which makes service rendering castes free to move to urban areas. However, remnants of *Jajmani* still keep certain artisans tied to villages despite the fact that the remuneration for their services is poor and the technologies employed by them remain primitive.

The priestly class has been able to transfer the *Jajmani* system to traditionally unfamiliar domain which have resulted, in an unequal relationship between the donor and acceptor families in matrimonial alliances. In traditional business communities, the parents/family of daughter has gifted away even industrial establishments and the acceptor families have been, thus, initiated into business which was not their hereditary occupation. Shau jains matrimonial alliances with Dalmias who became *Jajmans* are the new manifestation of this system.

Dalits or scheduled tribes were normally outside the caste system and were maintained as a reserve army of labour to discipline *Sudras*. According to 1981 census, there are 10.48 crores scheduled castes and 5.16 crores scheduled tribes. With the passage of time the caste system has grown more complex. There are so called "backward classes" who are above *Sudras* in caste hierarchy but do not fall exactly in the first three hierarchical orders of caste. In fact, taken together with the scheduled caste/tribes, backward classes and minorities constitute the bulk of Indian population.

It is argued that caste and class overlap and at least two/third of manual labour comes from the under-privileged classes enumerated above. This is also the official rationalisation for reservations in education, state patronage and jobs on caste basis rather than following an economic basis. There is a statutory reservation of around one/third seats in academic institutions, jobs in the organised sectors and in disbursal of assistance by banks/financial institutions. Mandal Commission has recommended reservations for identified backward castes and in some states preferential treatment is given in some respects to these backward castes. Of late, the policy of reservations has become a main bone of contention among the socially mobile work-force in urban areas/organised sectors.

The social fabric of India is sought to be characterised, outing across the traditional formulations of class analysis or caste analysis. Articulate social observers like Rajni Kothari are talking in terms of 'two Indians' created due to the particular model of social change adopted in India. The divide is among those who have access to power and those who are marginalised due to a model of national building which tries to dissolve all diversities—social, political, regional and cultural, to create one great monolith. Among the marginalised sections, Kothari includes the poor, the untouchables, the tribals, the backward classes, the lower castes, religious or linguistic minorities and women. Another variant of model owes its origin to the rise of Kisan power which talks of rural and urban divide. Of course, there are other studies which point that cultural traditions of India may blend with the demands of industrialisation and may not prove a stumbling block. In fact, it is suggested that the rise of an entrepreneurial class in India is closely connected with caste divisions.

On weighing the merits and demerits of caste system, it appears that caste has been a big inhibiting factor in industrialisation and modernisation of Indian society. It obstructs the mobility and utility of labour and creates bottlenecks in creating a free labour market. Caste inhibitions deter the higher castes from taking to manual jobs. Due to the caste inhibitions, optimum productivity of human resources becomes impossible. Support system provided by the kinship and caste network gets limited to trading castes and the *Brahmins* and *Kashtriyas* still disdain the idea of making compromise of their cultural superiority of material prosperity. Thus the enterpreneurial strata narrows down. The theory of *karma* dictated by birth kills the initiative and enterprise.

The influence of cultural values based on caste system could be salutory effect on the social division of labour, handicrafts and cottage industry but it is certainly detrimental to the development of modern business organisations based on detailed division of labour. The human resources drawn from caste-based societies are bound by the kinship ties which keeps them clinging to their traditional indentities and they donot internalise the organisational, secular or democratic culture. Universal outlook needed by the business systems operating in such a diverse society as India is also hindered because tradition outweighs the needs for modernisation of outlooks, attitudes and aspirations. Hierarchical structure based on caste in the society interferes with the organisation structures of modern business and makes the latter dysfunctional.

Caste and community divisions endanger the social stability of India. Communal and caste riots coupled with the ethnic and linguistic crises disturb the normal economic and business activities. Moreover, caste may impose restrictions on consumption habits of the adherents of the system and may restrict the industrial market. The participation of womenfolk in industrial labour force or professions is also adversely affected by the caste and community based value system. Happily, however, industrialisation and the growth of the tertiary sector in Indian economy has made some dent on traditional social fabric of the society and it is hoped that by the turn of Century when education and industry spread, the caste barriers will start crumbling.

Occupational Structure in India

The labour supply in an economy depends on the labour force, participation rate and number of people who are willing to work and the skill levels of the workers. In India there is around 24.46 crores working population available. Of these about 73.45 lakhs are working in factories. 77 lakhs are working in household industries. Main workers who are engaged for at least 183 days of productive activity are 22.25 crores. Of these, more than 68 per cent are engaged in agriculture as peasants or cultivators. If we also include marginal workers 70.6 per cent of working population is engaged in the primary sector, 12.9 per cent are employed in the secondary sector and 16.5 per cent in the tertiary sector. The percentage break up of population's employment has undergone a negligible change since 1901. In other words, the structure of the society seems to have undergone only a marginal change over last eighty years.

Organised sector accounts for about 2.5 crore workers forming about 10 per cent of the total working population. Of This 70 per cent of organised sector employment is on account of the public sector. In large establishments of private sector employment is, in fact, going down. In the governmental sector also disproportionate growth of the services sector is the major source of employment. Thus productive secondary sector has ceased to be a source of creating employment.

Unemployment statistics talks of the occupational preferences of the labour force. The educational and skill levels of working population are increasing but the employment available is not commensurate with their qualifications. About 10 crore pupils are receiving primary education, 2.5 crores stay till the middle stage, 50 lakhs receive secondary education and about 30 lakhs get higher education/technical/professional training. As per the registration on employment exchanges around 4.5 per cent of job seekers are either professionally or technically trained. Clerical or related services are preferred by around 5 per cent. Production workers are around 8 per cent. About 37 per cent of job seekers are either illiterate or have studied below matric and about 43 per cent have general education of graduation or above.

According to the Economic Census carried out in 1979-80, there were 183.6 lakh enterprises in India (except Assam). These employed 536.7 lakh persons. Among these enterprises 92 per cent were non-agricultural. Rural areas accounted for 61 per cent of the total enterprises. Hired workers in these enterprises were numbering around 290 lakhs which constituted 54 per cent of total employment. Thus wage labour is spreading even in the unorganised sectors.

From the discussion reported above, it is obvious that there is an ample supply of skilled as well as unskilled manpower in India. The productive sectors are not expanding fast enough to absorb the job seekers. The pressure for employment seems to be low on account of very low participation rate of women workers in wage labour. Only 16 per cent of rural women workers and 7.3 per cent of their urban counterparts participate in organised production or work in the service sectors. The dimensions of unemployment can be estimated from this fact, if all the women in age group 15.60 opt for work, there will be at least 15 crores more job seekers. Right now, these women are engaged in household jobs. The irony of situation, however, is that whereas such a large number of adults is unable to participate in work, child labour is not uncommon in India.

Per capita income in our country is increasing at a slow pace because only a few adults in the households are able to gainfully employ themselves. A *per capita* income of Rs. 711 as reported in 1985 is not sufficient for subsistence. So on the consumption front, the market which could be 80 crores million units shrinks due to non-availability of purchasing power. Capital intensive production is not a solution to the Indian employment problem, production has to be relatively labour intensive. But the latter calls for less sophisticated technologies and protection of traditional modes of production which may keep the occupational structure intact.

Joint Family System

Veteran sociologist IP Desai characterises that household as a joint family where more than two generations are living and the members are linked to each other by property, income and mutual rights and obligations. The modern urban or so called western nuclear family with only the parents and their non-adult children living together, is a relatively new phenomenon on Indian social scene. In fact, going by the tradition, the private property in means of production like land, capital, etc., are owned by what is characterised in law as a Hindu undivided family.

Joint family in India consists of grandparents, uncles—male offshoots of the family tree and their children of both sexes. The spouses of the males in the family tree are also a part of the joint family, besides the widowed and destitute adult female offshoots of the family. Normally, the family has a head (*karta*) who manages the wealth and income generated by the earning group of joint family members. Till the joint family holds together it uses the socialist principle of communal living 'from everyone according to his capacities to each one according to his needs'. There is a common residence, a common kitchen and the household work is divided among the family members, according to their ages and physical health. Generally, the members of a joint family believe in the same religion, observe similar ceremonies, festivities and adhere to the same customs and traditions. Respect for age is the cardinal principle on the basis of which such a productive unit operating agricultural or non-agricultural enterprises operates.

Joint family system has served Indian society well. In absence of state security, accidental deaths, premature diseases affecting the parents of non-adult children do not result in serious dislocations in the living of children. In a poor country like India, the families living on small plots of land or trading units are able to enjoy economies of scale for ensuring their subsistence level existence. The family responsibilities are shared according to the abilities of the member and one need not be master of all household responsibilities. In richer families enterprising youth are supported by their elders in building up new economic ventures. The concept of business house, the predominant form of apex business organisation in Indian private sector depends upon the joint family system. Sometimes, when the business empires expand the distant cousins and people in the kinship or caste network are also entrusted the responsibility of managing common property. Though the juridical forms of business may be companies or partnerships, in essence the closely knit joint family or extended kinship network manages a large number of business entities in prosperous households.

Joint family as an institution has checked the fragmentation of agricultural holdings and similarly the accumulated capital with prosperous families has been used in establishing large factory systems or trading networks. But it is being complained now that joint family kills initiative, inhibits personality development, denies privacy and becomes a home for idlers. This institution is also held responsible for unhappy homelives, uncontrolled procreation and population increase. It gives birth to the phenomenon of concentration of economic power and checks the professionalisation of Indian business. Family based houses in India are breaking. Dwajindera Tripathi reports the recent cases of Birlas, Mafatlals, Singhanias, Sarabhais, Shrirams, Goenkas, Bangurs, Modis, Thackersays and Morarjees succumbing to family divisions. Even lesser luminaries like the Piramals, Khataus, Amins, Kamanis, Morarkas, Jaipurias, Podars and Malhotras have fallen prey to this process of disintegration of joint families.

Industrialisation with developed means of transport and telecommunication may be bringing closer co-operation among village communities but is resulting in disruption of joint family as an institution. Decline of agricuture and trade as only occupation, spread of education and the increasing realisation of drudgery of household work coupled with western influences of egalitarianism among sexes have resulted in disintegration of joint families in urban area and emergence of nuclear families.

This phenomenon of nuclear families has opened enormous opportunities for new type of products. Normally husbands and wives living as a nuclear family are working and thus female participation in socially productive work has gone up. The household functions of cooking, washing and clothing are getting transferred to factory systems. Market for readymade entertainment, garments and foods has gone up. New electrical appliances and convenience goods are no longer luxuries in middle class households living as nuclear families. Demand for pressure cookers, gas stoves, refrigerators, automobiles, audiovisual entertainment, telephones, washing machines, vacuum cleaners, packed, fast and instant foods, convenience washing materials and readymade wear has gone up among middle class households.

Emergence of Middle Class

One of the consequences of our model of economic development is the emergence of a large segment of society which is loosely defined as middle class. The expansion of service sector in our economy and the protections granted to traders as well as rich or middle peasants in rural India, has created an intermediate strata in the society which neither can be described as ruling class or the underprivileged. These are people whose household income ranges from Rs. 20,000 per annum to Rs. 5 lakhs per annum. The number of such beneficiaries of the present regime is a few crores and in fact, our policy planners rather than talking of ameliorating the lot of poor are claiming from housetops that India will enter the 21st Century with a 10 crores large middle class. A few crores or ten crores is a sizeable number and if purchasing power is available with such large numbers, the demand constraints on Indian industry can be reduced to a very large extent. The products which we enumerated as the needs of nuclear families can be bought only by the middle class family. This segment of population of India is larger than many developed countries of the west and as such the domestic demand for goods of Indian business is going to expand, if the middle class keeps on growing.

On the supply side, the new stress on entrepreneurial development to reduce the pressure of educated unemployeds relies on recruiting the largest possible numbers from the middle classes for setting up new business units. Right now this segment of society consists of professionals, employees of organised sector, rich peasants and small traders. They provide the best possible education to their own wards and if self employment ventures are not provided to these educated youngmen and women, the strategy of developing a still larger middle class shall not work. It is with this view that financial and training inputs are being provided to increasing number of educated unemployeds. It is this very middle class which will also become the basis of information revolution and computerisation. The probability of such a scheme of co-opting middle classes into the ruling elite requires a very carefully designed strategy which has to guard itself against the anger of proletarianised or pauperised mass of Indians.

Socio-Cultural Trends

While managing business in India, we should be aware that though a single national market, India is a multinational country. Religion has a strong grip on the minds of people and our secularism is skin-deep. Even in conducting business affairs, our caste, communal or regional prejudices come to the fore. Scientific temper is not prevalent even among our educated elite. They eat, drink and dress as per the religious taboos or supernatural beliefs. Caste origins prevent some people from undertaking non-traditional professions. Business is still treated to be a preserve of *Vaishyas* or *Vanias* despite entries into various business lines by people from non-traditional castes. Material prosperity is not considered all that important and the philosophy of contentment blunts the achievement motivation of an average Indian.

Women are treated badly by their male counterparts and heavy dowries in matrimonial alliances are not uncommon. Though women are not treated to be equal partners in their parents' income, sometimes, factories are handed over as dowries. Quarrels in joint families can put the functioning of well run business establishments in jeopardy. Caste or kinship networks invade work places. Informal groups come into being on the regional or caste basis. Indian worker is the first generation factory worker and is not able to develop work commitment expected out of him. It is contended by a few sociologists that Indians are more loyal to their primary groups like caste and family than to their organisation. Alongwith modernising influences of industrialisation a process of Sanskritisation is going on in the Indian society. Secularism, democratic living have become a part of our society at a very superficial level only. Paternalistic or authoritarian social structures are more prevalent and our sectarian prejudices refuse to die even in factory or urban sort of settings. In fact, irrational rituals which were till early of this Century confined to only high castes are taking roots among *Shudras*. The religious fundamentalism among these productive but ill-educated castes assumes dangerous proportions as was witnessed in November riots of 1984 in Delhi. Even the tribes and *dalits* regard the religious orthodoxies, limited to high castes till recent times, as a sign of civilization.

A number of religion based organisations have come up in the country which are creating social strife and even the political stability of Indian union is threatened. All these seemingly remotely connected phenomenon have a direct bearing on management of business, as any businessman in Punjab can vouch for. Migration of labour from rural areas to urban areas and inter-state migrations, is another social phenomenon which we are witnessing in India. Though normally studies on migrants after partition of India have shown that they have flourished in business and brought material prosperity for their new habitats yet the social tension which this phenomenon creates is detrimental to smooth functioning of the regional economies. The interference of churches of various religions in social life of India also undermines the authority of the state and rule of law. Such chaotic conditions may not be conducive to the smooth functioning of any economic entity. Industrial relations are also governed by the wider socio cultural currents.

It is very difficult to encapsule all the social problems of India except observe that India is a country of social contrasts and every articulate manager has to be very receptive to social trends in such a volatile society where people are starving to death. The so-called welfare state keeps on talking of a number of social welfare programmes but the advantages of these programmes do not reach the poorest. The rates of crime, starvation, death, epidemics and natural disasters are alarming and

Indian society is, sometimes, characterised as a functioning anarchy.

Business in India till date is not very responsive to social obligations. The Union Carbide tragedy, however, stirred the masses in India, and a strong environmental movement is emerging. The popular pressure has forced the government to enact anti-pollution laws. The non-governmental organisations are resisting commercial felling of trees or wreckless mining of minerals for providing raw materials to industry. Similarly, supply of substandard quality of consumer items which was the normal practice in the Indian market is no longer all that easy. Though, there are no Ralph Nadars in India, yet, consumer movement has made a beginning. Restrictive trade practices and adulteration of edible products are being resisted by many voluntary consumer organisations.

Workers on their own have gone very conscious of their rights. The Gandhian model of trusteeship which guided the trade union movement till the early half of the Twentieth Century no longer stays as a dominant current of workers' movement. More militant trade union centres like Centre of Indian Trade Unions (CITU), All India Trade Union Congress (AITUC), Hind Mazdoor Sabha (HMS) have emerged to discard the class-collaborationist tactics of INTUC (Indian National Trade Union Congress) and BMS (Bhartiya Mazdoor Sangh). As a result of disillusionment with the pro-management and pro-government stance of all India trade unions, some local trade unions have been formed by Chrismatic leaders like Datta Samant which are making irresponsible demands. It is the latter set of trade unions which resulted in long-drawn strikes in Western India. Some regional and chauvinistic forces have also entered the industrial relations scene with demands like "sons of soil" oriented employment policy. The rise of middle classes is demanding professional, non-proprietory management based on specialised training rather than proprietory heritage based succession prevalent in Indian big business. The large companies like Reliance are so widely held that around one million Indian shareholders have invested in the company. Under such circumstances, ownership and control shall be automatically divorced. It will be difficult to perpetuate the control of promoters, if the shareholder activism gains ground in India. Annual General Meetings of the general body of shareholders in many companies are no longer rituals and the passive shareholders are making their presence felt. Similarly, professional management bodies like All India Management Association have evolved their own codes of conduct and professional managers refuse to toe the line of owning families. The complaints voiced by the traditional businessmen against products of management schools or MBAs owe their origin to the conflict between the values of the owner and the managers.

Traders, white collar workers and government officials are the other sections of society with whom business has a direct interface. On the margin, however, are the teeming millions of India who will keep on exerting pressure for growth with social justice. The anti-colonial anti-monopoly sentiment among Indians is rooted in the freedom movement and the big business and multinationals may not find business climate in India very hospitable.

Culture Ethos and Work Culture

India is a society in transition. Its oriental character tempts experts on cross-cultural studies to present models of human behaviour based on the predominant cultural ethos of Indian society. Recently, P. Singh and Asha Bhandarkar have advanced such a model based on seven cultural components of Indian psyche. Their basic propositions can be stated as follow :

(a) Need for a father figure presists with Indians even in their work places. This is based on the institution of *karta* in a joint family. In case the leaders in the organisational settings are able to project a *karta* like image, they can extract meaningful and purposeful superior/subordinate relationships by developing cohesive teams. This generates respect for powers of the superiors, if the latter are able to protect the interests of subordinates. The authority of superiors can be willingly accepted and most Indians may come forth to help the *karta* type superiors in attainment of the organisational/departmental interests. Negatively, if the boss is not able to behave as *karta* of joint family, it results in inadequate collective behaviour, with power games in which informal leaders from cliques and play their power games to challenge the formal bosses. Formal authority is challenged and supported is not extended to the boss which results in de-empowering behaviour and revolt against him.

(b) From the Indian experience of a longer childhood and more close family interactions, based on early close and intimate relationships in a joint family, the normal Indian likes to develop intimate relations even in his organisational life. In case such relationships can be fostered, cohesive work teams come into being and integration of individual's goals with the organisational goals becomes easier. This manifests in mutual understanding and respect among peers as well as smoother superior-subordinate interactions. Feelings of empathy towards colleagues and a sympathetic approach substitutes formal task-oriented behaviour. As opposed to this impersonal, informal role allocations are not able to breed intimacy. The formation of informal groups based on extra-organisational identities of language or region come into play. In industrial relations scene also the 'we' versus 'they' relationships come into being, resulting in confrontations and increased organisational conflicts.

(c) Respect of age and experience results in close weaving of knowledge with the on-the-job expertise. Thus different age groups or generations in the organisational hierarchy are able to function in harmony, in case the aged and experienced are able to create confidence among new recruits. Negatively, this value system promotes the seniority criteria of reward systems and ignores merit. Over-reliance on superiors, unquestioning loyalty to aged superiors and resentment against younger superiors, regardless of their merit are the various manifestations of these beliefs.

(d) Hero-worship or treating superiors as models of behaviour is also a childhood training and helps in smooth maintenance of hierarchical organisational structures for maintaining the power balance in organisations. But this may blunt creativity of individuals, building of teams, may be inhibited due to lack of delegation of powers and responsibility sharing. This respect for hierarchy may also result in lack of delegation of powers and responsibility sharing. This respect for hierarchy may also result in lack of achievment motivation among organisational members because low deviance and despise for rebellion are the valued traits among the employees.

(e) Security needs, of those reared in joint families and kinship networks, are high These may lead to bureaucratisation of organisation through risk avoidance and maintenance of the system based on passing the buck to elders. It may breed parasitism because the superiors are accepted uncritically and are required to handle all the tricky situations in decision making.

(f) Experiences of a self-sacrificing *karta* also bread the value of living by ideals. It may lead to comparative calm in organisations due to low ego and vanity problems. But the idealist values which an individual cherishes may become difficult to be accommodated in business organisations which have material pursuits.

(g) The psychology of entitlement is based on mutuality and reciprocity of obligations between various members of a family but since such families require only a few to sacrifice, this value has resulted in a psychology of craving for entitlements or rewards unrelated with the performance of members. Earning overtimes is a fashion with Indian workers and a general feeling exists among them that they are entitled to more than they are getting. This breeds uncalled for dissatisfaction among the organisational members.

These generalisations seem to be based on a rather personalised experience of the authors P. Singh, *et al.*, Besides the joint family system, which is treated as the basis of this cultural ethos, is not able to withstand the pressures of modernisation. The existence of the value system associated with joint family is also idealised. The value systems vary among religious groups, caste and community groups, regions or urban/rural residential status of the organisational members. The variety of Indian life is underplayed by enunciation of such a presentation of homgenised cultural ethos of Indians. M N. Srinivas cautions such analyses by reminding that "India...has a long way to go before its myriad castes, (creeds), communities, and ethnic groups are transformed into an integrated nation". But even "an integrated will not result in cultural homogenization for it must be repeated that India is and remains a multilingual, multireligious, multiethnic and multicultural country...". It may be pointed out the wave of Westernisation implying borrowing and imitating the aliens is still in evidence in India. Modernisation wave as a creative response to the problem of building on the great traditions of Indian society, to meet the needs of contemporary times is still weak and Indians are still "living in a revolution". Even the modern Indian godmen like Rajneesh combine Freudiad psychoanalysis with the vedic knowledge to propagate the ideal of our culture.

CASE IV

MANAGEMENT CULTURE OF BIRLAS

To keep the cogs of their ever-growing empire running Birlas are being forced to abondon the "referral system", the key to their management culture. Birlas have not only built a business empire, they have helped many Birla executives, especially Marwaris, develop satellite business groups like that of Saboos, Mandelias, Khaitans, Murarkas, Hadas and Kejriwals. Shared cultural values of Marwaris makes Birla executives a family. Once a person's loyalty is tested in the business, he is helped not only to rise in management hierarchy, his family members are also allowed to get employment with Birlas.

For every male member of Birla family, a new company is floated and three to four generations of Birlas have been manning top management positions of various Birla companies, rest of the companies are managed by the business associates. A Marwari, especially one hailing from within a small radius of Pilani, is favoured for recruitment to supervisory or management cadres of Birla family. Promotions are, however, strictly made on loyalty and merit determined by the financial integrity and acceptance of a principle of accountability displayed by the recruit. On the authority of Herdeck and Piramal, we quote Aditya Birla, one of the top functionaries of Birla group : "It is true, however, that the largest number (of managers) is of Marwaris. It is natural...there is an affinity and I will never feel embarrassed or compromised if there are more Marwaris... Is there any group which does not have more people of its own community ?"

Justifying and praising the paternalistic style of management practised by Birlas, a senior executive of the Century Mills, is quoted by the same authors.

"Working with Birlas, one gets extensive experience which one can use to help one's children. Working in such a tough environment, I know the available opportunities. Besides, over the years, influential trade contacts are made which can be utilised very profitably. Further may presence can get him (his ward) into the organisation, but he has to work his way up. He cannot automatically get may seat."

POINTS FOR CONSIDERATION

(1) Do you feel that Birlas are making the best use of

Indian Social Environment in managing their business ? Don't you think that management culture of Birlas is akin to Japanese ?

(2) 20 cases of major business splits have been reported with the disintegration of joint family system during 1970-87. In face of this evidence do you think that family based management has a future in India ?

FURTHER READINGS

1. Dube, S.C., *Indian Village*, London Routledge and Kegan Paul, 1953.
2. Ghurye, G.S., *Caste and Class in India*, Bombay, Popular Book Depot, 1957.
3. Hofstede, G., *Culture's Consequences : International Difference in Work-related Values*, Beverly Hills, Sage, 1980.
4. Kothari, Rajani, "Class and Communalism In India", *Economic and Political Weekly*, Vol. XXIII, No. 49, December 3, 1988.
5. Kuppuswamy, B. (Revised by Ravinder Kumar), *Social Change in India*, New Delhi, Vani Educational Books, 1986.
6. Menon, Narayana, "Traditional Culture, New Mediums, Interaction and Diffusion", Roach, Jame R. (Ed.), *India 2000—The Next Fifteen Years*, New Delhi, Allied, 1987.
7. Singh, P. and Asha Bhandarkar, "Cultural Ethos in the Organisational Milieu", *Indian Management*, October, 1988.
8. Srinivas, M.N., "On Living in a Revolution", Roach, Jame R. (Ed.), *op. cit.*
9. Subramaniam, V., *Managerial Class of India*, New Delhi, All India Management Association, 1971.

5
Business and Political System in India

India has borrowed the Westminster model of Parliamentary democracy. In fact, the India Act of 1915 and Government of India Act 1935 enacted by the Britishers were legislations which are the legitimate forerunners of the Indian Constitution. The Preamble of Indian Constitution secures to its citizens social, economic and political justice, liberty of thought, expression, belief, faith and worship, equality of status and opportunity and to promote among all fraternity assuring the dignity of the individual and the unity of the nation.

Fundamental Rights and Business Management

Possessive individualism was initially the philosophy behind Indian Citizen's Fundamental Rights but latter amendment to the right to property coupled with the directive principles of state policy make India a social democracy. A close scrutiny of fundamental rights in relation to functioning of business shows that Indian rights are not a carbon copy of the British model.

The word 'person' used in the right to equality in Article 14 also includes legal and juristic persons and, thus, business concerns when these are created under laws of land also become 'persons' in their capacity as artificial citizens. By allowing reasonable classification, Article 14 provides opportunity of protection to minors in contract and the equality of sexes is the ground under which Articles 15 and 16 provide for the same working conditions for women employees in factory employment. The provision of reservation of certain trades and services for the government is also an exception to the right to equality.

Similarly, right against discrimination does not prevent the government in providing reservations to scheduled castes/tribes, backward classes and even accord protective discrimination to women and children. The right to equality of opportunity, except a few exceptions, mentioned above makes it obligatory for private business and public services as not to discriminate on basis of sex, race, caste or place of birth. To bring the *shudras* and *dalits* in mainstream of public life and work-force, abolition of untouchability has been pronounced as a Fundamental Right.

Freedom of expression grants the advertising and marketing of commodities but restrictions can be placed on fraudulent claims made through these exercises of freedom of expression. Criminal or immoral activities or business infringing on other fundamental rights are not allowed under the freedom of profession, trade or business. In fact, Article 19(6) provides certain restrictions on free pursuit of these economic activities stipulated in Article 19(1)(g). Payment of minimum wages stipulated by the State cannot be construed as a violation of this right because reasonable restrictions can be placed by law on freedom of business. All Indians can carry on business in any part of the country. Workers, consumers, managers, suppliers or employers can form associations and unions. They can also take recourse to peaceful assemblies to get their grievances redressed under Right to Freedom.

Right against Exploitation has direct bearing on industrial relations scene. Article 27 specially forbids employment of children below the age of 14 years in factories, mines or any other hazarduous work. Religious sentiments shouldn't be hurt by conduct of any business. Beef processing can be a lucrative business but is not undertaken widely Minorities are guaranteed special rights of education and culture. Ultimately, in case of infringement of fundamental rights any citizen is free to move the Supreme Court.

The most controversial part of Indian Fundamental Rights is the 44th Amendment of 1978 whereby Right to Property was omitted from chapter on fundamental rights and was turned into a legal right. In fact, this amendment changed the character of Indian polity, at least constitutionally. Right to Property is the most sacrosanct right in the free market societies. This also altered the nature of our mixed economy and restricted the freedom of business. In essence, in India the freedom of business has been curtailed to an extent where the Democles' sword of nationalisation keeps on hanging over the head of private business. However, as we shall discuss later this threat is illusory rather than being real and businessmen have carried on their business, as before, by building up a proper rapport with the legislature and the executive.

Directive Principles of State Policy

The discussion on Fundamental Rights has made it abundantly clear that Indian state is not a silent spectator in free play of market forces. Realizing the economic problems that we are faced in India due to historical exploitation by alien rulers, the governments in Independent India had no option but to mediate the economic forces in the underdeveloped economy. The Directive Principles are, in fact, guidelines for the governments to conduct their affairs. In other words, they are imperative basis of state policy and public policy making in India draws inspiration from these principles. We list here the Directive Principles which have a bearing on the functioning of economy and micro-level economic institutions :

(1) All institutions of the national life should be geared towards equality and the government shall try to create conditions to minimise inequalities in income and wealth among its citizens.

(2) Common good shall be the guiding principle of economy and rather than concentrating wealth, property be distributed as to provide means of livelihood and equal wages for equal work.

(3) The State shall provide protective laws for workers, children, women and other worker sections. Proper working conditions, minimum wages, participation in management shall be secured for the working class.

(4) Environmental protection, education facilities for all and regard for religious sentiments like, ban on cow slaughter and restriction on harmful drugs and drinks are other provisions which may have implications for the functioning of business.

Interpretation of the Directive Principles has changed over time. Adherence to these is not as mandatory as the Fundamental Rights is. Abolition of fundamental right to property and an emphasis on distributional aspects in the functioning of economy make Indian union a welfare State. Right to property is only a legal right.

Though, the preamble of Indian Constitution declares that India is a Sovereign Socialist, Secular, Democratic Republic yet, the word 'socialist' shouldn't be taken too seriously especially when directive principles are the guidelines. Right to private property in means of production is not denied as is the case of socialist society. Private initiative and private enterprise have ample scope in India, if an influence can be generated on public policy making by the pressure groups of Indian businessmen.

Centre-State Relations

India is a union of states and the legislative as well as taxation powers are shared between the central and state governments. India is a country of wide heterogeneities, as such federalism has been enshrined in a constitution which, in essence, is unitary. Most of the vital economic activities are included in List I of Schedule VII which gives enormous powers to the Centre. The List II of the Schedule empowering States of the union include primary sector and service sector related activities, social welfare measures and public utilities are in the concurrent List III. List I includes activities like banking, insurance, stock exchanges, oil exploration, mineral explorations and all industries in defence and public interest, Import and export business and setting up of corporations. These are under the control of Central government, only residual powers with regard to manufacturing and mining sectors accrue to the States in the activities listed in List II. The concurrent List III again includes important economic activities especially the distributional aspects in the economy and here also the Centre normally has more powers than the States. Some of the entries in three lists are overlapping. Parliament has an effective control over manufactures and products of the industry whereas the supply of raw materials is largely a responsibility of the States. In essence, in the matter of economic and industrial regulation, Centre has the supremacy.

In taxation powers, taxes on income, wealth and other direct taxes are levied by the Centre, similarly MODVAT the tax on production is also levied by the Centre and prices for essential commodities are also fixed by the Centre. The States as well as the Centre can impose sales taxes. Custom duties are fixed by the Centre. The sharing of taxes between Centre and States is decided by the respective Finance Commissions appointed by the Central government. Various commentaries on public finance suggest that Finance Commissions in recent years have ignored the claims of the States and the distribution of resources is not commensurate with the increasing responsibilities of States. Centre also provides grants-in-aid but the Central Bank has gone very strict, on overdrafts by the State governments.

Though lip-service is paid to balanced regional development, the Indian Constitution stays unitary in character. The trend towards centralisation has gained ascendency after 1967. Despite creation of an Institution of National Development Council (NDC) in which States were adequalely represented, the planning for industrialisation has continued to be a spatial in character. The role of Central government has grown in spatial spread of industries. Even the regional pressure groups of business have to influence the public policy at the Centre. The so-called backward area industrialisation effort doesn't succeed due to inability of new business in generating necessary influence at the Centre in competition with big business. The Central public financing agencies have failed miserably in promoting balanced regional growth of industry.

Ashok Mitra one of the leading authorities on Centre State relations bemoans existing situation about resource mobilisation and devolution, in wake of Non-Congress (I) ministries coming to power in States. He makes a plea for mutuality and reciprocity in making resources available at both the levels. He also suggests decentralisation of resource devolution as well as mobilisation. What obtains is, however, "a piquant situation ; the Centre feels free to interfere into the spheres of resource raising which according to the Constitution, are the prerogative of the States, but is not willing to listen to the counsel of the States on matters which, while formally belonging to the Central list, deeply affect the interest of the States." At the time of appointing Ninth Finance Commission, it was suggested by some authorities on Public finance that there should be representative of the States on the Commission. Sarkaria Commission has done precious little about imbalances in attitudes of the Centre or States towards each other. In fact, the present government has come forth with its own brand of decentralisation by suggesting District Collector's office as the grassroots unit for decentralised development administration. The States are not satisfied with the arrangement of entrusting bureaucrats with the responsibilities which legitimately belong to elected representatives in democratic politics. Business has to closely monitor the demand for economic federalism and State autonomy, it has serious implications for micro-level management.

Chambers of Commerce and Industry

It is only in the context of generating influence on public

policy that the functioning of various chambers of commerce like Federation of Indian Chambers of Commerce and Industry (FICCI) and ASSOCHAM (Associated Chambers of Commerce) has to be understood. These chambers came into being as pressure groups of business and trade in a pluralistic model of liberal democratic polity. Stanley Kochanack has outlined the close co operation between FICCI, the pressure group of native business and Indian National Congress. This chamber was dominated by Marwaris and G.D. Birla was the moving spirit behind this group G.D. Birla had developed very good rapport with Indian National Congress and its leaders like Mahatma Gandhi and Jawaharlal Nehru. The growth of Birla house is, partly, attributed to this collaboration of the Birlas with the ruling party. Birlas were able to corner many licenses for themselves in diverse product lines, thus, pre emptying new entries in many industries. FICCI, stood for protective tariffs in favour of native business to keep the MNC's away from national market.

Associated Chamber of Commerce, in contrast, was a chamber representing more professional groups like Tatas and MNC's and, in fact, had better understanding with the Britishers than with the leadership of Indian National Congress during freedom movement. Traditionally, this chamber has advocated an open economy, as contrasted with FICCI's consistent crusade for protective tariffs. But one feature which both the chambers are united on is the support for a strong Centre because they are led by Pan-Indian big business. At the time of budget or plan making the representatives of both these chambers are invited. As the keen observers of Indian bussiness scene must have observed that so close is the nexus between chambers of commerce and the ruling party at the Centre, that recent eclips of FICCI and emergence of ASSOCHAM as dominant chamber is, partly, responsible for the regime of economic liberalisation in the recent times.

In fact the chambers do not represent the interests of all their members because business community in India is "far too plural, heterogenous and insufficiently mobilised to articulate a consistent set of class interests and values". Around 15 millions trading organisations, representing around one tenth of India's population, could find it more convenient to deal with the local/state level administrative structures. But the chambers have been able to mobilise their support in favour of the organised manufacturing sector. Similarly, around 14 thousand small scale units may also be votaries of devolution of resources to the states and decentralisation of political power but since the powers of reserving items for small sector lies with the centre, their organisations like the Federation of Association Small Industries of India (FASII) also joins the Pan-Indian big business in making a demand from strong Centre.

In such circumstances, "the industrial elite composed of India's large family controlled houses......has played the politically most prominent role" and for maintaining their monopoly positions, they depends upon their capacity to check the growth of a polycentric industrial regulation machinery. The existence of public sector units in infrastructural industries like Indian Railways also demands that such all-India undertakings be controlled by the Centre. Hence the Indian Constitution makers who had developed close co-operation with the Indian business have provided for a Constitution which is only federal in form but unitary in character. However, the regional pulls and pressures have been so strong in recent times that our ruling elite has been forced to do some rethinking on the question of State autonomy. Sarkaria Commission report makes a half hearted plea for more power to the States for a more balanced regional development.

Despite loud pronouncements and some populist politics which made Indian National Congress appear a multi-class party, the party, essentially, stands for protecting interests of the big business and landed interests. This coalition of essentially antagonistic classes is a product of our freedom movement, as discussed in Chapter on business history. Though the expansion of Indian market depends or radical redistribution of agricultural assets, especially through land reforms, the Indian National Congress has not been able to keep its promises made during the freedom struggle. The "economic miracles" of Japan and South Korea are partly on account of strict enforcement of land reforms and creation of a domestic market. In India, the chambers of commerce have been consistently demanding land reforms for activating the large Indian market but have been forced to revert to the supply-side economics due to reluctance of Indian National Congress in obliging them. As already discussed, Directive Principles of state policy have enabled Central government to play a very active role in regulating, supporting, promoting and starting business in the manufacturing sector of Indian economy.

The interventionist role of Centre and the ability of Indian Congress to retain power at the Centre has compelled the Indian business elite to fall in line with Congress policies of compromising with feudal and, sometimes, overseas business interests. "The political role of the industrial elite has been inhibited by its relative size, internal divisions, and the hegemonic role of public sector, but also by lack of ideological legitimacy" and a position dependent on the much larger agricultural sector and state machinery. During the freedom struggle, emerging business class had established close links with the dominant leaders including the Congress socialists. "Finance provided some leverage but it couldn't be translated into automatic influence" because mass support for the movement came from peasantry, working people and even some princes.

Election Process and Indian Business

Parliamentary democracy of the Indian type is a very expensive exercise for a poor country like India. During the debates on electoral reforms in recent times, state-funding of elections was debated but the ruling party was not in favour of such a measure. The talk of ceilings on expenditures incurred in contesting elections for the Parliament and legislatures is largely a paper exercise. After the 1957 general elections, the election costs have risen very fast. Whereas 1957 elections had cost, a paltry, Rs. 2.5 crores to the contessants and parties contesting the elections, the cost soared up to around Rs. 60 crores by

1967 and some estimates suggest that the cost of elections to contesting parties in 1984 may be to the tune of Rs. 500 crores in India. This figure looks realistic if the funds utilized by the ruling party from state coffers, its own funds and the individuals' contributions are taken into account. It is pertinent to note here that elections in a poor country like India don't mean the same as they do in relatively richer countries. At least, the margin of votes, which are perpetuating the rule of a single party, may be on account of outright purchase of votes by paying the poor voters in cash or kind.

More than one lakh units in organised corporate sector, with a total capital of around Rs 80,000 crores, and the black economy, which is estimated at Rs. 20 thousand crores, contribute to the election funds in a big way. When company donations were allowed, the legitimate donations of business, especially the big houses contributed sums, ranged from Rs. 1 to Rs. 25 crores in various elections. Estimates, however, suggest that legitimate company donations to parties accounted for mere 20 per cent of the total donations. Rest of the donations of business were to individuals, largely from the black income generated in the process of tax-evasion and other illegal activities of the business. Initially, especially in Nehru era, the business donations were collected through cheques and, thus, were fully accounted for latter, however, the process of collecting election funds became more decentralised. Central ministers, regional party leaders and the party treasurers collected funds from the various industrialised pockets of the country. The importance of Atulya Ghosh, C.B. Gupta, S.K. Patil and now Sita Ram Kesri in Congress party depended upon their fund collecting capacities.

It is argued by Stanley Kochanach that the floating of Swatantra party by Western Indian business houses and diversion of some of their contributions to election funds of the opposition parties like Jan Sangh and Congress (S) in 1967, resulted in the reduced majority of Indira Congress in Parliament and formation of SVD governments in the States. Tatas were very apprehensive of the socialist rhetoric and the populist measures like nationalisation of banks introduced by Mrs. Indira Gandhi in her first tenure as Prime Minister. G.D. Birla, the doyen of FICCI had counselled patience because he was sure that Mrs. Gandhi couldn't go very far with her radical utterances because she had to fall back on Indian big business for the election funds and he proved prophetic. During her second term as Prime Minister after 1971, her radicalism had been watered down. In her last term, before her assassination, Mrs. Gandhi had turned a votary of economic liberalisation.

Money Power and Economic Liberalisation

The mixed economy derived from Directive Principles and the abolition of right to property, as a fundamental right, during the Emergency were ostensibly aimed at justifying the word 'socialism' in new preamble drafted for Indian Constitution. In reality, the socalled 'License quota permit' Raj was enforced with a vangeance. Licenses, quotas and permits were freely traded by clever politicians like L.N. Misra. The election costs per candidate had scared to the limit of Rs. 10 lakhs in 1957 to one crore by 1971. Socialist pretensions were rendering the collection of funds difficult for Congress. Threats of nationalisation, raids and even jail terms for non-obliging businessmen became the order of day, during the Emergency period. Bonanzas for the obliging businessmen, like regularisation of illegally installed capacity, were offered as sops for donating liberally to Congress election funds.

L.N. Misra launched the "politics of big money" by the mid-Seventies, Sanjay Gandhi and P.C. Sethi followed the footsteps of the legendary "money bag". Ministers accepted bribes for giving governmental clearances in the name of party funds. Even some rich individuals/businessmen were offered party tickets for a price and those who were deprived of party tickets were given licenses, agencies and contracts as a compensation.

Frustrated with this state of affairs, Janata Government made a bid for economic liberalisation and initiated delicensing and decontrol measures. However, the emergence of *Kisan* power in Charan Singh era frightened the Indian business. The election costs during the 1980 elections had touched the Rs. 100 crores mark. Dismantling of controls was also viewed with suspicion by the traditional Marwari business because they didn't want to face international competition and new entries in various product lines. They again donated liberally to Indira Gandhi's party and it was back in power. She initiated certain measures to please the native business but by 1982 another element entered Indian business scene, especially after the negotiation of loan from IMF. As a part of IMF conditionalities, the export-led model became popular with the policy planners.

Meanwhile, some of the family members of Indian traders/businessmen had settled abroad and had been able to build business empires, partly, using the black incomes generated in the export-import business or defence deals. Swaraj Pauls, Dhirubhai Ambanis, Chhabrias, Hindujas and Mirjanis were the new stars of Indian business world. They laundered back the money made in international deals as non-resident investments taking advantage of the new scheme for liberal import of capital in free trade zones. They also attempted takeovers of business with the help of public financial institutions. They had a good rapport with the multinationals and some of them may have acted as frontmen for MNC's which were not still welcome in India. It is rumoured that after the assassination of Mrs. Gandhi, Rajiv Gandhi didn't make traditional party fund collections from native business. He relied more on these new stars of business, NRI's, for his election funds.

An era of economic liberalisation and open economy were seeming to have emerged in the right earnest. Opportunities were given to bring back black money into legitimate economic activities by cutting tax rates. But the overzealous. Finance Minister, of new Congress (I) government, V.P. Singh had taken his job too seriously. After allowing concessions to business, he expected compliance to tax laws and wanted to end the corruption, allegedly created by the government controls. Skeletons in the cup boards of the high-ups in the party were, however, soon evident. The Swiss bank and Overseas connections of party big-wigs soon came to light. Undue concessions and policy change to benefit particular business houses also became a subject of controversy. Privatisation of public sector or hiring of foreign consultants like M.S. Pathak were also seen to be a ploy for collecting party funds rather than measures for revitalisation of economy. For the first time in history of Independent India, the highest political office came for ridicule on account of shady business deals. Till this point of time, only money from Indian businessmen was playing its role in the Indian polity, now foreign money also started determining the Parliamentary politics in India. Scored by the new scenerio, the erstwhile votaries of economic liberalisation in Rajiv Gandhi government started seeing threats from political right and took recourse to socialist rhetoric.

After V.P. Singh's exit from Rajiv Ministry, the credibility of the ruling party had suffered due to a number of deals involving "kickbacks" or "commissions". In order to steal the thunder from opposition and as a part of the preparations for the next elections, the Rajiv government, with its newly acquired anti-big-business face, raided a large number of business houses for tax evasions. The business circles, however, cynically read it as a political message. It was commented that "raids may help loosen the purse strings of the industry" or may prove to be "the quickest and surest way of cleaning up his (Rajiv's) own image". But after the whole exercise was over, the biggest tax evaders were allowed amenesty, after they made amends with the ruling party bosses. The recent L.M. Thapar case is a shining example of Congress-big business nexus. As a part of their pseudo-socialist programme, the ruling party has also used its front organisations like INTUC to harass the businessmen, if need arises. Various business laws have been amended from time to time, depending upon the political convenience of the ruling party.

To sum up the discussion on business and politics in India, it may be remarked that mixed economy and government control are there too stay, not as an ideological commitment or on account of anti-business attitudes but as a part of pragmatic politics. The businessman in India has to learn to use this political environment to his best advantage.

Political Realities and the Opportunities for Business

Though, ours is a mixed economy, with lot of socialist talk in our Constitution, yet, private initiative is not suppressed in India. Businessmen who have been able to laisse with the politicians and bureaucrats have reaped dividends. Even the governments under control of Marxist parties cannot go very far in their commitments for centrally planned economy, as contrasted with free enterprise economies. India has a large public sector and economic planning exercises rather than the market forces determine the prices of majority of commodities. There are unlimited opportunities for entering diverse product lines and business can grow, if the ruling party bosses don't obstruct the growth. Only political vandettas by the ruling parties have resulted in limiting profit motive due to interference by the government. In fact, the government patronage has afforded protection to certain business houses to grow at the cost of others.

The history of Birlas and the recent emergence of Reliance Textiles, as the second longest corporate giant, are largely on account of G.D. Birla's and Ambani's ability to cultivate key political persons in the ruling party. Goenkas of Duncan fame have shown how a government led by Marxists is forced to ask them for co-operation in so prestigious a project like Haldia Petro-chemicals in West Bengal.

Public financing institutions have emerged as the dominant shareholders in most of the private corporations. When there are disputes in business families over control in these corporations, the ruling party and the ministers mediate. In the recent disputes within the Modi family, the Prime-Minister's Office directly intervened to retain K.N. Modi in the pivotal positions in the Modi empire. Swaraj Paul was persuaded to withdraw his investments in DCM and Escorts after Shrirams and Nandas evoked the blessings of ruling party bosses. Similarly in the takeover bid by Chhabrias, the government, through public financial institutions, helped them in removing the erstwhile, Chairman of Shaw Wallace. While allotting licenses, the donations especially underhand payments play a very crucial role. TISCO was allowed to remain in the steel industry or Tatas were allowed power production, on account of the good relationships of the house with the political regimes of Independent India.

The business interests of Ramnath Goenkas or Nusli Wadias suffered due to casting their lot with the opposition parties. Excise raids were conducted on many business houses but subsequently, the penal actions were shelved after the business corporations concerned were able to please the political powers. Illicit trade also flourishes under political patronage not to talk of legitimate business. The dominant consideration is working out business-politics relationship is the financial help which business can provide to organisational activities/election funds. Company donations to political parties have been legalised again but the funds shown as legitimate donations are the top of the ice-berg. The 'steel frame' of Indian administration looks after procedural formalities involved in clearing various business proposals and disbursal of subsides/concessions is the prerogative of the executive in India. Business in India can even evade its obligations to workers or society at large if they are able to work out right relations in the administrative structure of the so called developmental bureaucracy. Worker management relations is another interface of business-politics interaction. Multiple unions are an offshoot of multiparty system. Almost all national parties have their apex level bodies to affiliate trade unions. The managements help the trade unions backed by the ruling parties in establishing their bases whereas the leaders of these unions try to pay back, by adopting a conciliatory stance towards management. In an interesting study on trade unionism in India it has been proved how leading personalities of Indian National Congress helped Tatas in retaining a pro-management union in TISCO.

The proverbial red-tape also delays clearances for those

businessmen who can not grease the palms holding this tape. In fact, the business embassies created in Delhi by big business maintain guest-houses or hire accommodations in five star hotels, maintain fleets of cars and reserve managerial positions for the wards of key bureaucratic bosses.

The new breed of managers from business schools is hired by the traditional businessmen to maintain relationships with bureaucrats. Our bureaucracy and MBA's come from the same backgrounds, they have the same school ties of convent school, they are members of the same clubs and are able to interact more freely. The social skills of winning our bureaucrats/politicians is the key to business success in India. The bureaucracy-management relationship has turned further crucial with the government emerging as the major buyer of industrial products in India. Floating and awarding of tenders to particular business parties, sub-contracting developmental works and allowing permits/quotas has created opportunities for bureaucrats to share the booty which is a result of 'briefcase politics' being practised in our country. Business can ignore this political reality at its own risk. The state regulatory mechanism can easily be converted into a state sponsored business support system by internalising the politics of commissions and underhand payments by Indian businessmen. Industrial relations in the business organisations also reflect the acumen of managements in maintaining right political connections to discipline the work force. This may be done by either cultivating labour administration apparatus of the government or by striking deals with the political leaders who also serve as trade union leaders of multiple unions. Political parties are also creating their cells among the traders, the consumers and the environmentalists and the business has to keep track of the influential leaders in these sections who may whip up social movements impinging upon the smooth functioning of business.

CASE V

BUSINESSMEN IN POLITICS

Apart from the financial support provided to Indian

National Congress, the politics has seen the active participation of business tycoons like T.T. Krishnamachari, who was a minister in Nehru's cabinet in the important ministries like Commere and Finance. Walchand never concealed his disdain for Nehruvian Socialism. In fact, the western business houses floated Swatantra party in 1966 to contain the socialist rhetoric of Mrs. Indira Gandhi. It was at this time that Viren Shah of Bajaj group and long-time chairman of Mukand Iron & Steel Co contested 1967 elections, as a Swatantra nominee. He was of firm conviction that private business should directly exert its right to exist and grow in pluralistic liberal democracy of India.

Shah alongwith many opposition nominees got elected to Lok Sabha and it was with the support of private business that SVD ministries were formed in many states after 1967. He didn't give up his oppositional stance, while managing the second largest private sector steel manufacturing industry of India. Viren Shah was jailed alongwith George Fernandes for involvement in socalled "Baroda Dynamite" case during the Emergency. In 1977, Janata government came to power and Mukund Iron which was in doldrums in early Seventies kept on increasing its sales at 11 per cent per annum during the late Seventies. Viren Shah's activism in politics is, sometimes, blamed for the shody performance of Mukund Iron but he used his political acumen while handling 1983 strike in his company. Datta Samant, the volatile Bombay trade union leader had launched a strike in Mukund Iron and the strike paralysed the functioning of Kalwe Plant for more than a year. Viren, with his activist background and with a direct access to the workers, was able to get a court order in 1984 to hire new employees. While sales had plummetted to less than hundred crores in 1984, Mukund Iron was on its way to recovery in 1985. In fact, Shah had shown the way to the Bombay industrialists in handling such a dreaded trade union leader as Samant who was dislodged from the leadership of Mukund workers and the new union was led by a lady social worker who had very good relations with management. Others like

K.K. Birla have perferred to contest and win elections as independents.

POINTS FOR CONSIDERATION

Since politics conditions the functioning of Indian business, do you support active participation of Viren Shah in country's politics ? Does successful industrial relations management in India requires political activism by the top managers ?

FURTHER READINGS

1. Cherian, Dilip, "The Return of Raiders", *Business India*, 263, 4-17 April, 1988.

2. Dasgupta, A. and N.K. Sengupta, *Government and Business in India*, Calcutta, Allied Publishers, 1978.

3. Hardgrave, R.L. and Stanley A. Kochaneck, *India : Government and Politics in a Developing Nation*, New York : Harcourt, Brace, Jovanavich, 1988.

4. Herdeck, Margret and Gita Piramal, *India's Industrialists*, Washington, D.C. : Three Continents Press Inc., 1985.

5. Kochaneck, Stanley A., *Business and Politics in India*, Berkley, University of California Press, 1974.

6. ——, "Brief Case Politics in India", *Asian Survey*, Vol. XXVIII, No. 12, December, 1987.

7. Mitra, Ashok, "Resource Mobilisation and Devolution", *Social Scientist*, Vol 13, No. 12, December, 1985.

6

Corporate Legal Environment in India

Business as a corporate entity has number of social obligations. The state, in India, believes that business, on its own, may not discharge its responsibilities to the consumers, workers and society at large. So a number of laws have been enacted to reflect the demands of normative behaviour by the society from any business unit. Besides, the state is bound by the directive principles in the Constitution and has to regulate the functioning of business to ensure dispersal of industry and check the concentration of economic power. It is beyond the scope of the present exercise to enter into intricacies of mercantile or industrial law.

An environmental awareness exercise dictates that various laws directly impinging upon the functioning of business may be listed with a brief outline of the scope of these laws. At this point, it shall be pertinent to note that a company as an artificial citizen is bound by all the legal enactments of the land but our focus shall be only on those legislations which are specifically enacted for business and may be of a secondary concern to other citizens, not involved with managing a business. A summary review of various laws regulating conduct of business, viz., Industrial Development Regulation Act (IDRA), 1951, The Companies Act, 1956, Monopolies and Restrictive Trade Practices Act (MRTPA), 1969, Foreign Exchange Regulation Act (FERA), 1973 and Capital Issues Control Act is presented, to start with, company laws follow. Later, various labour legislations, consumer protection and managerial remuneration laws are reviewed. Ultimately, a brief introduction to mercantile laws like Contract and Sales of Goods Act shall be provided.

Regulatory Laws

IDRA, 1951 provides framework for industrial licenses and regulation of industrial investments in the country. This Act channelises investments and production of industrial goods, according to the priorities of National Plans. By restricting the established business houses' entries, the act is supposed to provide encouragement to new entries by small entrepreneurs. Regional imbalances in industrialisation are also sought to be rectified. There are a number of exceptions provided in the Act to the avowed aims of introducing compulsory licensing.

It allows exemption to big business in under developed industrial regions for production of new products and expansion of production. Some industries are exempted from industrial licensing. Delicensing provisions are changing from time to time but the firms in delicensed industry are supposed to register themselves with Directorate General of Technical Development (DGTD) and they have to follow the prescribed procedure by the Secretariat for Industrial approvals. The industries exempted from licenses include small-scale industries producing 872 reserved items and certain industries included in Appendix II, III and the industries, recently delicensed are listed in a new Appendix IV. Similarly, firms basing production on research of CSIR are also exempted from licenses.

The Government of India have constituted several inter-Ministerial Committees to consider applications for Industrial Licenses, Foreign Collaborations and Import of Capital Equipment under this Act. Initially, Letters of Intents are issued and these are converted in Industrial Licenses, after fulfilment of certain conditions by the abovesaid committees within a stipulated time frame.

MRTPA, 1969 regulates acquisition/merger/amalgamation by dominant undertakings defined in the Act and also provides for special permission for starting new undertakings and substantial expansions by these undertakings. A statutory body, Monopolies and Restrictive Trade Practices Commission (MRTPC) has been set up to entertain the applications from the listed monopoly houses for the proposals of business growth enumerated above. MRTPC is a quasi-judicial body whose decisions are justiciable. Restrictive trade practices, to check monopolistic trade through tied up sales, sole selling arrangements, etc., are to be enquired into by MRTPC, independently or by entertaining complaints regarding the use of these. The scope of unfair trade activities which can be enquired into is very wide and some of the provisions overlap with those of Consumers Protection Act. The aim of MRTPA, 1969 is to check countrywide and product monopolies, with a view to disallow concentration of economic power. The MRTPA clearances required by listed undertakings are in addition to IDRA clearances. The limits of assets of firms/groups inviting MRTPA provisions have been revised from time to time. The present threshold of assets qualifying for exemptions has been raised to Rs. 100 crores. A list of 27 industries was notified in 1985 which didn't invite provisions of MRTPA under sections 21 to 24 of the Act. Similar exemptions have been granted for setting up industries in backward areas and for export-oriented production.

Through proposed amendments to the Act, its scope may be restricted to unfair trade practices alone and the concept of inter-connected undertakings under the Act is also being re-examined. Re-endorsement scheme for capacity expansion and regularisation of illegally installed capacities have rendered MRTPA quite ineffective. Many studies, like the one by Rakesh Khurana on growth of monopoly houses, suggest that MRTPA, 1970 is just a decorative piece of legislation and with the enactment of Consumer Protection Act, 1988, the legislation aimed at checking monopolies has lost its teeth even in regulating restrictive trade practices.

FERA, 1973 normally covers the regulation of all those

transactions which have international financial implications. In particular, the following matters are regulated through foreign exchange control :

- —Purchase and sale of and other dealings in foreign exchange and maintenance of balances at foreign centres.
- —Procedure for the realisation of proceeds of exports.
- —Payments to non-residents or to their accounts in India.
- —Transfer of securities between residents and non-residents and acquisition and holding of foreign securities.
- —Foreign travel.
- —Export and import of currency, financial instruments, securities, jewellery, etc.
- —Trading, commercial and industrial activities in India of foreign firms and companies and foreign nationals, as well as acquisition of business undertakings and acquisition and holding of shares in Indian companies.
- —Appointment of non-residents and foreign nationals and companies as agents or technical/management advisers in India.
- —Employment, profession, etc., undertaken in India by foreign nationals.
- —Acquisition, holding and disposal of immoveable properties in India by foreign nationals and companies.
- —Acquisition, holding and disposal of immoveable property outside India by persons residing in India.

All transactions which involve foreign exchange directly or indirectly, require, under the Act, general or special permission of the Reserve Bank of India (RBI). General permission is granted by RBI for certain categories of transactions which are notified in the gazette and made known through circulars issued to commercial banks and others as authorised dealers of foreign exchange. A special permission, usually, indicates the necessity for prior approval of RBI.

Corporate Legal Environment in India

Under the FERA Act, all foreign investments quire the permission from the Reserve Bank of In ration proposals involving issue of shares to non borators which are in connection with the setting up of new industrial undertakings in India or raising of additional capital by existing undertakings also require the approval under the Act. The same is applicable to the issue of rights shares, bonus shares as also transfer of shares to the non-resident shareholders. Proposals involving technical collaboration with foreigners as well as remittance of royalties and technical fees also require the approval of RBI, after the proposals have been approved by the government. Remittance of dividends and repatriation of capital invested in India require the permission of RBI, under FERA Act. RBI's permission should also be obtained by Foreign Companies for permitting any Trade Marks, acquisition of the whole or part of any undertaking in India, opening of Liaison or Branch offices, appointment of agents, etc. However, under the Act, several liberalisations have been given to the non-residents for investment, with and without repatriation facilities, investment in new issues of Indian companies under 40 per cent scheme, investment in priority industries. Under 74 per cent scheme, deposits with public limited companies with repatriation benefits, acquisition of immoveable properties for residential purposes, for which, the provisions have amply been explained in the related amendment.

Company Laws

Though individual proprietory, extended family and partnership business concerns dominate Indian unorganised industry, yet the organised sector of industry had adopted corporate form of business. The social responsibilities balance sheet of the so-called 'small business makes one doubt the doctrine of "small is beautiful", the medium and large firms have been made to adhere to their responsibility to their shareholders and the government by enacting the Companies Act, 1956. The primary objectives of the Act include :

(1) While promoting or managing companies, a minimum level of business integrity should be presented.

(2) Due to the phenomenon of passive shareholders in corporate form, full and fair disclosure of information and effective participation to the shareholders should be provided.

(3) Government shall keep an eye on effective management of the company in the interests of shareholders and public at large.

Abolition of managing agency system in 1970 has changed the complexion of the original Act, alongwith many other amendments in the original Act of 1956. A corporate personality having limited liability in business and allowing transfers of shares in investment make a company an artificial citizen, with an assumed perpetual existence. There are special provisions for winding up the existence of this business entity.

Companies limited by shares, the most popular form, may be public or private company. Another form of company is a company limited by liability. The company with unlimited liability is third stipulated form in the Companies Act. 1956. A private company restricts the right to transfer shares, limits the number of shares to fifty and does not call for capital through public subscription. A private company may go public by removing the abovesaid restrictions. If more than one fourth of capital of a private company is held by one or more public companies, it is deemed as a public company.

In a Government Company, majority shares are held by the government at the Centre or in the States, or the both. A company is holding a 'subsidiary' company if the former controls half the voting power and exercises control over the board of directors over the latter company. A foreign company is incorporated outside India but is carrying on its business in India.

The Companies Act stipulates the process of formation of a company and drafting of its memorandum and articles of association. Shareholdings are to be raised through prospectus of the company and shareholders become members of the

Corporate Legal Environment in India

company. Company can also borrow funds. The process of convening meetings and conducting their proceedings, appointment of directors, remuneration and powers of managerial personnel, secretary, etc., are also provided for in the law. To prevent oppression of minority shareholders/debtors and prevent mismanagement, accounting, auditing and investigation processes into the affairs of a company, are also outlined. Winding up proceedings bringing the company to a close are also discussed in details by Indian Companies Act, 1956.

A major amendment to companies Act was enacted in 1974. The essence of amendment is as follows :

(1) Company Law Board has been entrusted with many functions which were preformed by High Courts earlier ;

(2) Definitions of groups, managing agents, secretaries and treasurers have been amended to check concentration of economic power ;

(3) The scope of deemed public companies has been enlarged by giving a new definition ;

(4) Transfer or acquisitions of shares among inter-connected undertakings under the same management have been restricted and investigation can be launched into beneficial ownership of shares ;

(5) A special unpaid dividends account has to be maintained and if dividends remain unpaid for three years, these are to be transferred to revenue account of Central Government ;

(6) Firms or persons are debarred from holding more than 10 auditing assignments with companies with paid up share capital upto Rs. 25 lakhs, audit assignments for companies with the share capital less than this ceiling can be upto 20 ;

(7) Prior approval of Central Government is needed for appointment/reappointment of Managing/Whole Time

Directors and the appointment of a whole-time Secretary is mandatory for companies with paid-up share capital of Rs. 25 lakhs and above ;

(8) If demand exceeds the supply of the produce of a company, sole selling arrangements are debarred. Certain restrictions have also been put on appointment of partners or relatives as directors of the company ;

(9) All employees of company drawing above Rs. 36.000/- per annum are to be listed in annual reports ; and

(10) Government's powers to intervene in company affairs in public interest have been increased. It can appoint unlimited number of directors on the board of the company.

Another amendment made in 1977 empowers government from granting exemption from the restrictions on inviting public deposits and a company has been allowed to denote upto Rs. 50,000/- to a charitable purpose/employee welfare. The degrees of company Law Board now can be enforced like those of a Court of Law. Most of the amendments to the Companies Act have been made on the basis of Sachar Committee Report but the recommendations of this Committee have been accepted only. partially.

The need to regulate the financial structure of joint stock companies and to protect the interests of the investing public has necessitated some control over capital raised by companies. Control under the Capital Issues (Control) Act. 1947, is sought to be exercised by means of approval of the Controller of Capital Issues (CCI) to : (*i*) issue of securities by companies, (*ii*) sale and purchase of securities by any person ; and (*iii*) advertisement making offer, public or private, for subscriptions or purchase of securities. Consent of CCI is required if the total capital issue by a company exceeds Rs. 5 million in a period of one year. The Central Government has been empowered to grant exemption under the Act in terms of which, it has issued Capital Issues (Exemption) Order, 1969, exempting certain issues of capital from the operation of the Act. The exemptions are applicable in the following cases :

(*i*) A private company which does not attract the provisions of MRTP Act.

(*ii*) A Government company which does not intend to issue securities to the general public.

(*iii*) A banking company or insurance company.

(*iv*) A public limited company not attracting the provisions of MRTP Act, if the issue made by it does not exceed Rs. 5.00 million.

(*v*) Amalgamation of two or more companies, provided the total paid-up capital of the amalgamated company, after the issue of securities, is not greater than the total paid up capital of the amalgamating companies.

(*vi*) The debentures taken up or bonds or promissory notes issued by the Central or State Government and financial and other institutions as specified.

(*vii*) Issue of securities for the purpose of subdividing or consolidation.

However, approval of CCI under the Capital Issues (Control) Act, 1957, is necessary in regard to the following :

—Issue of capital by MRTP companies.

—Issue of securities by a private company where an amount exceeding 20% thereof is or is to be subscribed by one or more public limited companies.

—Issue of securities to public by Government companies.

—Bonus issues by all companies.

—Issue of Preference Shares.

—Issue of debentures by public limited companies, except to the financial institutions.

—Issue of securities at a premium or discount.

—Issue of Capital in all other cases not specifically exempted under Capital Issues (Exemption) Order.

Where the issue of equity capital involves an offer for subscription by the public for the first time, the value of equity capital subscribed, privately by the promoters, directors and their friends, should be as under :

Total Issued Equity Capital	Percentage to be Subscribed by Promoters, Directors and their Friends
Upto Rs. 1.00 Crore	15% (minimum)
Upto Rs. 2.00 Crores	12½% (minimum)
More than Rs. 2.00 Crores	10% (minimum)

The rate of dividend on preference shares is not to exceed the rate notified by the Central Government which is presently 15% per annum.

Listing of securities is not a statutory obligation on the part of any company. However, under Section 21 of the Securities Contracts (Regulation) Act, the Government has power to compel a company in the public interest to get its share enlisted on the stock exchange. The listing requirements prescribe that a company should offer at least 60% of each class of kind of securities issued by it to the public. Out of 60% of the issued capital of each class of securities to be offered for public subcription, upto 11% in aggregate can be reserved for Government and quasi-Governmental agencies and a minimum of 49%, in any case has to be offered to the public. The conditions are relaxable in the case of existing FERA companies, established non-FERA companies, new companies with foreign equity participation new opportunities with non-resident Indian equity participation joint sector companies, etc.

The listing requirements also prescribe that :

—Issued capital of the company should not be less than

Rs. 2.00 Million. In respect of investment companies, the paid up capital should not be less than Rs. 10.00 million.

— The public offer should not be less than 1.2 million in face value if it is 60% or more of the issued capital of the company ; the public offer should not be less than Rs. 2.00 million in face value if it is less than 60% of the issued capital of the company.

— The public offer should result in a wide distribution of shares, i.e., 1,000 public shareholders for every Rs. 10.00 million of share capital. In respect of investment companies, the minimum number of shareholders other than promoters, should be 2,000 for paid up capital of Rs. 10.00 million and correspondingly higher number of shareholders for companies with proportionately higher capital.

Presently, the promoters can hold in respect of new issues, upto 70% of holdings during the initial stages of a project to match the desired level of promoters' contribution. This is, however, subject to the condition that the higher equity holdings above 40% will have to be divested within a period of three years form the date of commercial production by an offer for sale to the general public at the prevailing price not exceeding the average of three preceding years.

Recently, in order to encourage entry of more unlisted companies with good financial record in the Stock Exchange fold, the Government has decided that the existing closely held companies can also have their shares listed on the basis of two-stage public offer subject to some conditions.

Mercantile Laws

The laws relating to contracts, Sale of Goods, Partnerships, Negotiable Instruments, Arbitration, Insurance and Insolvency also come into play in the functioning of business world.

A contract is an agreement enforceable by law. There are two parties who agree to discharge certain lawful obligations to each other. Proposal and acceptance of one party to oblige the other legally for a lawful consideration forms a contract. It is further provided that only parties who are not minors of illegitimate persons or persons denied the right of free consent can enter into a contract. Compliance with legal formalities stipulated under Indian Contract Act is a must. Some agreements have been expressedly declared viod by law. Consideration is the most important evidence in deciding contract cases. Some contracts have to be registered with appropriate authorities whereas some of these must be reduced to writing. Contracts have been classified on the basis of enforceability, creation, extent of execution and form of the contract.

The Indian Law only recognises simple contracts, the formal contracts—the validity of which depends only on form are not recognised in India. Disputes can arise in the execution of contract on account of competence of parties, adequacies and legalities of considerations and mode of offer as well as acceptance. Boarding a bus, enrolling in a course, calling a taxi are various valid contracts which any common man enters in his daily life. In business life many more contracts with financially significant/important considerations and consequences are entered into.

A contract of sale is 'a contract where the seller transfers or agrees to transfer the property in goods to the buyer at a price' is the most usual contract in a marketing exercise. There may be a sale or an agreement to sell at a furture time. Like a contract, in Sales of Goods also, there are two parties—the seller and a buyer. Goods or moveable property is to be exchanged, at least, partly, in money prices. The general property/ownership of goods gets transferred in the process of a Sales of Goods Contract. Sale is distinguished from bailment (where only possession posses, not ownership), gift (where price is not charged), barter and exchange (goods exchanged for goods), mortgage/hypothecation (mortgage relates to immoveable property and hypothecation results in possession stay with the creditor). When a contract of sale is accompanied with a contract for work and labour, the court has to sit on judgement deciding the predominant object of sale. If it is moveable property then it falls under Sales of Goods Act and if it is work and labour which is predominant, the Act doesn't apply. Hire and purchase system popular in consumer durables/industrial goods is not a contract of sale. In hire and purchase, the buyer becomes owner only when all the instalments are paid, his capacity prior to that is of a bailee and he can set aside the contract but his payment of instalments, prior to setting aside, will be treated as hiring charges.

In a sale, goods can be specific, ascertained or uncertained, existing goods or future or contingent goods. Goods to be manufactured are future goods whereas the goods the acquisition of which depends on an uncertain contingency are contingent goods, *e.g.*, goods being transported by sea will be available to the buyer if the ship touches the port. Parishability of goods, ascertainment of price, document of title of goods, mercantile agent, insolvency are other important legal aspects of Sales of Goods Contract. Whereas a condition is something integral to such a contract, a warranty is only a collateral stipulation to main purpose of the contract. In case of a condition not being filled, the agreement is not endorceable whereas in case of warranty only damages can be claimed. For example, the sellers of electric gadgets issue a warranty that they shall repair the gadget free of cost if it falls in a stipulated span of time.

Though partnerships are not very popular in India, the Indian Partnership Act defines 'partnership' business "as the relation between persons who have agreed to share the profits of business carried on by all or any of them acting for all". Two or more persons enter into a partnership with mutual or agreement by all and the agreement must be about sharing profits of a business. The business must be carried on by all or one of the partners, acting on behalf of all the parties. Partnerships should be registered under law because in case of unregistered partnership, partners are deprived of many rights. The liability of partners in a firm is always unlimited. They can be held personally liable for the debts of a firm, the family property of the *karta* and other members also gets attached, in event of non-payment of debts by a partner belonging to the Hindu undivided family. The unlimited liability clause makes this form of organisation unpopular among businessmen in India.

The Essential Commodities Act, 1974, The Negotiable Instruments Act, Securities Regulation Act, The Laws of Insurance, Insolvency and Carriage of Goods which form the legal environment of business but are not being discussed in details. Direct Taxes (Amendment) Bill, 1987 seeks to amend the Income Tax Act, 1961 and other taxation Acts to provide for certain tax concessions for encouraging industries in selected sectors and in backward areas, for promotion of research and development, exports, etc. Tax concessions and deductions are given for promotional expenses, amalgamation with sick companies and attempts are made at avoiding double taxation, MODVAT (Modified Value Added Tax) has replaced excise duties precisely to avoid the double charging of excise on both the parts and their assemblies. In fact, the duties already paid on the inputs on which duties have been paid are allowed to be drawn back and duty on the final products only is charged. There are number of other duty drawback schemes to encourage exports or in order to pursue the priorities decided by Planning Commission. Direct tax laws are a major determinant of investment behaviour so a Long Term Fiscal Policy has been chalked out which rules out drastic alterations in tax rates.

Labour Laws

Labour is the most important factor of production in a manpower surplus country like India. With a large reserve army of working class, left to demand and supply forces in labour market, the lot of workers could be pitiable because supply is many times the demand for industrial labour. It is in this context, the welfare state in India has enacted a large number of labour laws. Some of the laws are aimed at preventing industrial conflict.

Factories Act, 1948 amended in 1976 is aimed at ensuring sanitary and safety conditions in working premises ; welfare of the workers in form of washing, eating, resting facilities ; provision of first aid arrangements and creches for children. Working hours of adult workers, holidays, shifts, overtime payments, rest intervals are also stipulated in the Factories Act. Conditions for employing women and young workers with a provision of providing paid holidays and damages in case of accidents are also contained in this Act. The Act also calls for installation of anti-pollution devices in the factories. The administrative machinery for enforcing working conditions like inspectors, welfare officers and certifying surgeons is also laid down in this piece of legislation. The Act applies to all working premises "(*i*) wherein ten or more workers are working or were working on any day of preceding twelve months, and in any part of which a manufacturing process is being carried on with aid of power or is ordinarily so carried on, or (*ii*) wherein twenty or more workers are working or were working on any day of preceding twelve months, and in any part of which a manufacturing process is being carried on, without the aid of power or ordinarily is so carried on but does not include a mine subject in the operations".

Industrial Disputes Act, 1947 amended in 1982 envisages the grievance redressal machinery comprising of (*a*) Works Committee, (*b*) Concilliation Officers, (*c*) Boards of Concilliation, (*d*) Courts of Enquiry, (*e*) Labour courts, (*f*) Industrial Tribunals, and (*g*) National Tribunals. The Act aims at regulating strikes, closures, lock-outs, retrechment and other work stoppages by providing for a mechanism of setting the demands of workers, etc. It provides for various penalties for acts on the part of employers or workers which are in contravention to the provision of the Act.

The growing complexity of industry requires the increasing use of machinery. Workmen operating the machines are liable to sustain injuries in accidents of various types. Since workmen are poor, it becomes vital to protect the worker from hardship arising out of the injuries caused by accident. A beginning in social security of labour was made in India when Workmen's

Compensation Act was brought in force in 1924. It provides for payment of compensation to workmen and their families, in case of industrial accidents and of certain occupational diseases, arising out of and in the course of employment and resulting in death or disablement. The Act has described scales of compensation for death, permanent total disablement and temporary disablement. It covers workers employed in certain specified hazardous occupations except, those who are covered under Employees State Insurance Act, 1948. The passing of Compensation Act has a salutory effect on the prevention of accidents by incorporating safety devices because compensation to be paid in the case of accidents is exemplary.

Among the social security labour laws, the passing of Employment State Insurance Act, 1948 is also very important. Till recently, it covered non-seasonal factories using power and employing 20 or more persons but now it is being gradually extended by the state governments to smaller factories, hotels, restaurants, shops, cinemas, etc., employing 20 or more persons. It covers employees drawing wages not exceeding Rs. 1,600 per month.

The Act provides for medical care in kind and cash, benefits in contingency of sickness, maternity, employment injury and pensions for dependents on the death of worker because of employment injury. Full medical care including hospitalisation is also being progressively made available to the members of the family of the insured persons. Retirement benefits in the form of provident fund, family pension and deposit linked insurance are available to the employee under the Employees Provident Fund and Miscellaneous Provisions Act, 1952.

The Trade Unions Act, 1926 provides for the registration of trade unions. Any seven or more members of a trade union may, by subscribing their names to the rules of the trade unions and otherswise complying with the provisions of the Act with respect to registration apply for registration of trade union under the Trade Unions Act. The Act gives protection to trade unions in certain cases against civil or criminal action. In fact, the Act is being amended, a bill, more comprehensive than the existing Industrial Disputes and Trade Union Acts is under the consideration of the Parliament. The bill provides for checking the phenomenon of multiple unions, wild cat strikes and abrupt lockouts. It also tries to discourage the politicisation of trade union movement by restricting 'outside' members in a trade union.

The payment of wages is governed by the Payment of Wages Act, 1936 and Minimum Wages Act, 1948. These Acts are not applicable in Sikkim. The payment of Wages Act applies to persons employed in any factory including the establishments declared as factories under the Factories Act, 1948 and in any railway and industrial establishments, such as tramway or motor transport service, air transport service, docks, inland vessels, mines, quarries or oilfields, plantations, workshops in which articles are produced and establishment in which any work related to the construction, development or maintenance of buildings, roads, bridges or canals, etc., is being carried on.

The Act applies to those who are in receipt of wage which average below Rs. 1,600 per month. According to the Act, employers cannot withhold the wages earned by worker nor can they make any unauthorised deduction. Payment must be made before the expiry of a specified day after the last day of the wage period. Fines can be imposed for only those acts of omission which have been approved by the appropriate government and must not exceed an amount equal to three per cent of the wages payable. If the payment of wages is delayed or wrongful deductions are made, the workers or their trade unions can file a claim.

The Minimum Wages Act, 1948 empowers the government to fix wages of employees working in specified employments. It provides for review and revision of minimum wages already fixed after suitable intervals not exceeding five years. The payment of overtime in schedule employment is also governed by the Act. Minimum wages presently are to be revised within two years or on a rise of 50 points in consumers price index, whichever is earlier. The Equal Remuneration Act, 1976 provides for payment of equal remuneration to men and women workers for "the same work or work of a similar nature" and for preventions of discrimination against women in matters of employment.

The right to share of the profits of a concern was conferred on the workers under the Payment of Bonus Act, 1965. The Payment of Bonus (Second Amendment) Act, 1980 provides for payment of a minimum bonus of 8.33 per cent or Rs. 100, whichever is higher, irrespective of whether there is allocable surplus or not. Bonus upto a maximum of 20 per cent of annual wages is payable under this law, in accordance with a prescribed formula. Bonus may be paid under a different formula linked to production/productivity in lieu of allocable surplus by mutual agreement between employers and the workers subject to a limit of 20 per cent. Bonus now has to be paid to upto the salary of Rs. 2,500/- per month but for those who have salary above Rs. 1,600, the bonus amount shall be the same as at the salary of Rs. 1,600/-.

Industrial Employment (Standing) Act, 1948 modified in 1963 outline model standing orders for establishment employing not less than hundred workers.

To wind up discussions on corporate legal environment, we have to make a mention of host of other legislations which directly or indirectly concern any business entity. Abolition of bonded and contract labour, redemption of past indebtedness, regulation of moneylender's activities, rent control, co-operative credit, marketing, etc., control of price and public distribution and restriction on dividend payments are a few of these laws. Consumers Protection Act, 1986 has come into force recently. The consumer pretection council and the related grievance handling machinery have been given a fresh lease of life. Consumer Dispute Redressal Agencies have been created at district, state and central levels. Sick Industrial Companies Act, 1985 provides for establishment of a Board of Industrial and Financial Reconstruction and as already pointed out in technological environment, we have four own patents law in the form of Indian Patents Act, 1970.

One is reminded of the famous quotation of Rousseu that "a man is born free but he is always in chains", while discussing the legal environment of business The stranglehold of various legislations on business seems to be so vicious that it appears that there is no freedom of managerial action. But that is the appearance, the practice is that all these laws are nothing more than a code for socially responsible behaviour on the part of employers, employees and managers. If they act in their enlightened self interest, this web of laws doesn't restrict them but protects them.

CASE VI

LEGAL WRANGLES OF CORPORATE WARS

When Swaraj Paul of Capro and Apeejay fame and with right political connections tried to takeover the management of Escorts and D.C.M., a legal battle followed in 1983 and 1984, the intricacies of corporate legal environments in India were unfolded and in fact, the presiding dieties of the highest court of land, while delivering their judgement doubted their own competence in delivering decisions on such complicated financial issues as share transfers and the Non-resident investments.

Escorts felt that the Central government shall come up with an ordinance if they insisted that Swaraj Paul's investments were violative of FERA, 1973. The government had flexed its muscles through Life Insurance Corporation of India, the latter forcing Escorts to register the share transfers in favour of Swaraj Paul. Escorts was blamed of violating the Indian Companies Act, 1956, and the spirit of Sales of Goods Act by refusing the transfer of those shares which have been purchased in the open capital market operations. Escorts owners, on other hand maintained that Swaraj Paul was guilty of FERA violations, so his purchases of their shares were not legal. Normally any company which feels aggrieved on this score moves the

Company Law Board (CLB). But sensing danger of an ordinance, if it approached CLB. Escorts managers moved the Bombay High Court under the impression that with the matter pending in the court and with the matter under the legal dispute, the government would have to think twice before issuing an ordinance along lines proposed, to favour transfers in favour of Swaraj Paul. In fact, the government got so panicky over Bombay High Court decision that the public institutions were pressurising Escorts not to challenge the government's ruling that the share purchases were illegal. Even after the Supreme Court judgement, it was this fear of the institutions which made them persuade Swaraj Paul not to pursue his case and an amicable settlement was arrived at.

POINTS FOR CONSIDERATIONS

Do you agree with observations of their Lordships in the case of LIC Vs Escorts that the financial matters related with corporate world were too complicated to be handled by the existing Courts of Land ?

It is advisable to grant various state regulatory agencies for the Private Corporation Sector a judicial status in matters relating to the business management of corporations ?

FURTHER READINGS

1. Ghosh, S.K. and Tapash Gan Choudhary, *Law of Monopolies and Restrictive Trade Practices in India*, New Delhi, Prentice Hall of India, 1980.

2. Khurana, Rakesh, *Growth of Large Business—Impact of Monopolies Legislation*, New Delhi, Wiley Eastern, 1981.

3. Maheshwari, R.P. and S.N. Maheshwari, *Principles of Mercantile Law*, New Delhi, National Publishing House, 1983.

4. Lal, B.B., *Elements of Income Tax* (8th Revised Edition), New Delhi, Allied, 1985.

5. Rao, Venkoba, *Commercial Reference*, Calcutta, Eastern Law House, 1980.

6. Sengupta, B.K., *Company Law* Calcutta, Eastern Law House, 1981.

7. Singh, Avtar, *Company Law*, (Eighth Edition), Lucknow Eastern Book Company, 1986.

8. ——, *Law of Contract*, Lucknow, Eastern Book Company, 1986.

7

Regulation and Control of Business

Communism and free enterprise economies are utopias, the former has a future and the latter is past. State was not so omnipresent in the era of *laissez faire* and is supposed to whither away when a communist society shall come into being. Right now what exists in the world is a variant of mixed economies. Socialist economies with their own versions of 'Prestrioka' are giving market a role in their economies whereas the Samuelsons like to describe even United States of America as a mixed economy. Neither governments plan every bit of economic activities through a centralised machinery nor are they silent spectators to the invisible hand of demand and supply forces. Russia and China are knocking at the doors of GATT, the international forum for free trade while USA refuses to oblige the underdeveloped world by withdrawing protective tariffs on textiles clamped in that country.

Even in India the Second World War proved to be a major watershed in Government-business relations. Socialist revolution in Russia was unfolding itself and so was state intervention in economic activities of capitalist economies in wake of the industrial depression. The Keynesian prescriptions became the basis of state investments in developing economic infrastructure. Government had forced war-time organisation of industries for the Allies in India, and was procuring locally manufactured goods. The two year period between the termination of War and dawn of Independence forced the government to deal with shortages that developed in large number of consumer items.

Regulation and Control of Business

It is a common knowledge the native Indian business itself had proposed a model of mixed economy through what is known as Tata-Birla or Bombay Plan of 1946. We have enumerated various laws governing the functioning of business in India in the chapter 6. These laws were framed on the basis of a consensus arrived at the necessity of state intervention and national planning. The objectives behind the planning experiment are :

(1) To channelise and conserve scarce capital and natural resources for a self reliant growth.

(2) To overcome poverty among weaker sections by making them available consumer goods as well as purchasing power.

(3) To reduce economic inequalities by checking concentration of economic power and industrial wealth.

(4) To protect the traditional skills and small scale industries.

(5) To encourage widely dispersed industrial growth.

(6) To save foreign exchange and break the dependence on foreign investments.

The government in India sets targets for economic growth to break the dependence on foreign business for capital goods needed by Indian industry and to provide infrastructure for industrial development it has itself set up large public sector units, it regulates the functioning of private corporate sector to check the growth of monopolies and overcome scarcity of consumer goods, it tries to encourage new entries and provide financial and training inputs to the entrepreneurs. As a planner apart from working out growth rates for five year periods, the government attempts to provide models for inter-sectoral transactions and it directly controls the achievement of targets in public sector. Thus its role as an entrepreneur running public sector companies has to dovetail with its activities as a planner. Its promotional role includes the supply of energy to industry besides efficient transportation and communication networks. It also provides key inputs like steel and non-ferrous metals. Financial support is also channelised through public financing institutions. Ultimately, it functions as a controller and regulator of all economic activities in private sector to gear this sector's functioning to meet the needs of Indian economy. It is this relationship between government and private business which shall become the focus of study in this chapter.

Industrial Policy of Indian Government

We have already outlined the legal framework for industrial development and regulation, in this section we shall concentrate on Industrial Policy Resolution of 1956 and the new Industrial Licensing Policy announced in 1973. The first Industrial Policy Resolution was enunciated in 1948 and is just of historical interest. The core of industrial policy is the Industrial Policy Resolution, 1956, which preceded India's planning for industrialisation which, in essence, started with the Second Five Year Plan. The objectives of the 1956 resolution derive from the objectives of state intervention/planning in India.

The resolution of 1956 has a preamble which states that :

"The adoption of the socialist pattern of society as a national objective, as well as need for planned and rapid development, requires that all industries of basic and strategic importance, or in the nature of public utility services, should be in the public sector. Other industries which are essential and require investment on a scale which only state in the present circumstances could provide, have also to be in the public sector. The state has, therefore, to assume direct responsibility for the future development of industries over a wider area."

The Resolution outlined schedule 'A' of the industries which were to be set up exclusively in the State sector ; schedule 'B' contains industries which would be progressively State owned and the private sector shall only play a supplementary role. All the remaining industries are left to the private initiative, preference again is to be given to new and small ventures.

Schedule 'A'

(1) Arms and ammunition and allied items of defence equipment.
(2) Atomic Energy.
(3) Iron and Steel.
(4) Heavy castings and forgings of iron and steel.
(5) Heavy plant and machinery required for iron and steel production, for mining, for machine tool manufacture and for such other basic industries as may be specified by the Central Government.
(6) Heavy Electrical plant including large hydraulic and steam turbines.
(7) Coal and lignite.
(8) Mineral Oils.
(9) Mining of iron ore, maganese ore, chrome ore, gypsum, sulphur, gold and diamond.
(10) Mining and processing of copper, lead, zinc, tin, molybdenum and wolfram.
(11) Minerals specified in the Schedule to Automic Energy (Control of Production and Use) Order, 1953.
(12) Aircraft.
(13) Railway transport.
(14) Air transport.
(15) Ship building.
(16) Telephones and telephone cable, telegraph and wireless apparatus (excluding radio receiving sets).
(17) Generation and distribution of Electricity.

Schedule 'B'

(1) All other minerals except 'minor minerals' as defined in the Section 3 of Minerals Concession Rules 1949.

(2) Aluminimum and other non-ferrous metals not included in Schedule 'A'.

(3) Machine tools.

(4) Ferro-alloys and tool steels.

(5) Basic and intermediate products required by chemical industries such as the manufacture of drugs, dyestuffs and plastics.

(6) Antibiotics and other essential drugs.

(7) Fertilizers.

(8) Synthetic rubber.

(9) Carbonisation of coal.

(10) Chemical pulp.

(11) Road transport.

(12) Sea transport.

It may be mentioned here that the divisions between public and private sectors in the policy are not 'watertight compartments'. Expansion has been allowed to schedule 'A' industries already existing in private sector. Similarly state sector has ventured into industries which were left to private initiative. Cooperation between public and private sectors was the favoured strategy for industrial growth and it is contended that 1956 policy had the seeds of what is termed as joint sector or national sector.

Besides, checking concentration of economic power and regional imbalance, the often repeated phrases in economic policy documents of Government of India : (*i*) fair and non-discriminatory treatment to private and public sector units where they co-exist ; (*ii*) encouragement to small industries were the objectives of all subsequent policy changes. The main thrust of the industrial policy announced in 1977 was aimed at widely dispersed industrial efforts in small scale and cottage sectors. It is under the influence of this policy that the reserved items for production in small scale sector which were 180 by

1977 were increased to 872 by January, 1984. Special encouragement was to be given to a newly conceived 'Tiny Sector', defined as units whose individual investment in machinery and equipment is upto Rs. 1 lakh and which is situated in towns with population of less than 50,000 as per 1971 census. Later, this limit for qualifying for the protections as tiny units was raised to Rs. 2 lakhs and 1981 census was made the basis of population for location of the industry. Commitment to Khadi, Handloom and Cottage Industries was also reiterated.

The Industrial Policy Statement of July 1980, had put a limit on investment at Rs. 20 lakhs in plants and machinery for small scale units, of Rs. 25 lakhs for ancilliaries. In 1985, these limits were raised to Rs. 35 lakhs for small scale units and Rs. 45 lakhs for ancilliaries. To encourage small scale industries, a number of steps were taken. These included strengthening of Small Industries Development Organisation and setting up District Industry Centres, Testing Centres, Tool Room and Product-cum-Process Development Centres ; providing facilities for export promotion, marketing in India, Ancilliary Development and Purchase of machinery ; conducting entrepreneurial and technical personnel development programmes and providing consultancy services. Small Scale sector's importance as enumerated in various policy documents includes :

(i) Creation of additional employment opportunities for relatively low investment ;

(ii) Increasing the share of mass and intermediate technologies for consumer and industrial products ;

(iii) Mobilisation of untapped capital and labour ;

(iv) Development of a large entrepreneurial class ; and

(v) Making of small sector production export-oriented.

Industrial Licensing Policy and Process

Industrial undertakings other than specially exempted, (e.g., small and ancilliary units, units with investment not exceeding Rs. 5 crores) are required to apply for license. Under the existing procedure, Letters of Intent, Foreign Collaboration Approvals, if any, and clearance for Capital Good Imports, etc., are to be issued within sixty days, if the licensing authorities feel that prescribed conditions for licenses are satisfied. In case of MRTP companies simultaneous applications have to be moved and the clearances can take upto 90 days.

New Industrial Licensing Policy of 1970 envisages the classification of industries into the core sector, the non-core heavy industries sector, the joint sector, the middle sector and the delicensed sector. The relicensed sector, small scale industries sector, the cooperative sector and the export-oriented industries sector are other classifications. As already stated Schedule 'A' industries of Industrial Policy Resolution are reserved for public sector. Both the core and non-core heavy industries sectors are presumed to be those undertakings which require investment of more than Rs. 5 crores. In the core sector private investments by the large industrial house and even MNC's is allowed. In the middle sector with investments ranging between Rs. 1 crore and Rs. 5 crores, new entrepreneurs are favoured. New projects in this category require licenses but the existing entrepreneurs do not require licenses.

Industrial Licensing Policy 1973 introduced the following changes in industrial licensing scene in India :

(1) A large industrial house was defined as one having assets of Rs. 20 crores and more. It was done to reconcile the different positions taken up by the Dutt Committtee and MRTP Act ;

(2) The exemption limit of new investments upto Rs. 1 crore was withdrawn from large business houses and dominant undertakings. Even when the investment was less than Rs. 1 crore, these houses/undertakings were required to seek a licence ;

(3) The list of core industries was expanded and the concept of non-core heavy industry sector in 1970 policy was done away with ; and

(4) Large business houses and FERA companies were allowed to produce mass consumption goods only in special cases.

In 1975, the government delicensed 21 industries and permission was given for an ultimated expansion beyond the licensed capacity to big business and foreign companies in 30 more industries. The trading of excess production was, however, to be controlled. In 1978, again liberalisation on in the so-called 'middle' sector were provided, the exemption limit for licenses was raised from Rs. 1 crore to Rs. 3 crores without any limit on foreign exchange spent on import of raw materials and components. In case of middle sector the upper limit of Rs. 5 crores was also waived for new entrepreneurs.

In 1980, automatic expansion of 5 per cent per annum in production upto a maximum of 25 per cent was allowed to all industries in Appendix I of IDRA, 1951. 5 more industries were allowed for investment by large houses and foreign companies. Industry was allowed to add 33.3 per cent more capacity over and above excess production of 25 per cent. Large and foreign business were allowed entry into many more industries, if they export 60 per cent of the produce for industries not reserved for small sector and the export obligation was to be 75 per cent, if the item belonged to those reserved for the small sector. The provision of enhanced capacity of 33.33 per cent was not to be made available to these business in the industries reserved for small sector and 72 other industries.

Considerations for Grant of Industrial Licenses

The guidelines for industries issued in 1982, by Government of India, outline the considerations while granting industrial licenses :

(1) Five Year Plans or annual plans shall determine the priorities for particular industry from time to time. The proposed investment should be conforming to licensing policies issued according to the priorities laid in National Plans ;

(2) A stock of existing licensed capacity as compared with

the projected demand for proposed manufactures shall be taken while licensing additional capacity ;

(3) The industries involving international trade shall be evaluated for impact on the balance of payment situations of the country ;

(4) Considerations of spatial dispersion shall also be taken into account while issuing licenses ;

(5) Import substitution potential of the proposed manufactures shall also weigh with license issuing authorities. The use of indigenous technical and managerial knowhow shall be a plus point ;

(6) The extent of ancilliarisation to promote small industry by a proposed industry shall be accorded favourable treatment ;

(7) Techno-economic feasibility with regard to size, raw material utilization, production processes, the environmental impact and the project time shall be fully examined ; and

(8) The track-record of established entrepreneurs in respect of the commitments fulfilled by them for earlier licenses issued to them shall be an important consideration.

Agencies of Regulation of Industrial Licenses

The Central Advisory Council (CAC) and Development Council as well as Monopolies Restrictive Trade Practices Commission (MRTPC) are the main bodies exercising regulation with regard to industrial licenses. The role of MRTPC is declining due to the present regime of liberalisation so we shall mainly discuss the role of CAC and Development Councils.

The basic function to CAC is to advise the government on the development and regulation of scheduled industries under IDRA. 1951. The council consists of maximum limit of thirty members with the chairman. All the members and chairmen are appointed by the Central government from among entrepreneurs, consumers, employees and experts on industry. CAC helps in working out capacity needed for products manufactured by scheduled industries. Similar development councils may also be appointed by the Government for individual industries.

IDRA also confers on these councils powers of investigation for ensuring compliance to licensing conditions, to assume management control of erring firms or provide relief from various controls and control the supply, distribution of goods as well as prices of licensee industries. The MRTPC was set up in 1970 under MRTP Act. In its discharge of functions for preventing concentration of economic power, it inquiries and provides opinion to the central government for various business expansion or growth proposals which may be taken into consideration in granting licenses or cancelling these to monopolistic or dominant undertakings.

According to the Capital Issues Control Provisions, every company, in addition to obtaining licenses has to seek the permission of Controller of Capital Issues to make an issue of Capital in India ; to make a public offer of sales of securities and to renew or postpone the date of maturity or repayment of any security maturing for payment in India. This permission is also required for right issues or bonus shares. Private Limited Companies, banking and insurance companies in order to invite public subscription shall seek the permission from the Controller. In other kind of capital mobilisation operations, they are exempted. Similarly, if the issue capital is less than Rs. 25 lakhs over twelve months, even Public Limited Companies may not take permission.

As already pointed out permissions of RBI are required in case of foreign capital investments under FERA, 1973.

Price and International Trade Controls

As already pointed out, in a mixed economy price formation is not left to the market mechanism. The government in India controls both internal and external trade. The controls on internal trade are mainly in form of direct or indirect price controls. The direct controls include administered pricing, dual pricing, subsidisation and the use of provisions of Essential Commodities Act.

Prices of key commodities, essential for economic development like steel, cement, coal, fertilizers, aluminium and electricity, are administered by the Central government. Prices are determined by Bureau of Industrial Costs and Prices (BICP) or inter-ministerial undertakings with a view to protect the interests of both producers and consumers. Sometimes, however, either of these two segments complains about unrealistic prices worked out by BICP.

In certain commodities of mass consumption like sugar, cotton textiles, paper and aluminium, dual pricing system has been adopted. A part of the output of these commodities, is procured by the government at a price lower than the market price, to be passed on to the weaker sections of the society. Rest of the production is left with the manufacturers, to be disposed off in open market. The criterion used in dual pricing is that government acquired portion of goods shouldn't be acquired at lesser than the cost of production.

In case the price at which the government wants to pass on commodities to weaker sections does not equal cost of production, government subsidises the producers from its budgetary allocations. At other times, to meet export obligations, subsidies are provided to the producers. Food/fertilizer subsidies are meant to help weaker sections and farmers.

The government has prepared a list of 60 essential items under ESMA, 1985. The production and distribution of these commodities is regulated by the government to maintain or increase their supplies and equitable distribution of these at fair prices. In emergency times, these items may be regulated to meet the defence needs. There are many other acts which have similar purpose and check illegal trade.

Monetary policy aimed at regulating supply of money and Fiscal Policy aimed at raising revenues have also a crucial role in price-determination in the Indian market. Indirect taxation and deficit financing have been singled out as the two main culprits for inflationary pressures, besides the practice of hiking administered prices too often.

The Import-Export Policy of the country has increasingly been geared to be export and production oriented. The international trade policy system covers the following :

(i) tariff policy of imports ;

(ii) import licensing system ;

(iii) exchange controls and exchange rate policy ;

(iv) export tax and subsidy ;

(v) import replenishment licenses against exports ;

(vi) cash subsidies for export promotion ;

(vii) the other export promotion measures like special credit facilities, duty drawback schemes, etc. ; and

(viii) indirect taxes on imports and domestic production.

The existing Export and Import Policy emphasises technology upgradation, with special emphasis on export promotion and energy conservation. The principal features of the policy are the allocation of permissible imports by categories such as capital goods, raw materials, maintenance imports, etc., among sectors and industries by means of an elaborate administrative machinery. Only those goods are allowed to be imported which are essential and are not available indigenously. Essentiality of goods have to be worked for all the categories while granting import licenses. Quota restrictions are imposed, regardless of international price comparisons to eliminate imports of goods which are domestically produced. Infant industry argument for tariff protection to domestic produce is gradually being abondoned and 1978 onwards liberalisation of imports has started. India is a party to General Agreement on Trade and Tariffs (GATT) but is opposing the recent moves of USA backed move for bringing services in purview of GATT.

The Import-Export Policy announced for 1984-85 had considerably liberalised the import of capital goods. 149 items have been added to the list of Open General License (OGL), 53 items have been taken of the list, 13 items have been shifted from one category to the other to make imports easier. The banned list (except beef tallow) has been abolished. The period of import license has been extended from 12 to 18 months.

Incentives provided for non-traditional exports have been increased and handsome export incentives are being provided but these shall be discussed in details on the promotional role of the State. The IMF repayment obligations has made India accept certain conditionalities and the subsidisation of exports and liberal imports of capital goods for export production, setting up free trade zones enjoying immunity from regulatory mechanism are a few measures which have been taken to increase exports. Exports have been taken up even ignoring the domestic demand for essential commodities like rice and textiles.

In a critical appraisal of import and export policy 1988-91, Charn D. Wadhva maintains that while the policy incorporates several innovations aimed at further trade liberalisation, these taken together are not enough to push Indian industry to strive to raise the international competitiveness of its products so as to achieve the twin objectives of efficient import substitution and efficient promotion. The major objectives of the policy are listed as :

(1) To stimulate industrial growth by providing easy access to essential imported capital goods, raw materials and components to industry and to sustain the movement towards modernisation, technological upgradation and making the industry progressively competitive internationally.

(2) To promote efficient import substitution and self reliance.

(3) To give fresh impetus to export promotion by improving the quality of incentives and their administration.

(4) To simplify and rationalise policy and procedures. 745 additional items have been put on OGL.

The import of selected capital goods shall be allowed without considering the indigenous availability. Import replenishment scheme is being extended even to traditional exports. However, for recognition of export houses, the provision have been changed and entrepreneur merchant exporter scheme has been abolished. Imports by NRI's have been made easier. Canalisation of exports through public sector agencies has been changed and 26 items have been decanalised.

The Regulatory Mechanism of the Government

The Planning Commission and Programme Implementation Ministry are apex bodies for planning, direction and control of Indian economy. They have responsibilities for inter-sectoral transactions and working out the targets of savings, investments, production in all the sectors and they also keep an eye on prices and balance of payment position.

The Ministry of Industry has the exclusive responsibility for industrial development but then for some key sectors of Indian industrial economy and for infrastructural facilities, there are separate ministries. That is why, the concept of inter-ministry bodies have been evolved. The Ministry of Industry has further divisions in the form of Department of Industrial Development and Department of Heavy Industry/Public Sector undertakings.

The Department of Industrial Development formulates and implements Central Government's Industrial Policy under the guidance of Planning Commission. IDRA, 1951 provisions are also implemented through the department. The department administers certain allocated industries directly. The Secretariat of Industrial Approvals in the Department processes applications of industrial licenses, foreign collaboration and import of capital goods. There is a special desk for formulation of industrial and licensing policy. The Industries division is a promotional and administering division for certain allocated industries. The financial management of industries ministry is looked after by the Finance Division of the Department. As is usual with all Ministries, there is an Administration and General Division for personnel in the Department.

The Department of Public Sector Undertakings looks after basic and capital goods industries in public sector. Capital goods are controlled by this Department.

Directorate General of Technical Development (DGTD) gives technical consultancy to the various Ministries/Departments. It is a private organisation specialising in technology, exports and imports, foreign collaboration and about tariff structures. The organisation has two functional wings Engineering and Non-engineering. It doesn't deal with industries of iron and steel, textiles, jute, sugar and vanaspati.

DGTC has regional offices at Madras and Calcutta which provide advice to entrepreneurs, Joint Chief Controller of Imports and Exports, the Department of Customs and other organisations. It co-ordinates functioning with the provincial directorates of industries in all states. The Technology Information Centre in DGTD collects information on technology which is used for processing proposals of foreign collaboration, choice of technologies and entrepreneurial guidance. This Technology Development Division in the directorate functions as Secretariat of Technical Evaluation Committee which examines international and as well as national transfers of technology and state of technology in the country.

Department of Industrial Development has an Economic Adviser's office which collects and compiles macro-economic statistics on foreign exchange position and its allocation; for raw materials, industrial production, wholesale prices; the tariff structures to stimulate investment; employment with the categorisation of natives and foreigners. Industrial statistics like capacity utilization, wholesale price Index are generated on monthly basis and help the policy makers in designing appropriate policies. Bureau of Industrial Costs and Prices

Regulation and Control of Business

(BICP) advises on administered, dual prices and market movements of prices, alongwith costs of production and measures to reduce costs and increasing productivity. Directorate General of Industrial Contingency (DGIC) insures industrial peace by preparing contingency plans. It overlooks labour situation and provides civil and/or paramilitary or police assistance to strife-torn industries. Directorate General of Supplies and Disposals (DGS&D) is the government's central purchasing organisation and procures governmental needs at all levels of the government. Of course, certain agencies of government are autonomous of DGS&D. DGS&D accepts tenders, decides rate contracts and running contracts and enters into price contracts by the selling agencies.

Most of the agencies mentioned above and agencies related with small industry, Ministries of Civil Supplies and Commerce play a role which is not just regulatory but promotional to industry. Even regulation and control of industry with a macroeconomic perspective amounts to protection of industry and preventing the economic sickness, presently afflicting Indian industries.

Summing Up

In a sample study of 752 companies conducted by Corporate Study Group of IIPA, the researchers feel that Industrial Licensing System is incapable of restricting overcapitalisation in organised private sector. The emphasis, or late, have been only on quick clearances, without a serious contemplation on the consequences of licensing uncalled for capacity in an economy which is essentially demand constrained. Salient features of the present day licensing of industrial capacity, brought out by S.K. Goyal's group are :

(1) Follow up of licenses has been unsatisfactory resulting in low utilisation of installed capacities. In two thirds of the cases studied, capacity utilization was lesser than 60% which resulted in higher capital-output ratio. MRTP and FERA companies performance, in this

regard, is especially disappointing because these companies are supposed to be over-regulated, as per the supply side critics of Indian industrial policies.

(2) It seems that resources generated in the name of licenses for priority sector production are diverted by MNC's to take up production in their non-priority sector productions, because the latter may be more profitable. 102 companies in the sample were producing far in excess of authorised capacity for non-priority goods whereas their production for priority sectors showed underutilization of capacity.

(3) The reporting of physical production by the companies doesn't follow any standard or uniform pattern as to show the real progress with regard to the implementation of licensed capacities. Even after ILIC and Hathi Committee reports unauthorised production of certain banned or harmful items has continued in the socalled over-regulated Private Corporate Sector in India. Export obligations or priority sector production are suffering on account of lack of a proper feedback mechanism to keep the licensing authorities informed.

(4) It seems that it is non-regulation of production, distribution, pricing and quality of goods which has resulted in the present chaotic situations. Monopolies have been created and new entries have been very few. Economic sickness and high costs of industrial production are the results of an indequate regulation and control procedure and it is not *vice versa* as is made out by the proponents of economic liberalisation.

But despite these studies by competent groups of experts, liberalisation of licensing has been going on, as is evident from 1982 policy. BM, in a recent commentary in Economic and Political Weekly (June 25, 1988) on the politicians, and Prime Minister's emphasis on liberalisation observes : "The criterion of essentiality of new investment, Indian and foreign, in terms of mass needs and self-reliant growth, is being decisively extinguished. The process will fit very well with investment pattern and production structure which has no relevance to the needs of the broad mass of the Indian people."

CASE VII

EXPANSION OF CAPACITY FOR SODA ASH

With the increased demand for Soda ASH, a vital input of fertilizers, many business houses made applications for creation or expansion of capacity for the manufacture of this product. In fact, at the height of 'green revolution', Soda Ash promised to be a very profitable product. In the early Seventies, many houses were granted letters of intent by the Industries Ministry of Government of India.

Tata-chemicals was already manufacturing Soda Ash and secured the permission of the government to double its capacity. But this was not enough to meet one million tonnes demand of this product at that time. Tatas could barely manufacture half a million tonnes after receiving approval of the expansion of their capacity in two instalments in 1971-72. Birlas made applications for a new undertaking and expansion of capacity by Saurashtra Chemicals, a Birla Company which was already manufacturing Soda Ash. The government rather than honouring letters of intent issued to other parties allowed expansion of capacity taking the capacity with Birlas to 0.3 million tonnes.

Thus our licensing authorities including MRTPC allowed the two largest houses in the Private Corporate Sector attain a virtual monopolistic position in this vital input for our agricultural economy. With the subsidies on fertilizers and near oligopolistic situation in the Soda Ash production, the prices charged by these for this critical input by two houses were not internationally competitive.

In the late Seventies when the demand for Soda Ash increased, the government allowed imports of this input. Bulgarian firms were supplying the input at much lesser prices.

At that time Birlas and Tatas made a common cause for protective tariffs decrying the open door policy in imports followed by the government. They alleged that international firms were dumping their product whereas the domestic capacity was going unutilized. This, of course, was an exception to the liberalisation of external trade for which our top houses stand in the Eighties.

POINTS FOR CONSIDERATION

(1) Does this instance prove to you that Dutt Committee conclusions about regulatory policies aiding concentration in our country are justified ?

(2) Can the import-export policy in India be based on the international divisions of industry on the principle of comparative cost advantage as is suggested by Import-Export Policy 1988-91 ?

FURTHER READINGS

1. Amarchand, D., *Government and Business in India*, New Delhi, Tata McGraw Hill, 1984.

2. Corporate Studies Group, *Functioning of Industrial Licensing System*, New Delhi, IIPA, 1983.

3. Dasgupta, A., and N.K. Sengupta, Delhi, Allied Book Agency, 1985.

4. Government of India, Department of Industrial Development, *Guidelines of Industries Part I—Policy and Procedure*, New Delhi, 1982.

5. — —, *Guidelines of Industries*, New Delhi, Ministry of Industry and Civil Supplies.

6. ——, *Report of Dagli Committee on Controls and Subsidies*, New Delhi.

7. ——, *Seventh Five Year Plan 1985-90*, Vol. II, New Delhi, Planning Commission.

8. Industrial Finance Corporation of India, *Investing in Industries in India—A Guide for Resident and Non-Resident Indian Entrepreneurs*, New Delhi, 1984.

9. Wadhwa, Charn, D., "Import and Export Policy 1988-91, A Provisional Appraisal", *Economic and Political Weekly*, Vol. XXIII, No. 26, June 25, 1988.

8
Industrial Support System in India

Government-business relationship in India is double edged. On one hand, the governmental agencies regulate and control the functioning of business. The focus in this chapter is, however, on promotional and supporting rolle of the Government of India. The supportive role of the government consists of providing direct incentives such as cash subsidies, tax concessions and concessional finances to meet the fixed and working capital needs. Besides, the government provides infrastructural facilities for industrial development. It is rightly argued that public sector in India is not a competitor but a collaborator of private sector in Indian mixed economy. Public sector undertakings also meet the capital goods needs of private sector.

Government in India provides a transport network to facilitate the movement of raw materials and finished products of private industry. The roads, railways, airways as well as waterways network largely owes its origin to the initiative of the government. Indian Railways is the fourth largest in the world and is, in fact, the spinal cord of Indian market/economy. The tariff structure of Indian Railways and its emphasis on goods transportation facilitate private industry's easy access to the large Indian market. More than one million wagon loads of freight move over the nooks and corners of the country, every month.

Similarly, both the Central and the State governments

supply coal, electricity and petroleum products to meet the energy needs of private industries, at rates lower than the ones charged for domestic consumption. The electricity generated every month is 18,616 million kilo watt hours, as per statistics available in the beginning of 1989. Though plant-load is low in Indian electricity generating units yet the situation is gradually improving. The growing Indian business has access to power at quite cheap rates, notwithstanding the power cuts which are largely on account of increasing needs of power in agricultural sector. Non-conventional sources of energy are also being explored as highlighted in technological environment of business. Captive power generation by industrial units is also being promoted.

The postal and telecommunication services are also provided by the government and with the new technology missions of Sam Pitroda, the telecommunication network is showing marked improvements. Water needs of private industry are also provided by the governmental agencies. Social housing schemes, developed industrial plots, estates and townships are made available to entrepreneurs by the Central Government as well as State Industrial Directorates.

Incentive Schemes for New Ventures

Various schemes have been introduced to help small and medium scale industries in the private sector. It seems reasonable on the part of the government to let the established business fend for itself through internal generation of resources while providing more support to new ventures. It is argued that Vizag Steel Plant constructed at the cost of Rs. 7,500 crores could employ 20,000 persons. A similar investment in small scale sector may provide employment to one million people. Among the various incentives and subsidies provided to entrepreneurs in different parts of the country a mention of a few is in order here.

Tax Incentives

The taxation structure in India is being constantly changed

to give incentive to private savings and investments. Among the incentives and concessions announced in this regard, the following is an illustrative list :

(a) New industrial ventures including ships, hotels and business of repairs of ocean going vessels or other powered crafts are exempted for a period of 8 years (10 years, in the case of co-operatives) from income tax to the extent of 25 per cent of the profits earned by them, in the case of companies and to the extent of 20 per cent of such profits, in the case of other entities. Complete tax holiday, in lieu of all other tax concessions is also available to industrial undertakings set up in Free Trade Zones, for an initial period of five years.

(b) New Industrial units and hotels, set up in the areas declared backward, are allowed a deduction equal to 20 per cent of the profits or gains derived by them while computing their taxable profits. This concession is available for 10 years from the date of establishment of the industry.

(c) A deduction, on account of investment allowance, is allowed at the rate of 25 per cent of the cost of new plant and machinery installed for generation and distribution of electricity or any other form of power, for construction, for manufacture of an article or thing except those considered to be of low priority. For checking pollution, the control equipment is allowed upto 35 per cent deduction for tax purposes. However, 75 per cent of the allowance has to be used for modernisa- of machinery over a period of ten years.

(d) Depreciation allowance upto 100 per cent is provided on 7 broad categories of industries. The rate applicable is $1\frac{1}{2}$ times of the cost for machinery installed after 31st March, 1980.

(e) For indigenous technology-based plants and machinery, investment allowance is 35 per cent in respect of the installations after 30th June, 1977.

(f) Entire expenditure on scientific research is allowed to be deducted from the income to be taxed. Similarly, one per cent of export turnover, in the previous year can be deducted, 5 per cent of incremental export turnover over the immediately preceding year as compared with the previous year's turnover is also allowed deduction.

(g) There are provisions for amortisation of project, feasibility reports and capital costs.

(h) 60-100% of the intercorporate dividends earned by the companies of the various types is allowed to be deducted from the taxable income, to avoid double taxation.

(i) There are arrangement for carry forward and set off of accumulated business losses and carry forward on unabsorbed depreciation in case of amalgamations for turn-around of sick companies.

(j) Indian companies transferring technologies to other companies enjoy tax exemptions on the incomes generated by such transfers.

(k) There are exemptions from income tax of interest on new capital investment bonds in specified financial assets, investments, etc.

(l) Initial equity capital, of new companies, is also granted exemption from Wealth Tax for five years.

(m) Any foreign investor loaning to Indian enterprises doesn't incur tax on interests. Similarly, there are tax concessions to foreign technicians and experts and Non-Resident Indians (NRI's).

It can be concluded from the numerous tax concessions in direct taxes that Direct Tax Laws are designed in India to promote savings and investments. A comprehensive Direct Taxes Legislation is on anvil in India. The salient features of the Direct Taxes (Amendment) Bill, 1988 are :

(1) Deductions from income under Section 35, *i.e.*, of payments made to the Associations or Institutions carrying out scientific research, rural development or conservation of natural resources are being allowed again.

(2) Fees received by foreign companies giving technical services in respect of defence agreements will be exempted from taxes, irrespective of whether the services are rendered in India or elsewhere.

(3) Income from NRI bonds purchased by NRI's shall also be exempted.

(4) Further concessions on R & D expenditure for research institutions/institutions of national importance have been proposed.

(5) Investment allowance will be made available for machinery installed after March 31, 1988 at 20 per cent on cost as reduced by the amounts drawn from deposits made for this purpose.

(6) In order to encourage hotel industry, the deduction under Section 80 (c) will also be available on shares of hotels. Similarly some tax concessions are also allowed to hotel/travel industry with regard to services provided to the foreign tourists.

(7) Some provisions aim at strict compliance of tax rates and laws.

Estate duty has been abolished. Besides, there are various concessions in central as well as state sales taxes to small industries. MODVAT or value added tax can also be construed as a Tax concession in duty structure to the extent that double excise duties have been avoided. Special features of tax concessions to the NRI's can be summarised as follows :

—Income from units purchased out of funds remitted from abroad or from non-resident account is free from income tax.

Industrial Support System in India

—Balances held in non-residents external accounts are free from wealth tax.

—Moneys and values of assets brought into India at the time of return to India for permanent settlement, are exempted from wealth tax for a period of seven years.

—Investment in new equity issues of companies in the priority sector is free from wealth tax.

—Investment in certain notified saving certificates including 6 years National Savings Certificate is free from income, wealth and gift taxes.

—Gifts made out of non-resident external incomes are exempt from income tax.

—Remittances to India out of foreign incomes are exempt from income tax.

—Investment income from foreign exchange assets is chargeable to income tax at a concessional flat rate of 22.5 per cent, inclusive of surcharge.

—Non-resident returning to India for permanent settlement can also retain their foreign bank accounts, foreign securities abroad and immovable properties subject to certain specified provisions.

—Non-resident medical practitioners/scientists, etc., returning to India for permanent settlement can import professional equipments/instrument upto a value of Rs. one lakh without an import license subject to certain conditions.

—Non-residents can seek priority in allotment of scooter, tractors, etc., against their remittances/savings in foreign exchange, subject to the specified provisions.

In fact, a number of amnesty schemes to promote bringing back of wealth amassed outside the country or in the domestic black economy have been announced so that this money can be channelised to promote industrial growth in India.

Backward areas are receiving top priority for overcoming uneven development of industries. Industries have been classified into three categories for providing investment subsidy. 25 per cent of capital investment is provided as subsidy, subject to a maximum of Rs. 25 lakhs for more than hundred identified 'Zero Industry Districts'. 15 per cent of the investment subject to a maximum of Rs. 15 lakhs for 55 backward districts of category 'B' shall be provided as subsidy. In another 246 districts, concessional finance and 10 per cent subsidy subject to a maximum of Rs. 10 lakhs is provided.

Concessions for nucleus plants providing for ancilliarisation, assistance to state governments for infrastructural development, allowing MRTP/FERA companies to set up industries and provision of freight subsidies, etc., are other measures for industrial development for the backward areas. Price support to the extent of $17\frac{1}{2}$ per cent higher prices charged by small scale industries and 5 per cent for large industries are given by various State governments. The State governments of Andhra Pradesh, Maharashtra and West Bengal have also been able to rope in sizeable non-resident investments.

Institutional Framework for Developing Small Enterprises

An elaborate institutional framework for entrepreneurial development has been created especially to assist Small Scale Industries (SSI's). There are a large number of Central, State and District level institutions which assist SSI's. The premier organisations at the Central level are :

Small Industries Development Organisation (SIDO)

SIDO is an apex body for policy making, co-ordinating and monitoring the development of SSI's. It provides extension services to these units all over the country. Other responsibilities of the organisation are :

(1) Preparing programmes and policies for the development of small industries.

(2) To maintain a liaison with State government industrial directorates to co-ordinate Central and State efforts for development of SSI's.

(3) To co-ordinate the efforts of Planning Commission, financial institutions and large industries in supporting small undertakings.

(4) To prepare and implement programmes for developing industrial estates and District Industry Centres (DIC's).

The organisation provides help in procurement of raw materials, machinery, technical expertise to small units in consultation with other agencies. Its extension network consists of 26 Small Industries Service Institutes, 32 Branch Institutes, 40 Extension Centres, 4 Regional Testing Centres, 10 Process-cum-Product Development Centres, 17 Field Testing Stations and 2 Training Centres. It helps ancilliarisation and marketing in both domestic and international markets.

National Small Industries Corporation (NSIC)

NSIC supplies machinery and equipment to small enterprises on hire-purchase basis and assists them in procuring orders for various items for the governmental purchases. It also distributes scarce raw materials. It not only asssists the marketing efforts but undertakes direct marketing of SSI produce. It develops technology at small scale and provides training in selected trades. It also exports turnkey projects for small industries development.

Small Industries Extension and Training Institute (SIETI)

SIETI provides consultancy service, research facilities and training facilities. It also trains the trainers of SIDO. It undertakes training programmes for more than 1,000 participants, on an average, during the last few years. Small Enterprises National Documentation Centre collects information for small business, and has branches in various regions of India.

Central Institute of Tool Design takes up tool production

technical consultancy and training in this area. It also maintains a technical information cell for SSI's. *Institute for Design of Electrical Measuring Instruments* provides technical knowhow to instrument manufactures. *Prototype Development and Training Centres* at Rajkot, Okhla, Howrah and Madras sell machine tools, execute job orders and by developing prototypes transfer these to SSI's for commercial production. They also train skilled workers taking up production of the Centres' prototypes.

NIESBD

A National Board for Enterpreneurial Development and a National Institute for Entrepreneurship and Small Business Development (NIESBD) were established in 1983 for laying down policies, reviewing the programmes and co-ordinating the activities and the programmes of various agencies in the field of entrepreneurship development of different target groups. The Institute has been organising and conducting training programmes for motivators, trainers and entrepreneurs, preparing model syllabus of training of entrepreneurs. It also conducts research and organises meets to promote entrepreneurship.

Other Promotional Agencies at Central Level

Indian Investment Centre and eighteen export promotion councils have been established for setting up joint ventures abroad and the promotion of the export of specific commodities or groups of products. The councils advise Union Government in respect of its export policies, undertake international market surveys, organise trade fairs, delegations and exhibitions. They also undertake standardisation of quality, publicity and arbitration in a bid to promote exports. Besides, *Commodity Boards* have been set up for export of our traditional items. They undertake generic promotion for Coffee, Tea, Cardamon, Rubber, Coir, Silk, Handicrafts and Handlooms.

KVIC's (Khadi and Village Industries Corporations) have been been set up to promote cottage industries. *Indian Institute of*

Packaging (*IIP*) undertakes value engineering, standardisation, demonstration, testing and trading in the field of packaging as well as packing. *Export Inspection Council* (*EIC*) advises industry about quality specifications in international markets. State Trading Corporation (STC) and Minerals and Metals Trading Corporation (MMTC) take up trading and procurement of certain specified items in international as well as domestic markets. As already suggested CSIR, NRDC's Institutions of Technology and other state sector training organisations develop technology, train manpower for industry. Institutes of manangement, university departments and Entrepreneurial Development Institute are also largely financed from the state exchequer.

State Level Organisations

Apart from the directorates of industries which provide for basic infrastructure for industrial estates, townships, in pursuance of various national/provincial level industrialisation programmes. They also organise training programmes and provide common facility services like industrial project appraisal agencies and stores for key inputs.

State Industrial Development Corporations are also set up for procurement of raw materials and marketing assistance. In some cases these undertakings also have their own production units and are assigned with management of particular industrial complexes for SSI.

Besides, there are corporations/boards for providing infrastructural support, finances and marketing assistance to industry in the States. The main district level institutions through which Central and State governments undertake industrial support functions are District Industry Centres (DIC's). There are around 400 DIC's covering all the districts in the country. It is, in fact, suggested by some studies that DIC's can function as Single Window Industrial Support Systems (SWISS) for self employment programmes like SEEUY, Village and Cottage Industries as well as small scale sector in rural industrialisation.

Industrial dispersal, in the Gandhian sense, can be insured if DIC's are able to carry on their training, financing or promotional functions efficiently. They have been provided with adequate administrative machinery to act as foster mothers for healthy and sick small units.

Public Financial Institutions

Development banking includes a network of institutions designed to mobilise resources from public at large and channelise these to the priority sectors, outlined in the economic policy of Indian government. There are specialised institutions for looking after the needs of primary sector like National Bank of Agricultural Development. Industry mobilizes resources from varied term lending institutions like Unit Trust of India (UTI), Life Insurance Corporation (LIC), and General Insurance Corporation (GIC), besides public financing institutions like Industrial Development Bank of India (IDBI) which are specially assigned the role of meeting long term needs of the Industry. The commercial banking system supplies the short-term working capital needs of the industry. The development banks have a number of objectives like stimulating an investment climate for industrial securities, providing risk capital or long term credit and assume the role of venture capital firms for financing the new entrepreneurs. In essence the development banks support private initiative to fulfil the needs of industrial development in India.

The Industrial Finance Corporation of India (IFCI) was set up as the first industrial development bank in 1948. Subsequently, with the enactment of the State Financial Corporation Act 1951, the provincial level counterparts of the national corporation came up in some states. *National Industrial Development Corporation (NIDC)* was the second term lending institution at national level and was set up in 1954. To handle foreign exchange loans from World Bank and other international agencies, *Industrial Credit and Investment Corporation (ICICI)* came up in 1955, IDBI followed suit in 1964. Later in 1971, *Industrial Reconstruction Corporation of India (IRCI)* was established. The more recent among the public financing institutions are *Export Import Bank of India* (*EXIM*) 1982, and *Industrial Reconstruction Bank of India* (*IRBI*) 1985. Besides insurance business was nationalised and organisations like LIC and GIC came under the control of government. UTI also holds the shares of public limited companies and it came up in 1963. There have been realignments in the business of various public financing institutions and the contemporary framefork of institutions is discussed in the following paragraphs :

Industrial Development Bank of India (IDBI)

IDBI is the apex financial institution and coordinates, directs and monitors operations of Central and State level financing institutions for industrial development. IDBI, on its own finances all types of industries engaged in manufacture or processing of goods, mining, transport, generation and distribution of power, etc., both in public and private sectors. As a developmental bank, it also assists the creation of a new class of entrepreneurs. The assistance pattern of IDBI shows that on an average 75 per cent of its assistance goes to the private sector, 10 per cent to the co-operative sector and rest to the public sector. The sources of Bank finances include share capital, borrowings from the Government/RBI, market borrowings, foreign currency borrowings, deposits from companies, repayment of past assistance and sale of investments. The Bank tries to work for the goals of checking concentration and regional imbalance in the industrial growth of India. The promotional measures of Bank include floating of Technical consultancy organisation, loans for various kinds to SSI's, assistance to technicians and for modernisation of industries.

In fact, IDBI channelises the support to the industries through other term lending institutions at the national and provincial levels. IDBI had disbursed financial assistance to the tune of Rs. 12,000 crores by 1985-86. The largest part was provided through refinancing of State Financial Corporation loans to industry. The industrialised states of Maharashtra and Gujarat were the largest beneficiaries of IDBI operations, followed by Uttar Pradesh and Tamil Nadu. In the form of loans, its average during the Eighties has been about Rs. 30 crores annually. With LIC's withdrawing from the capital market, IDBI has emerged as the major underwriter of capital issues. It has also subscribed to the share capital of SFC's IFCI, ICICI, UTI, IRCI and Technical Consultancy Organisations.

Industrial Finance Corporation of India (IFCI)

IFCI supplements medium and long range capital needs of a wide range of industries. It grants loans both in Indian and foreign currencies, takes up underwriting operations for capital issues and guarantees deferred payments of machinery whether procured domestically or internationally. Besides new projects, IFCI finances renovation, modernisation and diversification plans of existing units. Foreign currency loans are provided only for import of capital goods. The corporation has assisted around 2000 projects with a sanctioned amount of Rs. 2,500 crores. Sources of its finances includes share capital ; retained earnings ; repayment of loans by borrowers ; sale/redemption of investments ; borrowings from the market by issue of bonds ; borrowings from IDBI ; Central Government, foreign credit agencies and capital markets. IFCI plays a major role in providing concessional loans to traditional industries like cotton and jute textiles.

IFCI promotes measures to increase productivity of human and material resources by supportive measures for entrepreneurs through technical consultancy organisations. IFCI is the main agency of commercial borrowings in Euro Currency markets.

Industrial Credit and Investment Corporation of India (ICICI)

ICICI, in contrast to other organisations of development banking, only concentrates on assisting private sector. The sources of its funds include loans from Government of India, IDBI, lines of credit extended to India by World Bank. foreign loans as well as borrowings in domestic market. It provides scarce foreign currency loans and provides underwriting facilities. It helps in creation, expansion and modernisation of private sector companies and participates in equity of private sector. ICICI also provides managerial, technical and administrative services to the industry. The share capital of Corporation is around Rs. 27 crores rupees. Textile industry is the top beneficiary of loans, followed by non-electrical machinery. ICICI underwrites fixed interest bearing securities of the established companies and concentrates on large capital issues.

In 1983, the Corporation started leasing finance, counselling for industrial investment to NRI's. It is also taking up merchant banking and operates soft loan schemes for traditional industries.

Industrial Reconstruction Bank of India (IRBI)

IRBI basically aims at curing the problem of industrial sickness in India. It has become a statutory corporation in 1985. It takes over sick and closed industrial units after feasibility studies, assists them financially for both long term and working capital needs to revive them and nurse them to corporate health. IRBI is a joint endeavour of IDBI, LIC, ICICI and public sector banks.

Export-Import Bank of India (EXIM)

EXIM was established in 1982, with a view to finance export-import trade with the help of other institutions extending credit for international trade. The issued capital of EXIM till 1984 was Rs. 127.50. The bank is empowered to grant credit to commercial banks/financial institutions for purpose of refinancing export/import operations. It accepts, collects, discounts, rediscounts, purchases, sells, negotiates bills of exchange or promissory notes both in India and internationally to promote international trade. It can open, grant, issue or confirm letters of credit and collects bills and other documents drawn, thereunder. EXIM also acts as a merchant banker for export-import unit. It may provide finance as equity participation by Indian companies in joint ventures abroad. It deals in foreign exchange.

The sources of EXIM funds constitute borrowings in the capital market. It also earns from trustee securities and lodgement of bills and promissiory notes for commercial transactions. It also avails long-term credit from RBI. If required, it can go for commercial borrowings in the international markets.

National Bank for Agriculture and Rural Development (NBARD)

Established in 1982, NBARD extends credits for short term, medium term and long term requirements of rural industries, especially in the handloom and co-operative sectors. It also helps consultancy and research for rural industrialisation programmes while concentrating on agricultural/rural development programmes. It also co-ordinates the functioning of rural credit agencies for optimising the affectiveness of lending operations.

State Financing Corporations (SFC's)

SFC's are the major institutions for ensuring balanced regional development of industry. Since Central Public Financing Institutions tend to be biased in favour of large industries in the industrialised States, backward area development programmes and assistance to small and medium industries is largely channelised through SFC's. SFC's have a role similar to Central level institutions in providing term loans to the entrepreneurs in their respective States. They provide capital assistance to technician entrepreneurs and make available foreign exchange to their clients in the respective States, by making use of World Bank credit extended to them.

Financial Assistance by Public Financing Institutions

The details of financial assistance disbursed by various institutions for three years appear in Table 8.1.

Apart from the small units, liberal term-lending facilities also exist in India for large and medium size companies having investment above Rs. 3 crores. IDBI, ICICI and IFCI act as a consortium for finances to set up new projects as well as for expansion, diversification, modernisation and rehabilitation of

TABLT 8.1

Institution-wise Details of Disbursement of Assistance by All-India Financial Institutions During the Years 1983-84 to 1985-86

(Rs. in Crores)

Sl. No.	Institutions	Disbursements 1983-84	1984-85	1985-86
1.	IDBI	1,763.86	2,006.19	2,768.74
2.	IFCI	224.46	272.88	403.89
3.	ICICI	334.20	392.73	482.17
4.	LIC	140.90	161.54	261.87
5.	UTI	139.34	236.24	528.85
6.	GIC	84.54	110.54	107.34

Source: Minister of Finance, R S. Uns. Q. 2712, dated 19th March, 1987.

existing industrial units. Whereas the term lending institutions meet the block capital requirements of the industry, the requirements of working capital of the industry are met by commercial banks. A wide range of activities from food processing, manufacturing and technical consultancy are eligible for financial assistance both in the form of participation in equity as well as loans. Loans are available in both Indian and foreign currencies. Priority is, however, given to labour intensive, indigenous technology based, energy saving, export promoting units and the units located in backward areas.

The category 'A' districts in notified backward areas can get loan assistance upto Rs. 5 crores and underwriting facilities for amounts upto Rs. 2.5 crores. Similarly, category 'B' districts qualify for loans upto Rs. 3 crores and under writing assistance for half the amount. For 'C' category districts, loans upto Rs. 2 crores and underwriting arrangements upto Rs. 1 crore are made by Financial Institutions at Central level. There are two project specific and area specific schemes for financing even the infrastructural projects in industrially backward districts. State financing institutions also provide financial assistance for both industrial undertakings and infrastructural ventures, at concessional rates of interest.

For modernisation of the existing units, loans upto Rs. 4 crores are available at interest rates of 11.5 per cent as compared to 14 per cent normally charged by the financial institutions. Only 10 years old units are eligible for assistance under this scheme and the loans are given for technology upgradation in various facilities for manufactures or export oriented production. A similar scheme also operates for the energy units which help in development of renewable energy systems. The rate of interest charged from these units is 12.5 per cent. 100 per cent export oriented units can claim a rebate of 1.5 per cent on the loans from financial institutions.

Norms and Conditions of Financing

The financing norms prescribe viability of the project and promoter's competence in implementing. Growth prospects in the future and social cost-benefit analyses are also undertaken in clearing a project for financial assistance. The debit-equity norms and promoters' contribution for varied projects are different. Normally, 10-20 per cent promoter's participation in equity and a debt-equity ratio of 2 : 1 is standard yardstick. Listing of stock for shareholders is regulated by Security Contracts (Regulation) Act, 1956.

There is a differential interest rate structure for the loan assistance provided by public financing institutions. The institutions retain an option to convert 20 per cent of loans/debentures into equity in some cases of default. Certain schemes, however, are exempted from convertibility clause. Certain loans provide for equitable mortgage or hypothecation of assets of the company seeking loans. Loans have to be paid back in 7 to 10 years.

Apart from underwriting, public institutions also make direct subscription to the small and medium-sized capital issues. The underwriting commission is 1.5 per cent on the publicly subscribed amount and 2.5 per cent on the devolved amount in case of debentures. In case of shares the commission is 3 per cent. Consortium approach, with joint financing of projects by the institutions is getting very popular but in some cases there is a lead institution looking after the financing for particular type of projects.

Single window clearance in the joint financing scheme requires the applicant to approach one of the institutions and all the institutions participate in project financing. The lead institutions may get the power of attorney on behalf of other institutions in negotiating with the applicants.

Bridging loans, with conditions of fulfilling certain conditions later on, can be provided as project finance to certain projects-in-progress. Bridging/Interim loans can be had by supplying very brief information and shall become the part of the proper loan, after all prerequisites are fulfilled. Bridging loans, against public issue of share of capital, are also provided. The institutions also offer consultancy support, support for market surveys, seed capital assistance, support for human resource development for management, technological and entrepreneurship. Apart from the normal follow up procedures, the institutions have created a category of Nominee Directors who oversees the proper utilization of the financial assistance provided to the companies.

Role of Commercial Banks in Financing

The working capital needs of the industry in India are largely supplemented by short-term or medium-term loans from nationalised commercial banks. RBI oversees the provisions of working capital needs and State Bank of India has been functioning as the Lead Bank of meeting short-term financial needs of industry since 1965. Short-term limits of credit are extended for a period of six months on the basis for furnishing a guarantee.

The three methods suggested by Tandon Committee, for different stages of meeting working capital needs of an industrial project, determine the Maximum Permissible Bank Finance. Working capital gap in case of the first two methods is assessed by deducting current liabilities (except bank borrowings) from current assets. 25 per cent of this working capital gap becomes the minimum stipulated limit of net working capital, in the first method. Permissible Bank Finance may be worked out on the basis of deducting the minimum limit from the gap or by deducting the projected net working capital form working capital gap. In the second method, 25 per cent of current assets is deducted from the gap. The third method is not very popular but is considered to be more desirable by Tandon Committee. The Clore Committee appointed in 1979 favoured the second method of financing.

But a recent study on working capital suggests that the industry was not able to shift even to the second method not to talk of the third. It is being suggested that banks have to exercise a check over the sanction and use of bank finance to meet working capital needs. The borrowings are being allowed, according to different norms for different industries. The banks have decided to grade borrowers and decide the Minimum Lending Rate (MLR), according to this grading. RBI prescription of 16 per cent is not being adhered to. In grading the borrowers from categories ranging from C to A plus, bebt/equity, inventory and liquidity ratios are taken into consideration, alongwith the borrowers dealings with their banks. Around Rs. 10,000 crores of advances were outstanding from various types of small industry by 1986.

The entrepreneurs especially the small ones claim that the banks are ignoring their needs and are too strict about the follow up procedure for utilization of short-term funds. But it is always desirable to have more realistic projections of working capital needs and strengthen the capital base of firms to break the exclusive reliance on bank finances or governmental subsidies. The share of industry in total advances of commercial banks has gone up from one third in 1951 to about one half of the total credit by the late Eighties. Commercial banks with their 53,000 branches and deposits of Rs. 1.66 lakh crores can be the major vehicle for decentralised industrial growth. Commercial banks have also started merchant banking operations and their extensive network of branches can do a lot in mobilising savings of the vast masses in India for investment in risk capital.

Indian Capital Market

Ultimately, a word about capital market in India. There are 15 stock exchanges in India, but the bulk of capital was raised till 1980 from stock exchanges of Bombay and Calcutta. However, now Delhi has emerged as a strong centre for capital market culture, despite the fact that Kanpur and Ludhiana exchanges have also started functioning in northern India. The number of listed companies with the exchanges at the end 1985 was 4,744. The listed capital of the companies is of the magnitude of Rs. 13,000 crores with a market value of Rs. 27,000 crores.

The primary market is performing rather sluggishly, if we take the business of 1986 onwards. Only about 15 per cent issues get overscribed to the extent of 125 per cent. The public financing institutions are the major buyers of industrial securities, followed by the companies and the individuals. Whereas Bombay and Calcutta had more than 2,000 companies listed, new exchanges like Ludhiana had still less than 100 listed campanies. Public financing institutions enter the capital markets at the times of series disturbances in the functioning of the stock exchanges, in order to stabilise business. New financial instruments of debentures/convertible debentures are getting popular with Indian investors. The financial institutions and the government have emerged as the true partners of the private industry by assisting the business in raising capital through various means. They are indeed the major stabilising force in the turbulent stock market dominated by the speculators in India.

The Securities and Exchange Board of India (SEBI) has been set up in 1988 as the apex body of Indian capital market. It aims at promoting the healthy and orderly development of the securities market. SEBI has proposed a comprehensive legislation to consolidate and rationalise the provisions of Securities Contract (Regulation) Act, Capital Issues (Control) Act, and the Companies Act. The board shall go a long way in protecting small investors and for invigorating the securities market in India.

In the preceding paragraphs, we have provided a short review of the industrial support system. In 1988, the government has announced a scheme of Venture Capital Companies/funds which, as is witnessed in the West, is a bold step in direction of promoting widespread entrepreneurship among Indians. These companies shall be floated by national level banks and public financing institutions to meet the risk capital needs of entrepreneurs. In India, the entry of non-traditional castes/communities in the industrial world depends on the efficiency of the above mentioned Industrial Support Systems.

CASE VIII

THE GUARDIANS OF BUSINESS

Apart from rendering all sort of financial help to the private business the Public Financial Institutions come to the rescue in all types of adversities. The new role of these institutions, of course, is that of community leaders who decided the family disputes over property, of all those belonging to their community.

"IFCI initiates Modi parting meets" reads the caption of a news item in an economic daily. Not that Modis, one of the leading business houses of India, are allowing IFCI to meddle with their business affairs, without any consideration. The institutions own majority equity holdings in companies like Modi Rubber. In normal times, when the company was performing well, they took a back seat, allowing the Modi clan to run the show. But once the K.K. Modi branch and K.N. Modi branch of Gujar Mal Modi's family free developed serious differences in running the affairs of business companies, the institutions could not be silent spectators. They saw nominees of one branch trying to vote out the Chairman who belonged to the other branch.

It was reported in the newspapers that even the intervention of Prime Minister's office couldn't bring reproachment among the family members. The battle between two factions was so bitter that IFCI, Chairman, Mr. D.N. Davar felt that the parting of ways will be in the interest of both the factions. The interest of institutions was also at the back of his mind. Obviously, if the board meetings were to be held in an environment of suspicion and acrimony among the directors, this was going to cost the companies a great deal. The financial institutions as the largest equity holders were bound to suffer.

IFCI, is finding it hard to divide the Modi empires into two. In the flag companies of the group even foreign partners are involved. The institutions are increasing their equity holdings these companies and they are increasing the number of the nominees on the boards of these companies, to bring them to the proportion which equity holdings entitle them.

"It now remains to be seen whether IFCI will be successful in its latest bid, and whether there will be any fall out on the group if the two sides cannot agree on January 9, 1989. The Institutions have been called upon to play the role of "big brother" in many takeover battles and scores of partings, on account of the disintegration of joint families of the big houses in recent times.

POINTS FOR CONSIDERATION

Is it possible for the institutions to keep on settling family disputes of hundred odd big business families ? It not, what are the ways out ?

FURTHER READINGS

1. Chitale, M.P., "Finance for Industry", *Economic and Political Weekly*, April 26, 1980.

2. Gupta, L.C., *Readings in Industrial Finance*, New Delhi, D.K. Publishers, 1976.

3. India Investment Centre, *Specialised Financial Institutions in India*, New Delhi.

4. Kaveri, V.S., "Financing of Working Capital in Indian Industry", *Economic and Political Weekly*, August 31, 1985.

5. Khan, M.Y., *Indian Financial System—Theory and Practice*, New Delhi, Vikas, 1980.

6. Ojha, P.D., *Principle and Practice of Public Finance and Financial Administration in India*, Bombay, Vora & Company, 1980.

7. Rangaswamy, B., *Public Sector Banking in India*, New Delhi, Publications Division, 1985.

8. Reserve Bank of India, *Report on Currency and Finance*, 1985-86, Vol. I.

9. ——, *Report of the Study Group to Frame Guidelines For Follow-up of Bank Credit*, 1975.

10. ——, *Report of the Working Group to Review the System of Cash Credit*, 1979.

9

Public Sector in India

During the British Raj, only some defence establishments like ordinance factories and infrastructural facilities of railways as well as telecommunications were under the state control. At the time of Independence, it was clear to the Indian business and the political leadership the rapid industrialisation of India depends upon the provision of expanded infrastructural facilities. Basic and key industrial inputs to the private sector were to be provided at a subsidised rate. In order to attain self-sufficiency in industrialisation, technological dependence on multinationals for machines and industrial goods had to be broken. It was also felt that for maintaining the tempo of production, the energy sector has to grow at a fast pace.

Rationale of Public Sector

Indian native business was not large or strong enough to support the public utilities like the railways, road transport services, ports, posts and telegraph, power and irrigation projects. It was recommended in pre-Independence plan exercises that these services should be started as departmental undertakings by the government. These were to be financed wholly either by the Central or State governments Similarly, defence needs of the country also had to be manufactured in the state-owned establishment for security reasons. On the top of all these, the government was to establish commercial and industrial enterprises in capital goods, the finances for which may be provided in the form of the government's subscription to equity capital and loans. The argument was that the private capital was shy in investing on capital goods manufacture due to very huge investments with long gestation period, returns on which depended upon uncertain demand in a country with a low level of industrialisation.

It is in this context, that the reservation of core sector of industries like power, coal, steel, fertilizers, atomic energy and machine building was made for the public sector. Public enterprise came to be defined as an activity of the governments at all levels which required them to engage in production of goods, provision of services or running public utilities. A price was to be charged for these activities but the charge could not be decided just on commercial considerations, social benefits were to be the major criterion of pricing these rather than conventional cost of production yardsticks. Public sector was to control the commanding heights of Indian economy and generate surpluses for further expansion of the sector.

Types of Public Enterprises

In India, these enterprises have been categorised as departmental or unincorporated enterprises, owned, controlled and run directly by the public authorities and non-departmental or incorporated enterprises. Non-departmental public enterprise comprise (*a*) government companies (in which not less than 51 per cent of the paid up capital is held by the Central/State governments or partly, by the government and partly, by the subsidiaries of the government companies), (*b*) statutory corporations, (set up under special enactments of Parliament State Legislatures). The (*a*) type of enterprises are incorporated under Indian Companies Act, 1956. The guidelines for formation and incorporation of public sector were later revised to bring into being holding companies for various enterprises in certain key sectors like coal, steel and fertilizers.

While discussing the role and performance of public sector in India, we largely focus attention on non-departmental organisations under government control. The criteria used for distinguishing public enterprise activity from the conventional public administration function of the government are : Use of commercial forms of organisation and methods of accounting to determine financial performance, and control over productive capital in the form of equipment such as machines, plants and inventories. Guided by these norms, even the Committees on Public Undertakings formed by the Parliament donot cover departmental enterprises. Commercial banks and public financing institutions or non-banking companies taken over by the government temporarily are also not characterised as Public Undertakings. Joint sector units are a different genre of public enterprises and in fact, many large private corporate sector companies in India are also categorised as 'deemed' public companies because the majority shareholders in these is either the government or government-sponsored organisations.

However, management is also an important determinant of the types of public sector enterprises. Some are departmentally managed, others have their independent boards. There are statutory public corporations and there are enterprises which are organised as companies. On March 31, 1985 there were 221 central government public enterprises. Of these 152 were enterprises producing and marketing goods, 57 were rendering services of other types.

Central Public Enterprises (CPE's)—A Profile

Over the last four decades, the growth of public sector enterprises has been phenomenal in terms of investment, production, profitability and the range of activities. At the end of 1986-87, the capital employed in the central public sector alone stood at about Rs. 52,000 crores and the total sales turnover was Rs. 69,000 crores (c.f. Table 9.1). Total investment (including the project under implementation) was to the tune of Rs. 62,000 crores. The number of public enterprises had reached 228. An investment of Rs. 43,000 crores was envisaged in Seventh Plan.

Besides, there are more than 700 state level corporations with an investment in the range of Rs. 35,000 crores. The contribution of public sector to net domestic product had

TABLE 9.1
Investment in Public Sector

	Total Investment in Rs. Crores	Number of Enterprises
At the Commencement of the First Plan	29	5
At the Commencement of the Second Plan	81	21
At the Commencement of the Third Plan	953	48
At the End of the Third Plan (As on 31 March, 1966)	2,415	74
At the Commencement of Fourth Plan	3,902	85
At the Commencement of Fifth Plan	6,237	122
At the End of Fifth Plan (As on 31 March, 1979)	15,602	176
At the Commencement of Sixth Plan	18,225	186
As on 31 March 1981	21,102	185
As on 31 March 1982	24,916	205
As on 31 March 1983	30,038	209
As on 31 March 1984	35,394	214
As on 31 March 1985	42,811	221
As on 31 March 1987	51,931	228

Source: Bureau of Public Enterprises.

doubled from 10.7 per cent in 1960-61 to 21 per cent in 1981-82. The contribution of savings has also increased for Rs. 115 crores in First Plan to Rs. 600 crores in the Sixth Plan. It was expected to contribute Rs. 3,500 crores in financing the Seventh Plan.

But before we review the performances and pitfalls in view of the recent debates on privatisation, let us recapitulate that the public sector in India is the main instrument of endorcing the objectives of curbing concentration of economic power, ensuring regional dispersal of growth, providing the best possible working conditions, promoting exports and substituting import especially of capital goods. Public enterpises in India are undertaking projects of strategic importance for India's economic development which involve high overhead costs, locational disadvantages, high risks, no or negative returns, the returns are slow in accruing, due to uncertain project time. Table 9.2 shows the investments in the various industries which the public enterprises have undertaken. As the table indicates 8.40 per cent of the investment is locked in project at investment stage. About three quarters of the investment has gone into miscellaneous manufacturing units, 15 per cent into providing services of various types, mostly to assist the private corporate and small industries sector. It has invested only a fraction of its investment of consumer goods sector leaving this profitable sector to private initiative. Steel, coal, petroleum, chemicals fertilizers and pharmaceuticals are the sectors which account for more than 10 per cent investment, individually, and around half of its total investments.

Contribution of Public Sector

An investment of around 42,811 in Mid-Eighties brings a turnover of around Rs. 50,000 crores the value of export being Rs. 6,000 crores, *i.e.*, more than 10 per cent of turnover. The gross profit works out to be 4,637 crores, *i.e.*, 11 per cent of total investment. The public exchequer got Rs. 27,557 crores from public enterprises during the Eighties till 1984-85, about half of this amount was ploughed back into business. The number of enterprises making pre-tax profits increased from 109 in 1983-84 to 114 in 1986-87. During 1984-85, 60 enterprises have declared dividends as contrasted with 5 enterprises in 1983-84.

The overall net profit of CPE's in 1986-87 have shown 51

TABLE 9.2

Investment in Public Sector (Sector-Wise)

(Rs. in Crores)

Category	At the End of 1983-84 Invest-ment	At the End of 1983-84 Percentage of Total Investment	At the End of 1984-85 Invest-ment	At the End of 1984-85 Percentage of Total Investment
(1)	(2)	(3)	(4)	(5)
1. Enterprises Under Construction	1,747.18	9.94	3,596	8.40
2. Enterprises Producing and Selling Goods :				
(a) Steel	5,717.24	16.15	6,329.27	14.73
(b) Minerals and Metals	2,936.79	8.30	3,329.96	7.78
(c) Coal	4,068.40	11.50	4,741.74	11.07
(d) Power	2,510.71	7.09	3,810.78	8.90
(e) Petroleum	3,774.24	10.66	4,706.41	10.99
(f) Chemicals, Fertilizers and Pharmaceuticals	3,992.67	11.28	4,401.61	10.28
(g) Heavy Engg.	1,647.86	4.66	1,693.21	3.96
(h) Medium and Light Engg.	587.57	1.66	746.21	1.74
(i) Transportation Equipment	1,178.84	3.33	1,492.31	3.48
(j) Consumer Goods*	2.26	352.15	798.02	0.82
(k) Agro-based	0.10	39.83	36.20	0.09
(l) Textiles	858.03	2.42	1,094.78	2.56
Total (2)	28,106.57	79.41	32,738.26	76 47

*Hindustan Paper Corporation now appears in Enterprises under construction consequent on the formation of Hindustan News Print Ltd. to take over Kerala unit.

(Contd.)

(Contd.)

	(1)	(2)	(3)	(4)	(5)
3.	Enterprises Rendering Services				
(a)	Trading and Marketing Services	824.61	2.33	936.93	2.19
(b)	Transportation Services	2,149.81	6.20	2,583.19	6.03
(c)	Contract and Construction Services	265.84	0.75	370.49	0.86
(d)	Industrial Development and Technical Consultancy Services	94.19	0.26	104.67	0.24
(e)	Development of Small Industries	47.86	0.13	54.23	0.13
(f)	Tourist Services	90.67	0.26	91.37	0.26
(g)	Financial Services	1,835.75	5.19	2,071.94	5.19
(h)	Companies Registered Under Section 25	66.00	0.19	144.92	0.19
	Total (3)	5,419.73	15.33	6,357.74	14.85
Insurance Companies		121.00	0.34	118.50	0.28
Grand Total		35,394.48	100.00	42,811.16	100.00

Source: India 1986, Publications Division.

per cent increase over the profits in 1985-86. The profits increased from Rs. 1,172.5 crores to Rs. 1,768.08 crores. In fact, the overall profits of public sector have shown a steady rise since 1981-82 barring 1983-84. Percentage of gross profit to capital employed has remained steady at 12.5 per cent per annum on an average, despite the fact that this margin had increased by 137 per cent from 1981-82 to 1986-87. The percentage of gross margin to capital employed has also remained steady at a level of around 19 per cent. Percentage of net profit to capital employed was, however, only 3.41 per cent. The provisional flash results of 191 operating enterprises for 1987-88 show that these enterprises had earned an overall net profit of Rs. 1,748.43 crores. The turnover of capital enterprises has been increasing steadily as is evident from Table 9.3. However, percentage of sales to capital employed was around 133 per cent of capital employed in 1986-87, as contrasted to the peak of 166 per cent attained in 1981-82.

TABLE 9.3

Growth of Sales in Public Enterprises

(Rs. in Crores)

Year	Sales	% of Growth from Previous Year	Capital Employed	% of Sales to Capital Employed
1977-78	18,020	20.86	12,065	149.36
1978-79	19,061	5.78	13,969	136.45
1979-80	23,290	22.19	16,182	143.93
1980-81	28,635	22.95	18,207	157.27
1981-82	36,482	27.40	21,935	166.32
1982-83	41,989	15.09	26,526	158.29
1983-4	47,272	12.58	29,851	158.36
1984-85	54,784	15.89	36,382	150.58
1985-86	62,360	13.83	42,965	145.14
1986-87	69,015	10.67	51,931	139.90

Source : Bureau of Public Enterprises.

In terms of physical production around 98 per cent of coal production in India, 100 per cent of lignite and petroleum crude, 78 per cent of saleable steel, 100 per cent of copper, lead, half of the nitrogenous fertilizers and 100 per cent of telephones as well as teleprinters were produced in the public sector in the Eighties. The central public sector employed around 22 lakh persons by the Mid-Eighties, with an average income of Rs. 25,000 per annum for each worker. In fact, public sector accounts for the lion's share of increased employment in the organised sector industry. 6.28 lakh workers had housing facilities and the expenditure on social overheads was Rs. 630 crores by the Mid-Eighties which works out to Rs. 3,000 per annum per employee. There were around 1,648 ancilliary units of public enterprises in the year 1984-85.

Sales had multiplied four times during the decade of 1977-78 to 1986-87. Sales as a percentage of capital employed in manufacturing enterprises had grown from around 124 per cent in 1985-86 to 162.6 per cent in 1984-85. This ratio had touched the highest of 174.3 per cent in 1983-84.

The top ten corporations of the public sector had increased their investment to around Rs. 40,000 crores by 1986-87 and they made a profit of 1,974.08 crores during the year 1985. However, their sales turnover was not satisfactory, indicating a low capacity utilization. The star performer among the public sector units during twelve months of 1985 was Oil and Natural Gas Commission which showed around 20 per cent profits before tax. The other corporation in oil sector also performed well. Coal India Ltd., the perpetual loss marketing unit during the last decade has also turned around in 1985. So was the case with the other coal company, Central Coal Fields Ltd. At least 3 among the top 10, *viz.*, Food Corporation of India, National Thermal Power Corporation Ltd. and Rural Electrification Corporation Ltd., are in such sectors which can be properly defined as public utilities serving the common man, hence expecting large profits from these would be unreasonable. Similar in the case of Steel Authority of India Ltd. and Rashtriya Ispal Nigam. Hindustan Aeronautics Ltd. operates in strategic sectors of defence and civil aviation. The very nature of the sectors in which large corporations in public sector operate makes it obligatory on them to take into account social obligations.

According to a keen observer public sector enterprises, it is not very useful to consider the profitability of public enterprises in aggregate terms. The share of top ten enterprises turnover-wise had increased to Rs. 43,775 crores out of a total of 69,000 crores in 1986-87, thus, giving a share of 72.5 per cent to these giants. Similarly, the top ten of profit making enterprises accounted for Rs. 3,700 crores, *i.e.*, about 77 per cent of the total profit of Rs. 4,800 in 1986-87 for the profit making CPE's. ONGC and Indian oil accounted for around 57.5 per cent of total profit of profit making CPE's. Major loss making sectors during 1987-88 were coal, textiles, chemicals, fertilizers, pharmaceuticals and consumer goods.

But if we compare the statistics presented about top ten of public sector presented on 31.12.1985 and reported in Table

TABLE 9.4
Top Ten Central Public Undertakings

1. Oil and Natural Gas Commission	8,410.58	342.85	3,266.95	1,627.41
2. Steel Authority of (I) Ltd.	7,910.68	3,713.65	3,568.52	4.10
3. Food Corpn. of India	5,718.63	307.51	4,700.36	3.66
4. Coal India Ltd.	5,072.47	2,556.68	82.73	8.22
5. National Thermal Power Corpn. Ltd.	3,331.37	2,086.71	321.56	87.54
6. Indian Oil Corpn. Ltd.	3,000.02	123.27	9,792.40	162.35
7. Rural Electrification Corpn. Ltd.	1,727.61	141.00	110.40	22.23
8. Rashtriya Ispat Nigam Ltd.	1,771.40	1,480.06	—	—
9. Central Coal Fields Ltd.	1,681.42	262.85	670.60	9.64
10. Hindustan Aeronotics Ltd.	1,420.22	72.0	467.01	48.93
Total	39,993.40	11,086.60	2,29,805.3	1,974.08

9.4, with the top twenty houses in private sector, the profitability performance compares favourably. The twenty top houses showed pretax profits of Rs. 921.85 crores on a total capital employed of Rs. 20,936. However, if we compare the turnover the private sector outscores public sector.

Problems of Public Enterprises

Now that most of the public enterprises have completed the gestation period, it is important for them to generate internal sources. The Seventh Plan rightly expects internal sources to finance 2/3rd of the planned investment. This requires tremendous improvements in their performance. The major constraints on efficiency of public enterprises have been identified by various committees like the Arjun Sengupta Committee. These are as follows :

(1) The first and formost problem is lack of proper investment planning. Lag in project completion and low capacity utilization complicate this problem. Most of the large CPE's were able to finish the projects in periods ranging from seven to twenty five years. The cost of project increases due to continuous inflation and by the time the project is commissioned, the technology needs updating. But since there is shortage of funds, due to project cost overruns and satisfactory returns are not expected due to market entry costs, such updating is not possible.

(2) The optimum size of the industrial unit was overestimated in Indian public sector. Need for capital goods was worked on the basis of the vast market for industrial produce due to a large population. However, lack of distributional measures in rural assets made consumers goods industry demand-constrained and capacities were underutilized in the machine building sector. Another factor inhibiting unleashing of large scale private initiative was also a lack of infrastructural facilities. It was on account of faulty materials manage-

ment or lack of power and transport that sickness started afflicting Indian private sector and it had its impact on capacity utilization of basic, key and capital-goods industry. Underutilization of capacity in CPE's was a natural consequence.

(3) For the initial technological knowhow, public sector units had to depend upon foreign technology. Indian managers/bureaucrats had no experience in selection of righ technologies suited to Indian environment. Faulty choices of technologies were made. Inhouse R & D was inadequate with the result that even these technologies could neither be adopted, assimilated and absorbed. Thus technological obsolescence was high, productivity of capital was low, with the result that costs of production increased. As already pointed out, there were no funds for modernisation and even the preventive maintenance was unsatisfactory. The capital-output ratio in Indian economy is 6 to 1 and the operational costs have increased. When OGL lists were expanded to include capital goods which were being manufactured in Indian public sector, the demand for Indian goods decreased even in the domestic market. The case is best illustrated by BHEL, running out of power kit orders.

(4) Materials management is another area which is ignored by the public sector. In order to artificially push up capacity utilization, sometimes, excess materials are stored and since there is no immediate demand for the finished goods, the holding costs of inventory go up. On the other hand, if key sectors like coal and transport donot operate efficiently, all industries like fertilizers and thermal power stations suffer due to material shortages. The money which could be invested in expanding or modernising of production facilities is either locked in inventory or the demands is lost due to shortage of materials.

(5) Faulty manpower planning and personnel management is another cause of public sector in efficiency. Since the growth model of mixed economy didn't result in a very vibrant industrial economy, the employment in private corporate sector didn't pick up. In fact, private sector which employed more than 40% of the organised work force in the 50's is employing only 30% by 1980's. To accommodate the surplus work force, the public sector had to come forth to meet its obligation of creating employment, to the extent possible. At present, about 20 lakh persons and 1.3 lakh executives are working in this sector. Most of the undertakings are overstaffed. In order to increase productivity if they start taking recourse to more capital intensive technologies, the employment potential shall fall. So CPE's are caught in a paradox. Their growth is not satisfactory, technologies are out of date, they donot have any other means of accommodating surplus manpower which they are employing at present, even if their capacity utilization decreases further. Hence their wage bill keeps on increasing, at a pace faster than an increase in sales turnover, so costs of production stay high.

(6) The chain of decision-making is very long in the case of public enterprises, starting with the ministry/planning bodies, intermediaries like Bureau of Public Enterprises and the Boards of Directors are not free to decide the strategy of the firms. Their product-market scope is determined by the targets set by planning bodies. Even in case of administrative decisions about plant location or organisational restructuring, the top managements are not free. Under these circumstances, the time and cost escalations related with delay in decisions and the constraint of going for sub-optimal decisions cannot be avoided.

(7) Another problem afflicting public enterprises is the political interference, bureaucratic wrangling and petty politicking which forces the undertakings to languish

headless for long months. It is pertinent to quote Tony Joseph of Economic Times (dated January 2, 1989) in this respect "At any time there are a score and a half public sector undertakings without a chief. The exact number now is 31. If all the board level vacancies are included, it shoots to 65". It can be imagined what impact this has on the organisational effectiveness when CPE's stays without top management responsible for its performance. The problem of management succession at the top is so acute that most of the undertakings are rendered rudderless.

(8) The stranglehold of Indian Administrative Service over CPE's is another problem. Most of these personnel who man managerial positions in public undertakings are not trained to handle these jobs. Moreover, by the time any diligent officer learns to manage a particular type of business, he is shifted to another assignment which has nothing to do with business management. The socalled managerial revolution which was supposed to occur, as per the conception of James Burham, eludes Indian public sector. Professional managers and technocrats are not allowed full play in their fields of specialisations and become entrapped by rational-legal structures created by Indian bureaucracy. This obviously affects the performance of CPE's adversely.

Public Accountability Versus Autonomy

The functioning of any public enterprise is not only a matter of organising internal division of work. External environments, in the form of elaborate governmental machinery, directly determines the operations of public sector undertaking. The word "public" attached to the enterprise calls for fair and equitable dealings with the consumers, the suppliers, the distributors, the financial institutions and the shareholders. The Government machinery constituting legislative, executive and judicial orgnisations at various levels also directly regulates their business. The investment in public enterprises largely comes from budgetary allocations and the revenues for budget come from public at large. The values which are determined by a consensus among the pluralities in a liberal democratic model, demand that these public funds should be utilized as per the widely shared priorities. In a Parliamentary democracy like ours, the major institutions which endorce accountability of public enterprises are :

(1) Parliament.
(2) Executive/Ministry.
(3) Public at large.

The accountability is enforced through the following measures :

(1) Committee on Public Undertakings are a regular feature of reporting to the Parliament. These reports may explore the specialised aspects of public sector functioning or general functioning of these. These are debates, questions, approvals for investments and loans by the legislature and even special enquiry committees are set up for ensuring accountability of public enterprises.

(2) Audit by the statutory auditors, appointed by the executive, is another means of ensuring accountability. There may be audits of various types, financial, efficiency, propriety or social. Supplementary audits dictated by the contingencies can also be ordered. All records of money, materials, machines, manpower, etc., have to be put at the disposal of these audit parties and they scrutinize these minutely, sometimes, even disrupting the routine operations of public enterprises.

(3) In order to ensure accountability to public at large, Bureau of Public Enterprise (BPE) has issued guidelines to all undertakings about the preparation of their Annual Reports. These reports show financial results ; changes in accounting methods ; pricing policy and details about production as well as productivity. These

reports also give information about their contribution to exports and social welfare activities for workers of the undertakings.

(4) Controlling Ministry of public enterprises is the body which acts as a bridge between the Parliament and the enterprise. The Minister and his Secretaries keep on issuing general guidelines for policy formation and operation of these undertakings and in return, defends the top management's stand on the floor in the Parliamentary debates. However, policy guidelines are, sometimes, confused with operational manuals and the Ministry starts interferring in routine decisions of the enterprises.

The public enterprises at Central level have a regular interaction with the Central government so is the case with State enterprises. Since public enterprises were established as an instrument of Directive Principles of State Policy, this interaction is vital. The board of directors as well as chairmen have to seek prior approvals of the controlling Ministry in certain matters, in other matters they are to conform to directives, office orders or circulars. The boards and chairmen are usually selected by a Public Enterprises Selection Board (PESB) but the government can go outside the panel suggested by PESB. Thus the selection board has only powers of recommendation. It is alleged that the government wants to keep those appointed on tenterhooks so that they can become pliable to pressures. Apart from securing constant returns and reports, the government also supercedes decisions of top management in the case of statutory corporations.

Memorandum of Understanding

Memorandum of Understanding (MOU's) is the new device of ensuring accountability for public enterprises. According to this provision, MOU's commit the board of directors to achieve certain targets and more powers are delegated to them. In India, the boards are either Functional or Policy making. In case of the latter the number of part-timers is more than whole-time directors. Such boards can only exercise supervisory functions rather than taking up managerial functions. Mostly, Policy Boards delegate powers to the Chief Executive or the Chairman of the Board. The Secretaries of the Government try to get themselves appointed to board of directors, even if their departments/ministries have a remote connection with the functioning of the CPE's. This results in some Secretaries occupying multiple directorships which is an undesirable practice. Chief Executives are the key persons, it is their professional competence and only a customary acceptance by the ruling party can be the key to autonomy of public enterprises. It will be desirable to delegate adequate powers to the Chief Executive and his management team within the board policy framework of the government. The tendency of Chief Executives to identify themselves with the governmental bureaucracy should be discouraged to ensure autonomy.

In fact autonomy and accountability are directly related. More the autonomy of the enterprise, easier it is to fix the responsibility for better performance of the enterprise. Regular interference by MP's, Ministers and Secretaries will also afford opportunities to the Boards and Management of CPE to "pass on the buck" of responsibility. The parameters of criteria, results and behaviour expected from the enterprise should be clearly spelled out in the MOU's and these should be made the basis of evaluation. Frequent reorganisations of CPE's into sectoral corporations like Fertilizers Corporation of India and then into a number of independent units are aimed at improving the efficiency of CPE's. But the policy followed by the government is vacillating. It should be, however, kept in mind that the elected governments cannot be asked to completely divorce themselves of control of CPE's. The practice of controlled prices based on recommendations of BICP of Industries Department may be a major parameter of control.

The professional management of CPE's is vital and if the returns on investment donot improve, the chorus for privatisation shall be louder. Realising fully that no Indian business tycoons can take over departmental undertakings like Indian

Railways or CPE's like ONGC, the privatisation demand implies a call for neo-colonial exploitation by MNC's. But considering the fact that plan investment of CPE's is financed largely by indirect taxes and deficit financing, the inability of the enterprises in earning adequate return on investment shall amount to taxing the poor. So is the policy of showing profits in CPE's by forcing hikes in administered prices which has spiraling inflationary pressures and shall amount to reducing the purchasing power of common man in India. Thus even this hike cuts at demand for produce of industry in private sector and consequently, demand for capital and basic goods. The result shall be under-utilization of the capacity by PSE's and the consequent losses. Thus, cutting losses by cost reduction is the only key to success and survival of public sector in India.

Findings and Recommendations of Various Committees

The problem of economic sickness which has taken into its sweep around 1.5 lakh private sector units is spreading to large public undertakings also. The Ministry of Programme Implementation in a review of progress of 264 Central Public Sector Projects, involving an outlay of Rs. 65,000, revealed a very sorry state of affairs. It was found that 134 units costing Rs. 44,000 had reported delays and cost escalations. And because of this delay the cost of 134 public sector units had sought up by Rs. 17,088 crores. Obviously, such large cost escalations, at the project stage, become the major cause for subsequent economic sickness. Now that the Central government is facing a serious resources crunch, it will be no use to expect the government spreading its meagre budgetary allocations in expanding the public sector by starting new projects. The strategy is that of consolidating the position of the existing units. The government may have to use its resources to write off accumulated losses and expect the CPE's not to incur any further losses by professionalising their management. However, it will be of little use if the public sector looses sight of its superordinate goals because that will amount to privatisation of its management.

To examine the plight of public sector enterprises in India, the following extracts from Dr. Arjun Sengupta report may be quoted. The Committee observes :

"The expectation that the public enterprises as commercial ventures should 'augment the revenues of the State' and provide a return which can be used for further investment and growth has not been fulfilled. Even for units which were making losses because of the nature of products or because of their serving some specified social objectives, the efficiency of operation has often deteriorated. In actual practice, the freedom of operation of the management has been quite often curtailed or interferred with by formal or informal Government intervention. While the public enterprises were to be judged by their 'total results' in monitoring and evaluation system of the Government has not been adequate to the task. The strict enforcement of performance standard on the public enterprises would entail a new look at the Government-public enterprise relations is essential, if performance standards are to be enforced as it would not be realistic to expect results without giving necessary autonomy to the enterprises with regard to the decisions which affect such results."

Among the major recommendation of the Committee about reorganisation of PSE's are :

(i) careful dovetailing of plans in the public enterprises with the National Plan, only in a few core sectors of coal and lignite, crude oil, petroleum and natural gas, power, primary steel production, primary production of aluminium, copper, lead, zinc and nickel, fertilizers, primary production of petro-chemical intermediates ;

(ii) integration of plans of enterprises in the non-core sectors with National Plan should be "only in an indicative manner as for the private sector" ;

(iii) reduction of points of government's intervention without minimising the Government's right to have needed information for performance evaluation ;

(iv) the Holding Company structure (under the Sectoral Ministries) as a reasonable framework for the public enterprises' organisation, combining the objectives of centralised policy formulation with decentralised operation and management (where Holding Company could not be formed, the prevailing unitary companies should be reorganised into Apex Companies);

(v) the Holding Company in the core sector to specify its plan for investments, production, capacity utilization, profits, dividend for a period of five years and arrive at Memorandum of Understanding (MOU) with the government on mutually agreed basis;

(vi) reorganisation of various public enterprises in the non-core sectors into a few Holding Companies and Apex Companies under the sectoral Ministries that are to retain administrative supervision.

For financing and investment decisions, the committee proposed :

(i) two stage clearance of investment approvals by the Government for the core sectors (first, through the institution of a "Task Force' by the Public Investment Board to go into all aspects of manufacture by the public enterprises, needs for import and secondly, by a detailed scrutiny of technology, costs, etc.);

(ii) contribution of the government only towards equity for the financially viable enterprises in the non-core sectors;

(iii) the government to undertake additional equity contribution or reimburse the additional net cost of such activities in case of non-core enterprises used as agencies for other than commercial objectives ;

(iv) conclusion of a MOU's between the Government and the Holding or Apex Companies on the agreed plans for investment, profits, dividends for a five year period (with a periodic review every year);

(v) evaluation of financial performance of the public enterprises through criteria of gross margin on assets (for all enterprises), net profit on networth (for the core sectors and profit-making enterprises), gross margin on sales (in service enterprises), industry average for both gross margin on capital employed and the rate of net profit (in the non-core sectors);

(vi) monitoring of unit cost and productivity to be undertaken in the core sectors;

(vii) in case of project implementation in the core sectors, monitoring of such indicators as percentage utilization of plan funds, average slippage in outgoing projects; and

(viii) *suo moto* examination by BPE for capital restructuring and closure of such units which suffer cash losses for several years.

Besides, on personnel and sales management, the Sengupta Committee recommended that :

(i) determination of the basic wage structure of the public sector employees on industry basis for industry-cum-region basis by a Wage Commission/Wages Boards for a period of five years, with a clear component of earning linked with productivity (in addition to the basic wage);

(ii) evolution of a liberal compensation scheme for workers for those units where closure is recommended;

(iii) the Chief Executives and Functional Directors to be given a five years term; and

(iv) periodic revision of price controls and retention of such controls only where the nature of the product justified.

Ultimately, reduction of parliamentary, governmental and ministerial interference to day-to-day working of the enterprises was also recommended.

Arjun Sengupta Committee's recommendations are already being implemented. About a score of CPE's have already signed MOU's. CIL, the loss making coal giant has already started persuading 2 lakhs of old workers to accept voluntary retirement. The financing patterns of CPE's are showing a sea-change.

In a study on the possible sources of financing investment in public enterprises, Anand P. Gupta, shows that internal resources finance about 30-40 per cent of Plan investments on Central Public Enterprises (CPE's). Though budgetary support continues to be the major source of financing the plan investments, its contribution has decreased from 53 per cent in 1984-85 to 40.3 per cent in 1987-88 and is expected to go down to 36.8 per cent in 1988-89. As a percentage of GDP, the budgetary support to CPE's constituted 2.8 per cent in 1984-85 and has gone down to 2.2 per cent in 1987-88.

Gupta argues in favour of extra-budgetary resources like public enterprise bonds on the pattern of NTPC and IRCON. Bonds have already floated in the market by National Hydro Electric Power Corporation, Indian Telecommunications, Mahanagar Telephone Nigam, Neyveli Lignite Corporation and Indian Petro-chemical. Only 15, out of 250 CPE's have used these bonds but these Bonds account for 42.5 per cent of the funds raised for plan investment through extra-budgetary sources.

External commercial borrowings, Inter-CPE deposits, loans from Oil Industry Development Board (OIDB) and Oil Co-ordination Committee (OCC) or Steel Development Fund (SDF) are suggested as the alternate sources of raising funds. Gupta also advocates more loans from Public Financing Institutions to public sector and even goes to suggest equity participation not only by cooperatives but even by foreign collaborators. In fact, the latter prescription of allowing foreign equity amounts not only to privatisation but intrusion of multinationals (MNC's) from the backdoor.

This will defeat the very social objective of public enterprises. One wonders, however, why shouldn't public financing institutions charge lower interest rates on term loans advanced to public enterprises, when the latter are functioning in low profitability, high social priority and high technology areas.

Some critics of Sengupta Committee, however, feel that the committee has gone too far in its recommendations. Reference to indicative planning for non-core sector CPE's, participation by government only in equity of these CPE's, *suo moto* enquiries and subsequent closures with golden handshakes for employees are some measures which have raised eyebrows about the intentions of the committee. Handing over of management by some holding companies to foreign consultants have come for a severe criticism. Use of bonds for financing public investments may lead to private savings' channelisation to investment in equity. The state control as well as management of CPE's is, thus, facing serious threat.

Limits to Privatisation

Samuel Paul in a seminal contribution to the debate on privatisation in market economies and underdeveloped countries has taken a very balanced stand on the question. Among the negative features of public ownership and management, he enumerates, "high costs of production, inability to innovate and costly delays in delivery", diversion of goods of public sector for elite consumption and fast expansion of bureaucracy which may tax the resources of the governments. Paul, while enumerating types of goods refers to private, toll, common, pool and collective goods. It is in the latter three types, that public enterprises have emerged in India and analysis suggests that in case of fear of natural monopolies emerging, the government has to either control production directly or regulate it.

Divestiture as a means of privatising as is being done in the case of some public undertakings in India, doesn't seem to be a very feasible alternative. Normally, the governments want to dispose off loss making units, whereas private entrepreneurs are willing to buy out only profit generating ones. In the other alternative, *i.e.*, private provision of goods and services, the fact that 70 per cent of Indian population still resides in rural India makes it difficult for the private suppliers to reach out the poor people. In common utilities and urban transportation, private sector is already participating in India. But it is very difficult to imagine, in the given circumstances, that the sub-contracting of services like water supply in rural areas will be acceptable to private parties in India.

Paul, on one hand maintains that deregulation is desirable in underdeveloped countries, because "patronage, corruption and hunger for power are forces which contribute to over-regulation". On the other hand, it is suggested that in order that privatisation may succeed, a regulatory mechanism has to be devised for increasing competition through a feed-back system from the market. "Increased privatisation does, therefore, imply much more than shrinkage in the size of the government". The government-business interaction changes in case of privatisation but "regulation is still needed".

It is pertinent to point out that a strong anti-colonial attitude is a product of our freedom movement in India. Public sector has moved in, to replace the MNC's, largely as supplier of capital goods. The internal competence of India's industrial sector owes itself to major public sector initiative. The performance of private sector in India, appears to be better only on account of the fact that conglomerate groups have been diverting investments from consumer goods to luxuries or consumer durables. The wage-good sector which was primary responsibility of private sector in India has suffered and the vast masses in India still don't have access to the produce of industry.

Given the level of development in India, privatisation on the pattern of USA or UK is a remote possibility. The public sector undertakings have mostly come up of age in the seventies and in the last ten years, they have shown a steady improvement in their performance. If Arjun Sengupta Committee

Report, in the spirit of improving the performance of public enterprises, then it is welcome move. If the object of our planners is to bring privatisation through the backdoor, it would be like "throwing the baby with the bath-water". The politicians are not willing to oblige them either, due to the popular opinion in favour of public sector as contrasted with MNC's. The recently issued white-paper on public sector makes it abundantly clear. In fact, the public-private mix in our economy is closely related with the political regimes and it is futile to argue, like the *Wall Steel Journal*, that the word political-economy should be banned, on account of incompatibility of the two. As argued earlier, politics and economics cannot be divorced. In fact, the arguments for privatisation is the politics which MNC's have played for very long. In this context, we may quote V.R. Panchmukhi and Nagesh Kumar :

"In recent years, there has been a concerted effort on the part of the developed countries to have more effective access to the service activities in the developing economies. The demand for the inclusion of services in GATT framework implies that the giant MNC's from the developed world in the fields of banking, insurance, telecommunications, informatics, shipping, etc., would like to have a complete stranglehold on the most strategic infrastructural activities in the developing world". If it is as a part of the design of developed on countries, that the following argument is advanced by Samuel Paul, then any discerning Indian shall tend to disagree with the argument for privatisation. Paul observes : "The miracle chip revolution, the resurgence of the small firm in the arena of high technology and computerised planning, manufacturing and control systems are forces which call for an usually highly degree of innovation, internal flexibility and adaptiveness which conventional state control and incentive systems are unlikely to sustain".

The MNC's subsidiaries are probably the flexible 'small firms' which shall takeover service sector from the existing public sector units and given the fact that "the expansion of services has also been accompanied by a serious decline in corporate accountability......", the entry of MNC's in the name of privatising public sector shall be compromising our national priorities and goals. Public sector in these circumstances has enormous challenge which should be faced with all their might by all those who want to see it attaining "commanding heights" of Indian economy.

CASE IX

INDUSTRIAL RELATIONS IN PUBLIC SECTOR

How the government, especially the ruling parties at Centre can play with the industrial relations climate came to light in a public sector assembly type of a unit. The unit which was making profits in early Eighties turned into a loss making unit after 1983-84. The unit employ around 7,500 employees and is plagued by industrial disputes over a wage agreement, arrived in 1977.

This agreement had a history. The agreement was strongly objected to by Bureau of Public Enterprises (BPE) till 1975. This was, partly, on account of the fact that the union in the undertaking was led by Communists. The top INTUC leadership in the country was trying hard to break the influence of Marxist-led CITU union in this unit. It was strongly backed by Congress (I) leaders at the Centre because winning over the union of 7,500 workers could pay electoral dividends in the city where the undertaking was located. In order to play its cards at the unit level, the INTUC leaders won over once-powerful but rebel leader of CITU union.

In order to establish the leadership of newly formed INTUC union in the enterprise, the union government managed to get a new Chief Executive appointed. During the national emergency in 1976, fresh negotiations were started with this union but the BPE norms came in the way of substantial increase in wages. With the workers hopes dashed, they again rushed to CITU led union. With the majority of workers joining CITU union and the INTUC leaders sabotaging any agreement which the local level management was willing to arrive at with the workers, the industrial relations scene became so vitiated, that strikes and lockouts have become the order of the day.

POINTS FOR CONSIDERATION

(1) Do you think that the enterprise level management could avoid industrial conflict ?

(2) Given the present industrial relations climate, is there any hope of reviving the unit without stopping the political interference ?

FURTHER READINGS

1. Clairemounte, F.F. and John, H. Cavanagh, "Transnational Corporations and Services—The Final Frontier", *Economic and Political Weekly*, Vol. XX, No. 8, February 23, 1985.

2. Government of India, *Arjun Sengupta Committee Report*, December 31, 1984.

3. ——, *Transactions of the Public Sector, 1960-61, 1979-80*, New Delhi, 1983.

4. Gupta, Anand P., "Financing Public Enterprise Investments in India", *Economic and Political Weekly*, Vol. XXIII, No. 51, December 17, 1988.

5. Narian Laxmi, *Principles and Practice of Public Enterprise Management*, New Delhi, S. Chand & Co., 1982.

6. Panchmukhi, V.R. and Nagesh Kumar, "NAM—Economic Non-alignment at Stake", *World Focus*, No. 75, March, 1986.

7. Paul Samuel, "Privatisation and the Public Sector—Relevance and Limit", *Economic and Political Weekly*, Vol. XX, No. 8, February 23, 1985.

8. Ramandham, V.V. (Ed.), *Joint Ventures and Public Enterprises in Developing Countries*, (Yugoslavia), International Centre for Public Enterprises in Developing Countries, 1980.

9. Sapru, R.K., *Management of Public Sector Enterprises in India*, Vol. I, New Delhi, Ashish Publishing House, 1987.

10

Private Corporate Sector in India

India's planning for industrialisation has created a very diversified base of industries in the country. This progress has been possible on account of co-operation of the public and private sectors. Whereas capital goods industry has developed in the public sector, private sector has dominated consumers goods industry. Whereas small scale industry or the informal sector has contributed equally to the industrial development, we limit our attention to the organised sector. It has been stated earlier that company form of organisation has been popular with the Indian business especially the units engaged in manufacturing.

The number of companies which was around 29,000 in 1951, declined to 26,000 by 1961, especially the number of public limited companies came down from around 12,000 to 6,600 during this period. Enactment of Indian Companies Act, 1956 was the watershed in the private corporate sector of India. Though the total paid up capital had gone up from Rs. 1,000 crores in 1956-57 to 1,389 crores by 1961-62, the number of corporate entities had fallen down from 29,000 to 24,000 during this period and the number of public limited companies had fallen down from 8,771 to 6,399. The paid up capital increased from around Rs. 700 crores in 1956-57 to Rs. 1,100 crores by 1961-62 for the public limited companies.

Hazari's Study of Private Corporate Sector

It may be noted that unit of control and decision making in Indian private corporate sector is not a joint stock company but a business house. A business house is formed by the existence of common control through phenomena of inter-corporate investment, managing agency and multiple directorship. Hazari identified Twenty business complexes for the period 1951-58 which controlled 1,000 public and private limited companies. These complexes had physical assets of more than Rs. 5 crores, there were other houses which had smaller amount of assets. Thus, the fall in corporate entities during this period was on account of reorganisation by the business houses of their empires. Hazari maintains that whereas in 1951, the share capital of twenty complexes accounted for 29 per cent of share capital of private corporate sector (PCS, hereafter), this share increased to 32 per cent by 1958. Hazari talked of complexes constituted of inner core and outer periphery of corporate entities. To illustrate Hazari's conception further, the Tata Complex consisted of 102 companies in 1951 which increased to 120 companies in 1958 with a share capital of Rs. 108.23 crores. Thus Tatas accounted for 10 per cent of the paid up capital of the entire corporate sector in 1958. It is the example of Birla complex, however, which explains the phenomenon of decreasing number of corporate entities during the Fifties. The number of Birla companies decreased from 356 in 1951 to 298 in 1958. But it is interesting to note that during the same period their private companies had increased from 61 to 105.

Most of the business houses were diversified industrial groups. Whereas Tatas had investments in such basic and key goods industries as steel, power, engineering besides textiles; Birlas had interest in textiles, *viz.*, cotton, jute and woollen; paper and asbestos. Textiles continued to be the mainstay of many houses, besides sugar and paper. Hazari surveyed the pattern of shareholdings of 643 public companies controlled by 20 complexes in 1958 and RBI conducted a similar survey of 70 companies in 1959. There is a starking similarity in ownership patterns, as displayed by the two surveys. Whereas individuals controlled half the share capital, joint stock companies owned 35-40 per cent of share capital and public financing institutions had around 6 per cent of shareholdings.

In business complexes "the technique of holding controlling power is comparable to chain breeding process. The controlling companies in most cases make an initial investment to own wholly or almost wholly a principal company or companies. These companies initiate a breeding process...that takes care of nearly all subsequent controlling investments of significance, without calling forth further substantial investments from the controlling families".

Private Corporate Sector During Third and Annual Plans

The total number of companies during the Sixties again picked up and reached 28,678 by the year 1969-70, paid up capital increasing by around 50 per cent during the decade and touching a level of Rs. 2,188 crores. The number of public limited companies was around 6,400 all through the decade. The investment in public companies had gone up from Rs. 1,093 crores in 1961-62 to Rs. 1,741 crores in 1969-70. Manufacturing activities got an impetus on account of better infrastructural and capital goods facilities made available by the public sector. But it was felt that the grip of business houses and multinationals had further tightened over Indian private corporate sector. Since industrial stagnation had set in the Indian industrial economy in the Mid-Sixties, an accusing finger was pointed towards the growth of monopolies in Indian private corporate sector. Growth rates of industrial production which were averaging 7 per cent till 1965 abruptly fell down to 3.5 per cent per annum. Its amidst this scenerio of stagnating industrial economy, that a number of committees like, Monopolies Inquiry Committee and Industrial Licensing Policy Inquiry Committee were appointed to investigate the industrial regulation system and growth of the big business in India.

Monopolies Inquiry Committee Report

Mahalanobis and Hazari were the forerunners of the investigations necessitating and official inquiry into growing tempo of concentration in Indian industrial economy. The Inquiry Commission identified increasing capital intensity and related economies of scale, the institution of managing agency system and a general paucity of managerial and entrepreneurial skills as the basic causes of industrial concentration. The paucity of skills resulted in multiple directorships and the paucity of capital with masses was responsible for intercorporate investments. These two phenomena with the umbrella of managing agency system led to conglomerate growth of the established business houses and certain multinationals.

While investigating into productwise monopolies, it was found that in such common place commodities as infant milk foods, corn and wheat flakes, stoves and thermosflasks an oligopolistic market prevailed with a single to six producers controlling 80-100 per cent of the market. Toothpastes, cigarettes, sewing machines had less than ten producers controlling more than 75 per cent of the market. Evidence were collected about similar productwise concentration in bicycles, electric lamps, talcum powder, electric fans and soaps where a few producers controlled more than 2/3rd share of the total market for these products. Oligopolies lead to artificial scarcities and high prices. New entries in PCS were made difficult due to cut throat competition in form of resale-price maintenance, enforcement of exclusive rights in trading, appointing sole selling agents, tie-up sales, etc.

For country-wise-concentration, MIC used the test of ownership and management discarding Hazari's outer circle. In all 2,559 companies were examined for asscertaining control by group masters of 83 houses. Ultimately, it was found that these 83 houses own 1,609 companies. For controlling monopolies, MIC listed 75 groups which controlled assets to the tune of Rs. 2,605.95 crores and total paid up capital of group companies was Rs. 646.32 crores. In percentage terms, 75 groups controlled around 47 per cent of assets of PCS and 44 per cent of paid up capital. The top 20 houses among these controlled around one third of assets of PCS and 29 per cent of the paid up capital.

R.C. Dutt in his note of dissent to the main MIC report maintained that phenomenon of business houses causing countrywise concentration was more alarming than productwise concentration. He found managing agency system and family based succession to top managements, as the real barriers to professionalisation. He showed that houses like Tata, Birlas and Martin Burn were exerting more than 75 per cent of their control over independent corporate entities through managing agency system.

Subsequently, I.G. Patel Committee recommended abolition of managing system in 1970 and MRTPA, 1969 was enacted to check countrywise and productwise concentration.

Industrial Licensing Policy Inquiry Committee (ILPIC)

Popularly known as Dutt Committee, ILPIC reviewed the working of IDRA 1951. The committee attempted a comprehensive review of the functioning of licensing system for industries. Dutt Committee found MIC's definition of a business house unsatisfactory. Family for establishing family control comprised of wives, sons, daughters and senior employees of the group. Assuming that governments and public financing institutions were passive shareholders, ownership of effective equity was considered as an adequate criterion and a one by third share in effective equity was deemed fit to establish prevalence of family control. Besides, characteristics such as the majority of directors on the board, sole selling agency arrangements, common office premises of telecommunication facilities were considered sufficient to treat the companies interconnected. There were other evidences which rehabilitated Hazari's notion of outer circle companies as a second tier of the business houses The coverage of 775 companies for 20 houses was extended to 821 non-banking companies and 8 banks in the first tier and another 70 non-banking companies were included in the second tier. Assets of Twenty houses by the end of 1966 were Rs. 2.500 crores.

ILPIC found that big houses pre-empt capacities through multiple applications for licenses and the bureaucracy favoured private sector in the Schedule 'B' industries and even allowed big business to get licenses in Schedule 'A', otherwise reserved for public sector. Due to use of subterfuges for obtaining licenses and cornering licenses for profitable product-lines, big houses strengthened their stranglehold on PCS. Hazari also showed that 31.3 per cent of the total assistance disbursed by public financing institutions and banks went to the companies belonging to 20 top houses. This was partly due to the fact that all these institutions had representatives of big business as directors.

The ILPIC, thus came to a conclusion that hold of big business on PCS had increased with connivance of licensing authorities and public financing institutions. The concept of joint sector, convertibility clause and nominee directors were proposed to maintain effective regulation of private corporate sector.

Private Corporate Sector 1971-85

Table 10.1 portrays the growth in number and paid up capital of private, public and all companies. During 1970-75, an increase of around Rs. 1,000 crores in the paid up capital of PCS was observed. Public companies accounted for more than 70 per cent of growth in paid up capital, despite the fact that the number of private companies floated was around 11 times that of 832 public companies incorporated in the period. Slightly less than ten thousand companies were incorporated during this period. Average size of the public company had grown from Rs. 25 lakhs in 1971 to Rs. 31 lakhs in 1975, in terms of paid up capital. Similarly, average size of paid up capital per private company had increased from 2 lakhs to 2.3 lakhs in 1975.

The Fourth Plan was essentially a period of moderate growth for industries. In fact, the total number of companies registered in 1984-85 alone, was larger than the total number of companies incorporated during the entire Fourth Plan. Similarly the paid up capital of companies registered during 1984-85 was also double than that of the 1971-75 period.

TABLE 10.1

Number and Paid-up Capital of Non-Government Companies at Work in India During the Years 1970-71 to 1984-85

Sr. No.	As on March 31 of Year	Public Limited Number	Public Limited Paid-up Capital (in Rs. Crs.)	Private Limited Number	Private Limited Paid-up Capital (in Rs. Crs.)	Total Number	Total Paid-up Capital (in Rs. Crs.)	PUC Index No. with 1971 as Base Year
(1)	(2)	(3)	(4)	(5)	(6)	(7)	(8)	(9)
1.	1971	6,443	1,775.1	23,655	461.8	30,098	2,236.9	100
2.	1972	6,703	2,035.9	25,212	535.8	31,915	2,571.7	115
3.	1973	6,819	2,175.6	27,147	574.5	33,966	2,750.1	123
4.	1974	7,071	2,323.3	29,964	662.6	37,035	2,985.9	133

(*Contd.*)

(Contd.)

(1)	(2)	(3)	(4)	(5)	(6)	(7)	(8)	(9)
5.	1975	7,275	2,484.4	32,736	750.4	40,011	3,234.8	144
6.	1976	7,465	2,536.1	35,149	783.3	42,614	3,319.4	148
7.	1977	7,585	2,554.4	37,346	819.3	44,931	3,973.7	151
8.	1978	7,725	5,649.4	39,485	847.3	47,210	3,496.7	156
9.	1979	7,893	2,688.0	42,376	874.9	50,269	3,562.9	159
10.	1980	8,225	2,751.0	46,730	906.8	54,955	3,658.3	163
11.	1981	9,415	3,379.0	52,401	1,020.0	61,816	4,399.0	196
12.	1982	10,169	3,716.0	60,594	1,245.1	70,763	4,961.1	221
13.	1983	11,372	3,839.3	70,589	1,347.1	81,961	5,186.4	232
14.	1984	12,526	4,058.7	80,768	1,459.9	93,294	5,513.6	246
15.	1985	14,149	4,260.4	92,240	1,578.1	1,06,389	5,838.5	261

Source : Research and Statistics Division, Department of Company Affairs.

The period 1975-80 saw incorporation of around 1,000 public companies and an increase of Rs. 267 crores in paid up capital which was even lesser than half the increase in the earlier plan. Around 14,000 private companies were incorporated, accounting for less than Rs. 100 crores of increase in paid-up capital. Thus the total number of companies in PCS was around 55,000 by 1979-80 with a capital of Rs. 3,658 crores, which is Rs. 424 crores higher than that in 1975. No significant change in paid-up capital per public company was witnessed over this period, the average size of private companies, in terms of average paid-up capital per company, declined. The share of paid-up capital contributed by public companies declined to 63 per cent. Thus, 1975-80 was a period of very slow growth of the PCS and industrial climate was not conducive for private initiative.

In fact, these were the years when the terms of trade were sought to be altered in favour of primary sector at the cost of the secondary sector. Due to inflationary pressures, the purchasing power of Indian consumers had gone done, so industry was becoming more and more demand constrained. In fact, the number of public companies have doubled in 1971-85, largely planning effort during this period also laid more emphasis on development of informal sector of industry, the growth of the organised sector was tardy.

The Sixth Plan period, starting with the Eighties and terminating in 1985 has witnessed a phenomenal growth in PCS. More than 50,000 new corporate entities came into being recording a 93 per cent growth over the number in 1980. In fact, the companies registered during Sixth Plan were more than the existing companies, till the beginning of Fifth Plan and twice the number of companies registered during the preceding decade. Public companies increased by 72 per cent recording a 54 per cent increase in paid-up capital during 1980-85. In fact, the number of public companies have doubled in 1971-85, largely on account of the growth in the Sixth Plan. Paid-up capital more than tripled during the period 1971-85. The number of private companies grew almost four-folds in the period 197 -85. The paid-up capital grew 3.5 times during 1971-85 and recorded 74 per cent of growth during the Sixth Plan.

The average paid-up capital per company was slightly more than Rs. 30 lakhs in 1985 but the average size of private companies and the entire PCS had declined. This shows that the progress of PCS in terms of new incorporations has picked-up substantially in the Eighties and in the latter half of the Eighties average of around 15,000 new corporate entities were being registered per annum in the non-government sector. Over thirty years from 1956-57 to 1986 87, the number of registered companies had touched a figure of 1,40,000. The gross paid-up capital had increased almost four-folds during this period touching Rs. 40,000 crores in 1986-87. Out of these government companies, account for 75 per cent of the total paid-up capital. The paid-up capital of private corporate sector has barely touched Rs. 10,000 crores mark. Within the private corporate sector, business houses and corporate giants account for the bulk of corporate growth. In 1969-70, the number of companies with annual turn over of over more than Rs. 100 crores was only three, in 1986-87, this number had risen to more than a hundred.

Internal Stratification of Private Corporate Sector

Reserve Bank of India (RBI) carries on periodic studies on five sets of non-governmental companies which give in an idea about the relative contributions of large, medium and large Public companies, medium and large private companies and small private companies A census study of small private limited companies for the year 1970-71 was also conducted. It is interesting to note that the initial RBI survey of 1650 medium and large public companies, later extended to cover 1,720 companies, indicates that these companies account for a very large proportion of the paid-up capital of all public companies as is evident from Table 10.2.

Table 10.2 goes to show that on an average of 80 per cent of the paid up capital was on account of as small number as 1,760 medium and large companies as far as public companies are concerned. In 1980 about 21 per cent of the total companies accounted for 85 per cent of the share capital. Thus, the increasing number of public companies after this period is an

TABLE 10.2

Share in PUC of RBI Large and Medium Companies

Sr. No.	Year	PUC in Crores of Rupees of Public Ltd. Companies	PUC in Crores of Rupees of RBI 1,950/ 1,720 Companies	Percentage
1.	1971	1,775	1,598	90.02
2.	1972	2,035	1,643	80.70
3.	1973	2,175	1,652	76.00
4.	1974	2,323	1,712	73.60
5.	1975	2,484	1,814	73.02
6.	1976	2,536	1,899	74.88
7.	1977	2,554	2,030	79.48
8.	1978	2,649	2,159	81.50
9.	1979	2,668	2,269	85.04
10.	1980	2,751	2,343	85.40

Source : Data from RBI Surveys and Department of Company Affairs.

illusory guide to the growing strength of public companies in PCS. Only a few large and medium companies have accounted for at least three fourth increase of paid up capital at the start of the Eighties. In 1981-82, the largest 247 companies in Private Corporate Sector had a networth of 4.408.31 crores which was about 90 per cent of the entire paid up capital of the private sector. It is pertinent to note that networth is a better indicator for command over capital in case of established companies. If we attempt a study of assets, we find that the 100 largest companies percentage share in the 1,720. Medium and large Public Limited Companies is growing constantly and may be half of the assets in the Eighties, if we interpolate values on the basis of the trend of growing shares. Similarly, the 100 largest companies accounted for more than 30 per cent of the assets of entire Private Corporate Sector in 1981-82. Similarly 20 top houses also account for increasing shares of assets in private corporate sector which rose from 26 per cent in 1971 to 30.1 per cent in 1981-82.

The picture which emerges before us is that despite, the fact of proliferation of corporate entities in the Seventies and the Eighties, the concentration of economic power is increasing. The top 100 corporations account for one third of corporate wealth in PCS, the next 150 corporations account for further 15 per cent and 400 companies may account for 55 per cent of the assets and the share of around top 2,000 corporations may be to the tune of 80-85 per cent. The 20 big business houses assets are reported in Table 10.3.

TABLE 10.3
Assets of Top 20 Houses 1971-85

Sr. No.	Year	Assets of 20 Monopoly Houses	Index No. (With 1971=100)
1.	1971	2,700	100
2.	1972	2,916	108
3.	1973	3,318	123
4.	1974	3,928	146
5.	1975	3,630	172
6.	1976	5,290	196
7.	1977	5,846	217
8.	1978	6,248	231
9.	1979	6,618	245
10.	1980	7,641	283
11.	1981	8,300	307
12.	1982	8,987	333
13.	1983	13,376	495
14.	1984	15,815	585
15.	1985	20,236	749

From the time series constructed on the basis of the assets of Twenty Big Houses after the enactment of MRTPA, 1969, it is clear that the growth in assets was restrained initially because during the Fourth Plan period growth was only 72 per cent. During the Fifth Plan reflecting the general mood of Private Corporate Sector, the growth was only 64 per cent. Thereafter, during the Sixth Plan the assets have grown by 265 per cent. Thus, despite all claims of checking concentration of economic power, the top houses have recorded 7.5 times growth in their assets during the period 1971-85 which far outstrips the growth rate of entire private corporate sector. If we take 75 houses of MIC, it shall be revealed that these still command more than 50 per cent of assets of Private Corporate Sector.

The top business houses are diversifying their business. Companies like Reliance have gone for vertical integration. The growth of Tatas, Birlas and Modis has been conglomerate. The ten top houses have increased their assets of less than Rs. 2,000 crores to more than Rs. 18,000 crores during the period 1971-86. They have built empires which are 10-folds their assets in early Seventies. Tatas and Birlas alone account for assets around Rs. 10,000 crores by 1988, *i.e.*, about 12 per cent of the entire PCS assets.

Foreign Investments in India

An important feature of the developments in private corporate sector in recent years has been growing foreign collaboration arrangements. Although foreign investment and the collaboration are normally inter-related, foreign investment may take place without technical collaboration or *vice versa*. Reserve Bank of India Survery of Foreign Collaboration (1974) classifies companies into three types :

(*i*) Subsidiaries in which a single foreign company holds more than 50 per cent of equity capital ;

(*ii*) Minority companies, in which foreign company equity holdings are 50 per cent or less ; and (*iii*) Pure technical collaboration companies which have no foreign company equity participation but have technical collaboration agreements.

According to the information available by the beginning of the Eighties, 315 branches of foreign companies in India were functioning. The largest number of parent companies of these branches were incorporated in U.K. These branches accounted for about half the number of branches operating in India (152). USA based companies had 57 branches, Japan based companies had 19 branches functioning in India. The assets controlled by 247 companies for which information was available was Rs. 2,373.85 crores. Banking branches accounted for more than Rs. 2,000 crores of assets. Hence the assets of non-banking foreign branches were not significant. These were to the tune of Rs. 300 crores for around 250 non-banking branches by the beginning of the present decade. Indian subsidiaries of non-banking Foreign Companies which numbered 103 by 1980 had paid up capital of 212.85 crores and assets of 1858.62 crores. There were 29 wholly owned subsidiaries of foreign companies which accounted for around Rs. 7 crores paid up capital and around Rs. 70 crores of assets by the turn of the Eighties.

Foreign investments in India according to RBI surveys were around Rs. 680 crores by 1961 which increased to 1679.0 crores in 1971 and had reached Rs. 2,218.8 crores in 1980. U.K., U.S.A. and West Germany had major investments amounting to about Rs. 660, 592 and 245 crores. Remittances on foreign investment which were less than Rs. One hundred crores by the beginning of the 1970's reached Rs. 468 crores by 1982-83. Manufacturing accounted for half of the foreign investments, rest of these being in services, plantations and mining as well as services. Number of approvals for foreign collaboration which were averaging less than 200 per annum in the Sixties, were stepped upto more than three hundred by the late Seventies and are already averaging 1000 per annum by 1986. Despite enactment of FERA (1973), the industrial climate in Indian PCS continued to be very conducive to foreign investments. However, a preference has been shown for the socalled NRI investments in PCS who are substituting the traditional role of MNC's in the economies of the underdeveloped countries. According to the information provided in the Lock Sabha during 1984, '85 and '86, the number of foreign collaboration approvals were 752, 1024 and 956 respectively which involved foreign investments of Rs. 113, 126 and 107 crores in the respective years. These investments were Rs. 107 and Rs. 238 crores for '87 and '88. The foreign investments in India are estimated at more than Rs. 3,000 crores and around Rs. 500 crores per annum are being remitted on account of these investments. The assets controlled by the foreign companies are to the tune of Rs. 12,000 crores. The Indian corporate sector is opening up for international technology and capital. A large number of large companies (according to an estimate 55 among top 400) bear the names of collaborating MNC's, *e.g.*, Birla-Yamaha, Tata-Honeywell Modi Olivetti, DCM-Toyota. While in Mid-Seventies less than 10 per cent letters of intents being issued by Government of India had foreign collaborations, one third of all licenses being granted in recent years have foreign participation.

Financing Patterns in PCS

A sample study of new projects carried out in 1975 and 1984 yields the following light on the financing sources of PCS. In 1975, term loans from financial institutions contributed around 29.5 per cent of project costs, followed by equity capital which accounted for 26.14 per cent and loans from banks 24.91 per cent followed. Debentures accounted for less than 5 per cent of the project costs. By 1984, no noticeable change was noted despite the fact that banks contributed only 5 per cent of project costs. Debentures were able to raise 4.5 per cent of project costs. The contribution of the term lending institutions had increased to 40 per cent and equity capital also contributed 39 per cent of the project costs.

However, if the statistics for new companies and the new projects of existing companies is disaggregated, it is observed that debentures/bonds are becoming a very popular source of raising capital with the existing companies. Even in 1975, they contributed 9.33 per cent for the new projects of existing companies. Their contribution has increased 20.10 for the projects of the established companies by 1984 which matched the contribution of term loans from financial institutions, (*i.e.*, 21.26 per cent). With the innovations in industrial securities like convertible and partially convertible debentures, the capital issues market has become very active and is contributing more than half of the costs of the projects.

If the data on consents for capital issues is screened, it becomes clear that contribution of debentures to financing which was around 20-30 per cent of capital raised in the Seventies has registered a growth to the extent that 60 per cent or more of the money is being raised through public issues of debentures. In 1982-83, debentures accounted for 68 per cent of the total raised through public issues, whereas equity issues only raised 31 per cent of capital consents. We know that many debenture issues have been over-subscribed. Through the instruments like convertible debentures, Indian investors are being initiated into investing in risk capital of the PCS. The primary issue market has grown 30 times in just six years from Rs. 134 crores in 1980-81, to around Rs. 4,000 crores in 1986-87. The investors population has increased to 15 millions.

The ownership pattern of industrial equity shares in PCS as reflected through RBI surveys suggest that whereas in 1959 individuals owned 52 per cent of shares, the percentage declined to 45.6 in 1965 and further to 37.6 per cent in 1978. Share of joint stock companies came down from around 40 per cent to 33 per cent during 1959-78. Public financing institutions are a phenomenon of the Sixties and from negligible shares of about 6 per cent in 1959, they increased their share to 18.5 per cent in 1965 and owned 25.7 per cent of equity shares of the surveyed PCS companies in 1978. These institutions have increased their participation in equity capital through undertaking operations, convertibility clause and direct buying in the capital markets. A large number of corporate giants and big house companies like TISCO, ESCORTS, have financial institutions as the major holders of equity. That is why, now the institutions have a major say in the strategic management of private corporations with adoption of the consortium approach by institutions and the oppointment of nominee directors.

Profitability Performance of PCS Giants

Though profitability and sales performance varies from industry to industry, yet an aggregate picture is being presented here. We observe that the *Gross Profits as Percentage of total capital employed ratio* has varied from 12.5 per cent to 13 per cent for large and medium public companies from the years 1975-76 to 1979-80. The ratio of *Gross Profits to Net Sales* varied from 8.5 per cent to 9.2 per cent during the period for the same sample. The sample comprised of around 700 large or medium public limited companies in PCS.

It appears from the discussion, that the tendency of rates of profits to fall as capital intensity increases is being observed in the private corporate sector. Gross profits as percentage of total capital employed for Economic Times 250 giants declined from around 12 per cent to 9 per cent in the period 1980-81 to 1987-88. Gross profit as percentage of sales is more or less stable at 10.5 per cent. Net profit as percentage of networth peaked at around 14 per cent in 1981-82, and then steadily declined to 7.5 per cent in 1987-88, and then steadily declined to 7.5 per cent in 1987-88. As many as 54 giant companies out of Economic Times 236 giants, for which the data was available suffered losses in 1987-88. No dividends were paid by 52 companies, while 37 others reduced them. It is argued that it is the so called small sector or informal sector which is more profitable as contrasted with the organised private corporate sector of Indian industry, due to lower capital intensity. In discussions on public sector, we have shown that the profitability ratios have not been lower than PCS, at least during 1980's, except for net profit ratios. So, it is difficult to argue that PCS of India, especially the large companies are employing capital more profitably as compared to the public sector. The increasing incidence of sickness afflicting around 700 public limited companies, endangering the recovery of thousands of crores lent to them by the public financing institutions, is a further indicator that it is not the form of ownership or control but general health of the economy which determines the surplus generating capacities of all the sectors of our industrial economy. Increasing capital output ratio is the main culprit in the slow industrialisation of Indian economy.

CASE X

REORGANISATION OF UNILEVER SUBSIDIARIES

With the Indian Government's move to dilute equity of foreign parent companies in their subsidiaries in India, the Anglo-Dutch conglomerate Unilever adopted a noble strategy. A reorganisation of business between FERA subsidiary Hindustan Levers and Non-FERA associate Liptons India was taken up. The restructuring was a part of Hindustan Levers strategy of retaining higher foreign equity by concentrating on core sector and high technology business only. The Government of India in its policy pronouncement allowed majority participation for foreign companies in these sectors.

Liptons, till this point of time was a single line company dealing in packet teas. Hindustan Lever's dairy products, edible fats, vanaspati, refined oils, margarine, animal and poultry feeds business was transferred to Lipton's for a meagre sum of Rs. 15 crores in 1986. Thus Liptons was supposed to takeover the entire consumer goods business of subsidiaries of Unilevers in India. In this process, the company shall have more secure and diversified product lines. The regrouping of the commodities business would allow Hindustan Levers Limited to evolve a new corporate image. The company concentrated on manufacture of chemicals, agro-chemicals and other biotechnology based products. It may be pointed out that prior to the reorganisation, Hindustan Levers had taken over many small undertakings in consumer goods The total capital employed of the company was Rs. 223 crores and its sales turnover had reached Rs. 617 crores in 1985, as contrasted with total capital of Rs. 65 crores and sales turnover of Rs. 188 crores, a decade back. It was for a very meagre consideration that the most lucrative of Levers business was transferred to Liptons to serve the interests of the parent company Unilever.

POINTS FOR CONSIDERATION

(1) Don't you find the reorganisation of business by Unilever associates as discriminatory to the Indian shareholders of Hindustan Levers ?

(2) Doesn't the employment of such techniques to circumvent the public policy makes it impossible for the government to regulate private corporate sector ?

FURTHER READINGS

1. Chandra, N.K., "Monopoly Capital, Private Corporate Sector and Indian Economy—A Study of Relative Growth, 1931-76", *Economic and Political Weekly*, Special No., 1979.

2. Ezekiel, Hannan, (Ed.), *Corporate Sector in India*, New Delhi, Vikas Publishing House, 1984.

3. Hazari, R.K., *Industrial Planning and Licensing Policy*, Planning Commission, New Delhi, 1967.

4. Herdeck, Margret and Gita Piramal, *India's Industrialists*, Washington, D.C., Three Continents, 1985.

5. Government of India, *Report of Monopolies Inquiry Commission*, New Delhi, 1965.

6. ——, *Report of the Industrial Licensing Policy Inquiry Committee*, New Delhi, Department of Industrial Development, 1969.

7. ——, *Directory of Joint Stock Companies*, 1980, New Delhi, Directorate of Company Affairs, 1980.

8. Goyal, S.K., *Monopoly Capital and Public Policy—Business and Economic Power*, Bombay, Allied Publishers, 1979.

9. Reserve Bank of India, *Reports on Currency and Finance*, Bombay, 1971-88.

10. *Supplements on Private Corporate Sector Corporate Giants, Economic Times* (1973-89).

11

Small, Village and Cottage Industry

The importance of labour intensive technologies, decentralised development of industry is obvious in a large and thickly populated country like India. Small, Village and Cottage Industry is construed to be the means of absorbing manpower and overcoming imbalance in regional development. Industrial Policy Resolutions, from time to time, have been reiterating the protective measures and support systems needed for small scale industries, village handicrafts and cottage industries. In fact, in 1977 when Janata Party government tried to devise a Gandhian blueprint of industrialisation, they made bolder assertions about decentralised development of small and village industries.

Objectives and Strategies for Development

In 1980, the Industrial Policy Resolution of the new Congress (I) government devoted ten paragraphs on small industry while declaring allegiance to economic federalism. Setting of Nucleus Plants, ancilliarisation effects of these plants and raising the limits of investments for redefining the scope of small scale units and ancilliaries were the highlights of the 1980 resolution. System for financial support, supply of critical inputs and marketing of produce of small scale industries were the other measures proposed by the new policy. Handlooms, handicrafts, khadi and other village industries were to receive great attention to achieve a faster rate of economic and employment growth.

Small scale sector is aimed at contributing towards ensuring social mobility by improving the economic and occupational profile of the people at large. This sector would :

"(a) assist in the growth and widespread dispersal of industries ;

(b) increase in the levels of earnings of artisans ;

(c) sustain and create avenues of self-employment ;

(d) ensure regular supply of goods and services through use of local skills and resources ;

(e) develop entrepreneurship in combination with improved methods of production, through appropriate training and package of incentives ;

(f) preserve craftsmanship and art heritage of the country."

The changed strategy enunciated in the Seventh Plan is to improve productivity, enhance quality, reduce costs, restructure product mix through technological upgradation and modernisation of traditional manufactures. Increased capacity utilization by improving credit facilities, raw material and power supplies and giving access to domestic market through standardisation and publicity of products shall be able to overcome the problem of economic sickness to a very large extent. An effort shall also be made at human resource development aimed at improving the lot of all skill classes dependent on small scale industry.

Plan Outlays

Despite the proliferation of development agencies and increase in number of items reserved for small scale sector, small industry has not received very large financial allocation in the plan outlays of industry as is reflected in the Table 11.1.

From the Table 11.1 it is clear that leaving apart the first plan which had very meagre outlays for industry as a whole, the attention given to small scale industries as is reflected by Plan outlays was not adequate. The outlays for small and village industry declined from 16 per cent to around 6 per cent of the

TABLE 11.1
Plan Outlay on 1951-1990 Industry

Plan	Outlays (Rs. Crores)			Percentage of Columns 3 to 4
	Industry and Minerals	Village & Small Industry	Total	
(1)	(2)	(3)	(4)	(5)
First Plan	55	42	97	43.0
Second Plan	938	187	1,125	16.0
Third Plan	1,726	241	1,967	12.5
Annual Plan	1,510	126	1,637	7.7
Fourth Plan	2,864	243	3,107	7.8
Fifth Plan	8,989	593	9,581	6.2
Annual Plan	5,384	256	2,639	9.7
Sixth Plan	15,002	1,945	16,948	11.4
Seventh Plan	19,708	2,753	22,461	12.3
Total	53,176	6,386	59,562	10.7

Source : Seventh Plan Document, Planning Commission.

outlay of industry as a whole from the Second to Fifth Plans. Thereafter, it started picking up and was 12.3 per cent of the total outlay for industry by the Seventh Plan. On an average, for the period 1951-90 the small and village industry was receiving an average 10.7 per cent of total industry allocations. These outlays work out to 1.5 to 4 per cent of the total outlays of public sector in various plans. The outlays after Fifth Plan may seem to be satisfactory but the fact has to be noted that outlays for industry in general had gone down by then. Small industry received 1.5 to 2.1 per cent of total plan outlays in public sector for the period 1966-90. It is estimated by some sources that even if private sector investment in small sector is taken into account, this will also work out to be 3 to 5 per cent of all development outlays for forty years period, 1951-90.

Growth of Unregistered Sector

In fact, the so-called small sector is defined by using a negative criterion. All those units which are not registered under Indian Factories Act, 1948 are assumed to be small scale manufacturing units. According to National Accounts Statistics, the growth of manufacturing in unregistered sector is portrayed in Table 11.2.

TABLE 11.2

Contribution to Net Product of Unregistered Manufacturing as a Share of Munufacturing Sector

(Rs. Crores, 1970-71 Prices)

Years	Unregistered Manufacturing	Manufacturing	Percentage of Columns (2) & (3)
(1)	(2)	(3)	(4)
1950-51	775	1,674	46.3
1960-61	1,244	2.918	42.6
1970-71	1,745	4,619	37.8
1975-76	2,161	5,557	38.9
1980-81	2,633	7,057	37.3
1981-82	2,697	7,402	36.4
1982-83	2,752	7,580	36.3
1983-84	2,916	7,813	38.3

Source : Government of India, National Accounts Statistics.

We note from the Table 11.2 that at least 37 per cent of total product of the secondary sector is contributed by the unregistered manufacturing. Since the share of manufacturing sector in the total net national product has ranged from 10-16 per cent and is averaging at around 15 per cent in the recent years, unregistered manufacturing contributes 4-6 per cent of the Net National Product. According to more recent estimates, unorganised manufacturing may be accounting for about the half of total industrial produce.

According to estimates for 1984-85 the number of small scale units is more than 12.5 lakhs as contrasted 8.05 lakhs in 1979-80. The production at current prices of small sector units was 50,520 crores in 1984-85, as contrasted with 21,637 crores in 1979-80. Thus the production at current prices has gone up by 2.3 times from 1979-80 to 1984-85. At 1979-80 prices, however, the production of small sector is Rs. 34,065 crores in 1984-85 and, thus, the real increases in production over five years is 57 per cent. Over this period, the employment has gone up in this sector from 67 lakhs to 90 lakhs, thus registering around 50 per cent growth. Exports of this sector have increased from 1,226 crores to Rs. 2,580 crores and have doubled during the Sixth Plan period.

Contributions of Village and Small Scale Industries (VSI)

Two sample surveys were carried out in the Seventies for ascertaining the state of small industry. RBI conducted a sample survey of small enterprises to estimate their growth and structure. 16,636 units were selected for the survey but of these information could be made available for 12,356 units. Later, National Small Industries Corporation (NSIC) sample survey data of 1979 was collected. This data focussed on the problems of small sector like marketing of inputs, nature of competition, pricing, etc, These surveys became the basis of assigning small sector a crucial role in the Indian industrialisation in the Eighties.

There are three types of small units as per the plan documents of Government of India. The traditional industries outlined include Khadi, Village industries, handlooms, sericulture, handicrafts and coir. The modern manufactories include

TABLE 11.3
Output/Exports/Employment of Different Categories of Village and Small Industry

Category	Production (Rs. Crores) 73-74	79-80	84-85	Exports (Rs. Crores) 73-74	79-80	84-85	Employment (Lakh Persons) 73-74	79-80	84-85
Traditional Industries	2,183 (16.10)	4,447 (13.10)	7,726 (11.75)	314 (3.68)	1,231 (54.0)	2,208 (48.0)	102 (58.0)	131 (56.0)	165 (5.23)
Modern Industries	9,180 (51.94)	24,885 (64.51)	5,944 (86.63)	538 (63.2)	1,050 (46.0)	2,350 (52.0)	50 (84.4)	78 (33.3)	122 (38.7)
Other Industries	2,237 (16.44)	4,206 (12.54)	1,061 (1.61)	—	—	—	24 (13.6)	25 (10.7)	28 (9.0)
Total VSI	13,600 (100)	33,538 (100)	65,730 (100)	852 (100)	2,281 (100)	4,558 (100)	176 (100)	234 (100)	315 (100)

Source: Seventh Five Year Plan 1985-90, Volume II, New Delhi.

chemicals and chemical products. basic metals and alloys, machinery, machine tools, metal products, parts except machinery, rubber, plastic, petroleum and coal products ; the distinguishing feature being use of non-traditional skills and machinery for manufacture. Then there is a group of miscellaneous industries which cannot be grouped as being strictly traditional or modern. In all, around 850 items are reserved for manufacture in small scale sector. The achievements of different sectors of village and small industry (VSI) are summarised in Table 11.3. The table shows that traditional industries are loosing importance as far as total output of VSI is concerned. Their share has come down to 11.75 per cent from 16.10 per cent in the last decade. Seventh Plan document, however, expects that the same share will be retained by the terminal year of Plan, *i.e.*, 1989-90.

As far as modern sector is concerned, it has increased its share from one half of the output a decade back to 87 per cent of the total output. The targetted growth for 1989-90 also aims at retaining about the same share. The contribution of the other groups is being increasingly marginalised and shall be to the tune of one per cent by 1989-90. Exports of VSI have increased 5-folds over the period 1973-74 to 1984-85. Traditional industries had peaked in their share of exports in 1979-80 with a 54 per cent contribution and the share came down to 48 per cent in next five years and is further expected to come down to 45 per cent. Around 30 per cent of output of traditional sector was exported in 1984-85. In contrast though the share of modern sector was larger in exports, this sector exported only 4 per cent of its total output. The share of the modern sector in total export of VSI is expected to go upto 55 per cent by 1989-90

Employment in VSI has increased by 78 per cent from 176 lakhs to 315 lakhs in the period 1973-74 to 1984-85. Main contributor to this export has been the modern sector which empolyed one third of persons employed in VSI in 1979-80 and in 1984-85, its share has gone up to 38.7 per cent. But it seems that the planners are not very hopeful in this sector increasing its share in employment due to the increasing capital/output ratio. The share of the modern sector is expected to plummet down to 30 per cent by the year 1990. The employment potential of traditional industries, in contrast in much higher. All through the period traditional sector has been dominant employer and is expected to employ 2.18 crores in 1989-90 which will be around 55 per cent of the total employment of VSI, the average percentage has been projected on the basis of past experience. A point of caution, however, needs to be mentioned here, the others sector employed around 10 per cent of persons in VSI and its marginalisation may have an adverse influence on employment potential of this sector. The statistics for the unregistered manufacturing sector corresponds to modern sector of VSI.

Financial Sources for VSI

The rationale behind promoting VSI is to provide employment to the largest possible numbers, despite the fact that technologies being utilised may not be most modern. But the development of modern sector in VSI shows that the technology is being upgraded in small sector, especially through plans like development of ancilliary industries around a nucleous plant. Small units, generally, may have higher costs of production, due to non-availability of economies of scale but due to lower capital intensity the units are able to absorb more surplus manpower. Track record of small units, as far as payment of wages is concerned, is disappointing and the units also generate lesser surplus per worker, *i.e.*, labour productivity is low in these units.

If one goes by statistics provided by the planners, the governments in India have been able to sustain the small sector units in face of competition from the organised industry. The elaborate support system developed for sustaining SVI have been discussed in chaper 8. The Table 11.4 shows the financial assistance disbursed through commercial banks and State financial corporations. The guiding philosophy behind lending to small sector is that the loans should be need-based not security-based, this is justified on account of the employment potential of this sector.

TABLE 11.4

Financial Assistance to Small Scale Industries

Commercial Banks

As on	Number of Units ('000s)	Bank Credit (Rs. Crores)
December 1979	681	2,632.77
December 1980	794	3,136.48
December 1981	961	3,953.09
December 1982	1,050	4,464.32
December 1983	1,225	5,050.58
December 1984	1,413	7,238.47
December 1985	1,570	7,462.51

Source : India Annuals, Publications Division, Government of India.

State Financial Corporations

		Funds Disbursed
1979-80	15,278	114.08
1980-81	26,447	157.39
1981-82	28,178	210.71
1982-83	28,510	290.17

Source : IDBI, Reports on Development Banking.

Commercial Banks, apart from providing composite loans under self-employment schemes also give term loans to small industry at concessional rate of 12.5 per cent for backward areas and at 13.5 per cent for other areas. They also sanction credit limits to industry and limits upto two lakhs carry an interest rate of 14 per cent. Loans upto Rs. 20 lakhs have to be processed within a period 4 to 8 weeks. The number of small scale industry accounts as on March, 1986, had increased to about 16 lakhs and credit had gone upto Rs. 7,561.36 crores. There was a sea transformation from pre-nationalisation era, in 1969, the commercial banks had only 51 thousand accounts of industry with credit at the level of Rs. 5.49 crores. Number of accounts after thirty years is expected to be 35 times of that in 1969 and the loans have increased 1600 times.

The Seed Margin Money Scheme and Small Scale Industries Guarantee Scheme are two other schemes introduced recently to assist small industry. The former aims at making funds available to State governments to make venture capital available to small entrepreneurs, the latter guarantees the repayment of the borrowed money to the term lending institutions. Various subsidies being provided to the entrepreneurs have already been discussed.

Commercial Operations of Small Units

Though the majority of small producers market their output directly to the firms in the private sector, small scale sector and public sector in descending order, the governments as buyers give special preference to the purchases from these units. The NSIC Survey of 1900 units indicates the different marketing channels used by small scale industry. It is interesting to note that as many as 963 units, *i.e.*, about half the sample units benefit from government/public sector buying and the price preferences given to them. Majority of surveyed firms (61 per cent) are manufacturing industrial products and as such their main buyers constitute the private corporate sector and governmental undertakings. It seems that not more than 20 per cent units are ancilliaries despite the fact that NSIC sample is biased in favour of modern sector of industry. Nucleus Plants resulting in ancilliarisation effect is a policy measure conceived in 1980, *i.e.*, after the 1979 survey.

A nucleus plant would concentrate on assembling the parts subcontracted to small scale ancilliary units. These plants are also supposed to help the ancilliaries in updating their technologies besides, procuring bulk of their product. This was an important step in building a link between the small and large in our industrial sector, the former is not left to succumb to the market power of the latter, the two are supposed to co-operate.

It is worthwhile mentioning here that the organised sector is not only an important customer of small scale sector, it also supplies raw materials. According to NSIC survey, 31 per cent of small units procured their raw materials from private sector firms, another 29 per cent procured materials from public sector firms or agencies, it is only 40 per cent of the industries which procure their raw materials from sources other than organised sector of industry. The 40 per cent include the units which base their products on produce of primary sector. The ancilliarisation as a two way relationship, *i.e.*, of supply of raw materials and procurement of finished product had not progressed as is evident from the fact that only 5 units reported that they were engaged in 'job-work'.

The reservation of items for small scale sector aimed at eliminating competition from the large native as well as overseas business. The NSIC Survey showed that the policy had worked because 87 per cent of units faced main competition from other small producers. Of course, one/third of the surveyed units felt that they may have competitors from organised sector or private sector units. Pricing was done on cost plus principle largely, and the competitive price characteristic of free market was also in vogue. As many as 70 per cent of the entrepreneurs used cost plus prices. However, there were more than one principles used in price fixation.

Capacity Utilization and Economic Sickness

The majority of small scale units operate only one shift, though the shift may be of longer than eight hours, due to lack of trade union pressures. The quartile distribution of capacity utilization shows that 8.49 per cent units utilize less than 25 per cent of capacity, 38.30 per cent utilize from 25-50 per cent of capacity, 23.61 per cent have capacity utilization between 50-75 per cent whereas only 28.71 per cent has capacity utilization of 75 per cent and above.

The detailed classification of industries given in NSIC survey shows that small sector produces a relatively limited range of products using simple technologies. There is no relationship between the size of the units and the number of customers. They utilize barely 50 per cent of the capacity but since they use cost plus principle of prices the overheads are accounted for.

"Comparison of profitability between the private corporate and small scale sectors and within the small sector across size class of units is revealing since the findings are at variance with some of the accepted views on this issue. Profitability within the small sector is inversely related to size of the units as measured by the original value of plant and machinery. Further, profitability in the small scale sector as a whole is higher than that in the private corporate sector. The result could be attributed to lower wage costs and fiscal concessions to the small scale sector."

Principal characteristics of small and large factories is depicted in Table 11.5. While summing up evidence of Annual Surveys of Industry, IMD Little observes. "The surveys didn't provide evidence that small firms employ resources more efficiently......than large firms, nor even that they are relatively more labour intensive. If our research can be held to suggest anything about size and economic or social desirability it is that beauty is to be found mostly in the middle of the size distribution." Thus small is not beautiful according to the studies of factory sizes and their relative efficiency.

How does one explain the high mortality rate associated with VSI. From the statistics reported from various sources, it is clear that the village community based household or cottage production is not able to grow in competition with the factory sector. In fact, the units in traditional sector cannot survive

TABLE 11.5

Principal Characteristics of Small and Large Factories, 1966-67, 1974-75 and 1982-83

(Percentage)

Characteristics	Part A 66-67	Part A 74-75	Part A 82-83	Part B 74-75	Part B 82-83	Part C 74-75	Part C 82-83
(1)	(2)	(3)	(4)	(5)	(6)	(7)	(8)
1. Number of Factories							
Small	92	78	81	84	83	76	77
Large	8	11	8	5	7	2	1
Other	—	11	11	11	10	23	22
Total	(49,346)	(64,217)	(93,166)	(64,217)	(93,166)	(64,217)	(93,166)

(Contd.)

(Contd.)

(1)	(2)	(3)	(4)	(5)	(6)	(7)	(8)
2. Fixed Capital							
Small	8	6	6	9	7	5	4
Large	92	93	94	90	93	68	72
Other	—	1	—	1	—	27	24
Total (Rs. Cr.)	(5,855)	(11,922)	(41,006)	(11,922)	(41,006)	(11,922)	(41,006)
3. Productive Capital							
Small	NA	8	8	13	9	6	5
Large	NA	91	92	86	91	64	71
Other	NA	1	—	1	—	30	24
Total (Rs. Cr.)	NA	(17,932)	(57,326)	(17,932)	(57,326)	(17,932)	(57,326)
4. Number of Employees							
Small	36	31	33	39	35	14	15
Large	64	66	62	58	60	45	43
Other	—	3	5	3	5	41	42
Total (in Lakh)	(48)	(61)	(80)	(61)	(80)	(61)	(80)

(Contd.)

Small, Village and Cottage Industry

(Contd.)

(1)	(2)	(3)	(4)	(5)	(6)	(7)	(8)
5. Output							
Small	30	22	22	30	24	14	13
Large	70	77	77	68	75	40	44
Other	—	1	1	2	1	46	43
Total (Rs. Cr.)	(8,715)	(26,099)	(86,238)	(26,099)	(86,238)	(26,099)	(86,238)
6. Value Added							
Small	22	15	15	22	17	8	8
Large	78	84	84	77	82	51	54
Other	—	1	1	1	1	41	38
Total (Rs. Cr.)	(2,045)	(6,081)	(16,674)	(6,081)	(16,674)	(6,081)	(16,674)

Notes: — Means NIL/Negligible; NA=Not Available.

Source: Central Statistical Organisation, Government of India, Annual Survey of Industries, Summary Results for Factory Sector for 1966, Table 5, p. 10.

without technology upgradation. Technological obsolescence, inadequate and irregular supply of raw materials, lack of organised marketing channels, imperfact knowledge of market conditions, unorganised nature of operations, inadequate availability of credit, constraint of infrastructural facilities including power and managerial as well as technical skills have been identified as the causes of economic sickness and high rate of mortality.

In fact, the so called self-employment projects are non-starters. The mortality rate may be as high as 95 per cent, in self-employment ventures working with composite loans. As of December, 1985, 16.42 lakh small units have been provided bank credit amounting to Rs. 7,829 crores, of which 1.18 lakh units (7 per cent) have been found to be sick with outstanding bank credit of Rs. 1,071 crores (7 per cent). Of these sick units only 7,800 (7 per cent of all sick units) with outstanding bank credit of Rs. 245 crores (23 per cent of credit locked) were considered by the banks as potentially viable. Of these viable units, 2,200 with outstanding bank credit of Rs. 176 crores were put under nursing programmes by financial banks. The number of sick units in small sector has further grown and, in fact, as compared with 20,326 units in 1979, the number has grown to 1,28,687 by 1986. The bank credit locked with these sick units has grown to Rs. 1,184 crores and only 10 per cent of the units are considered revivable. But incidence of sickness is even more alarming with the organised sector where around 1,000 medium or large units have locked bank credit to the tune of Rs. 2,500 crores.

Problems of Small Entrepreneurs

Various empirical studies have pointed to the problems encountered by the entrepreneurs which results in the failure of many new venture in India. The first major problem is regarding the proper identification and selection of feasible projects. Though, a large number of techno-economic consultancies are trying to identify projects and prepare techno-economic feasibility reports, yet, these half baked exercises leave much to be desired. Wrong choices of technology and improper forecasting of the demands is not uncommon.

Secondly, despite all utterances, various clearances needed for starting any manufacturing unit delay the project completion and results in cost-escalations which small entrepreneurs find very difficult to bear. Long project times create liquidity problems, raise production costs, hike the break-even points and increase the debt burdens.

Inadequate finances, especially finances needed to finance working capital needs, are not uncommon in small industry. Non-productive expenditure, aimed at cultivating the institutional bureaucracy, and lack of proper internal organisation of the business also hampers efficient functioning of small units.

Lack of basic infrastructure inhibits the setting up of small units in backward, semi-urban or rural areas, despite announcement of so many concessions. Power failures, inadequate telecommunications and transportation facilities are not uncommon even in the so called industrial estates/townships. Lack of adequate communications hinders information flow between markets and factories as well as between the latter and suppliers of raw materials. This communication failure obstructs smooth production and distribution of the industrial produce.

Lack of housing facilities for workers also creates problems especially when multiple shift production is needed. The provisions of anti-pollution laws makes certain localities unfit for industrial locations and it is impossible for a small entrepreneur to install anti-pollution devices. Water supply and swerage or waste disposal systems created by local authorities are utterly inadequate.

Since small industries are sought to be promoted in townships, backward and rural areas, the operation of these factories becomes costlier due to lack of local availability of technical manpower and technical services for preventive maintenance and repairs. The unskilled casual labour drawn from rural areas does not severe their connections with agriculture, as their primary occupation, and during the cropping or sowing seasons, labour is not easily available. This results in underutilization of installed capacity.

Multiple clearances have not only to be sought at the time of setting up a industry. According to Raj Krishna there are 86 legislations and 28 agencies which the industry is supposed to deal with all through its period of operation. May be the number is smaller for unregistered sector. The number of promotional organisations for SVI is very large and the co-ordination among these agencies to provide Single Window Service to entrepreneur is a distant dream, as yet.

As is well known many critical inputs of manufacturing are produced in the public sector and are distributed through governmental agencies. Unless an entrepreneur is very good at public relations, the supply of these inputs is irregular and short which disrupts the smooth functioning of production process.

The ancilliaries in India are faced with peculiar problems. Normally, ancilliaries cater to the needs of one mother unit whereas, the vendor development departments of the mother units always have access to alternate sources of supply of various parts or subassemblies needed for their production. This dependence of ancilliaries on single mother unit creates problems of unequal relations and unfair treatment of small units by the so called nucleous plants. Similarly, in case of production to meet the demand of institutional buyers also, a small unit may find assured market situation comforting in short run but this can prove to be fatal for the unit's survival in the long run. Tax laws especially on excise duties are very complicated with plethora of notifications and trade notices, small units find it very hard to cope with and, sometimes, penal excise payments lead to sickness and ultimate liquidation of small units.

The officials manning support systems for small industry

are inadequately trained. They function as the agents of regulatory mechanism rather than as agents of an industrial support system and consequently, the small businessman is constantly harassed by these bureaucratic functionaries. Despite loud talks of improving quality to make produce of small industry flat to compete in the domestic as well as the export markets, the common facilities provided to entrepreneurs for testing, standardisation and quality improvement are meagre. In fact, marketing front is the weakest in case of small scale units. Large private and public sector units delay payments to these units and the credit institutions are also callous to this problem and refuse to lend a helping hand in marketing nor do they wait for repayment for their loans.

Developmental approach to administration faces its biggest challenge in the present exercise of entrepreneurial development being taken up as a national task. Various suggestions with regard to professionalising developmental bureaucracy to match its changed responsibilities have been made by a number commissions. Administrative Reforms Reports suggests a number of changes in personnel policies and practices. Without going into details of proposed changes, it is pertinent to mention here that the entrepreneurs with their ideas shouldn't be trapped in the intricate administrative apparatus. The industrial support system has not only to promote new units but also help 'turn around' measures for sick small units. The banker-borrower relationship in case of small entrepreneurs leaves much to be desired.

A supporting official for entrepreneurial developments can only succeed in merging 'his overt identity with them (entrepreneurs) by showing empathy (not sympathy) with their problems and life conditions'. Disadvantages of high costs in small industries can be overcome, if government incentives as subsidies are disbursed as effective promotional measures.

Since the industrial culture has still to emerge in India to ensure, a regular supply of new entrepreneurs, entrepreneurial development effort based on Schumpetarian premises is receiving a big impetus. The effort is geared to create an entrepreneurial class of 50 lakh self-employed job creators. The target group for identifying job creators has been extended to unemployed educated manpower in the country. But if the small industries are to progress, it is essential to understand the problems of small entrepreneurs and redress them through an elaborate support system created for this purpose. Rather than being overenthusiastic only about new ventures, the problems of existing small ventures also need to be attended. Without removing the structural obstacles in the way of effective demand in domestic market, we may not be able to sustain the existing number of small scale units.

CASE XI

SMALL INDUSTRY : REALITY AND MYTH

As a part of its entrepreneurial guidance programme, a management school in North India has been following up the setting up of new ventures. The following are a few instances that reveal the myth and reality of small business in India.

The quote a success story, Shashi Bhushan's entrepreneurship exercise can be narrated. This young management graduate hailing from a family of edible oil wholesalers, considered many projects like solar heaters, micro-electronics and publishing but ultimately, settled at a project which was based on his family business. He hired a shed in the industrial area of Chandigarh, with a seed capital of Rs. 50,000 and liberal aid of financial institution started crushing oil-seeds. The small amount of edible oil which his small unit could produce was easily sold through family whole-sale agency. Latter, he accumulated enough capital and was able to start modern processing of oil-seeds in a hired factory premises. He, in fact, had bought an established oil mill with its brand name.

This youngman was later able to procure an industrial license for a Vanaspati plant and was able to persuade two of his batchmates of the management school and a rich farmer of

Punjab to pool capital. Now he is managing a private limited company with a turn over of Rs. 5 crores. The entire process of transformation of a tiny sector unit into a medium scale industry was completed in the decade of 1974 to 1984.

Prompted by Shashi Bhushan's success, many other MBA's started small ventures. Krishan was able to set up an ancilliary unit for Eicher Tractors, nearby the parent unit in industrial township of Parwanoo, near Chandigarh. He was liberally assisted by State Financing Corporation. He was relying exclusively on orders of Eicher but intended to diversify. Meanwhile, due to credit squeeze by commercial banks, the demand for tractors in green revolution belt fell down, the mother Eicher unit was not able to meet the increased wage demands of its labour due to recession in tractor market. There was a prolonged labour trouble, the aftermath of which was that Eicher decided to close its Parwanoo unit. Krishan's ancilliary also came to a grinding halt, at a time when his rescheduled repayment of loans advanced by State Financial Corporation has started. The failed entrepreneur was in a fix which is obvious in such circumstances.

Kulwinder, a rich farmer of Punjab didn't want to take a job despite his doctorate degree. He set up a small unit manufacturing nuts, bolts and nails, near flourishing industrial town of Ludhiana. He was also given a term-loan by the State Financing Corporation.

He met the expanding working capital needs through the savings of family's agricultural income but couldn't manage it, at a stage, when the unit had gone beyond the break even capacity. He tried to get a credit ceiling sanctioned but the dishonest bank officials demanded commissions which Kulwinder was not willing to pay and as a result the capacity utilization of his factory started declining and he didn't have enough savings from business or agriculture to keep the machines busy.

In contrast, Ashok another MBA managed to get a sales agency of tractors from a nationally reputed tractor manufacturer and is able to make a deccent living with his earnings from business showing an upward rise year after year. Similarly, Rajan who had invested in real estate including hotels was also expanding his business. Others who joined the established trading or manufacturing business of their families are able to use their expertise in expanding the volume of the operations of their established family concerns.

POINTS FOR CONSIDERATION

(1) Do you think that trading or service industry is more profitable business for small ventures as compared to manufacturing?

(2) Is it family background or institutional support which has resulted in success/failure of small enterprises in the case?

FURTHER READINGS

1. Dawar, Ram, *Institutional Finance to Small Scale Industries*, New Delhi, Deep and Deep, 1986.

2. Development Commissioner, Small Scale Industries, *Small Scale Industries in India : Policies, Programmes and Institutional Support*, New Delhi, 1980.

3. Government of India, *Statement on Industrial Policy*, New Delhi, July 23, 1980.

4. ——, *Reports of the National Committee on Backward Areas Development*, New Delhi.

5. ——, *Reports on Industrial Dispersal*, New Delhi, October, 1980.

6. ——, *General Issues Related to Backward Area Development*, New Delhi, November, 1981.

7. Little, IMD, "Small Manufacturing Enterprises in Developing Countries", *World Bank Economic Review*, Washington D.C., January, 1987.

8. Nagaraj, R., "Some Aspects of Small Scale Industries in India—Findings Based on Two All India Sample Surveys", *Economic and Political Weekly*, Vol. XX, Nos. 41 & 42, October 12 & 19, 1985.

9. Sandesara, J.C., "Small-Scale Industrialisation : The Indian Experience", *Economic and Political Weekly*, Vol. XXIII, No. 13, March 26, 1988.

10. Vepa, Ram, K., *Small Industry : The Challange of Eighties*, New Delhi, Vikash Publishing, 1983.

12

Changing Economic Environment

India is an economy in transition. A news like India achieving an industrial growth as high as 8 per cent in 1988 makes one optimistic about its future. The growing rate of savings, *i.e.*, 25 per cent on an average during the recent years, record production of 170 million tonnes of food and decline in percentage of population below poverty line all are promising features of the economy. But the optimism cannot be sustained for very long.

The long range GDP growth rate has been stable at 3.55 per cent even till 1987-88, recent increases on account of disproportionate growth of tertiary sector notwithstanding. The growth rate of agricultural output is 2.6 per cent when the population dependent on agriculture stays at 69 per cent. Accounting for growth of population in rural areas and the Gini's coefficient (measuring inequality) at 0.65 per cent, the rural poverty rate has stayed above 50 per cent and the urban poverty rate is not lagging far behind. *Per capita* income in 1987-88 grew by 1.4 per cent as compared to 1986-87. Even, if we accept our planners' optimistic view that the overall growth rate shall rise to 4 per cent and through population control measures, "our *per capita* income would be only $ 371 ; it would take an overall growth rate of about 4.5 per cent before poverty would begin to diminish, even then *per capita* income would be only $ 574 at the end of the Century". The Gross Domestic Product stood at around Rs. 293 thousand crores and *per capita* income at around Rs. 3,300, at current prices, by 1987-88. In 1977-78, official estimates of poverty in absolute numbers stood as 31 crores to 37 crores which according to 1983-84 data was around 32 crores and if this trend continues there will be 40 crores below the poverty line by the year 2000 A.D. It is well known that one of the two illiterates of the world would be in India, by the turn of the Century, so skill levels of the population would be very low and the problem of unemployment shall persist.

The savings ratio being at around 25 per cent, according to the development economists should have launched full scale transition of the economy to a higher stage but the capital-output ratio which has risen to 6 : 1 ; has neutralised whatever positive impact this increasing savings rate could have on economic growth. According to the new index of industrial production, the industrial growth rate has substantially picked up and index of industrial production (1980-81=100) had reached 180 by middle of 1988. The industrial growth rates for the four years of the Seventh Plan are shown to be above 8.5 per cent. According to Prof. Raj Krishna's estimates, this growth rate can increase the capital stock at a rate of seven per cent, if we are able to sustain these growth rates over the next 12 years, we would be able to reduce unemployment considerably. Of course, this will not be by way of absorption in the modern sector of industry because capital intensity of this sector is continuously rising. The increase in employment will take place in the informal small scale sector which at present also is the major employer in secondary sector. The multiplier effect of high industrial growth especially through the small industry can dramatically reduce unemployment. The recent emphasis on entrepreneurial development can be explained in this context.

Developmental Perspective—A Planning Commission View

The gross domestic product, at factor cost according to the Seventh Plan, is targetted to grow at an average rate of 5 per cent over the period 1985-2000. The rate of capital formation is expected to be 26.4 per cent of G.D.P., with step up of domestic savings to 25.8 per cent and a contribution of 0.6 per cent from the foreign savings (current account balance). Manufacturing, electricity, gas and water supply are expected to grow at rate of above 7 per cent over the entire period. Services sector's average growth is aimed at around 6 per cent.

The sectoral composition of gross value added at factor costs is 36.9 per cent for agricultural sector, 14.6 per cent for manufacturing. If we include and electricity and water supply, the share of secondary sector can be estimated to be 20.1, but if we exclude these the infrastructural sector/service sector accounts for half of the value added. The service sector is accounting for as large a share as 31.2 per cent. In fact, most of the growth in the so called services sector is not directly productive. It is aimed that by the turn of Century, manufacturing will increase its share to 20 per cent, a hope which is not sustained by the growth experience of Indian economy in the last four decades.

The rosy picture painted by the Planning Commission of the possibilities of Indian economy can be captured through the effect the development scenerio is going to have on quality of life (see Table 12.1). Obviously, the entire exercise seems to have been prompted by the political vision of Rajiv Gandhi government, whose slogan 'towards Twenty-First Century' has become an object of ridicule among the serious economists and political scientists. It seems that the needs of people, as visualised in Table 12.1, have become the basis of forecasting the growth scenerio, the analysis is neither rooted in the objective realities of our economy nor cognizes the political constraints on the growth process. Lot of statistical juggling, especially redefinition of growth indices and choice of base years, justify the forecasts of socio-economic indicators of change depicted in Table 12.1.

Commenting on the visions of the authors of the developmental perspective for 2000 A.D., observations like the ones made by Surendra J. Patel in his Presidential Address to Indian

TABLE 12.1

Socio-Economic Indicators of Change (1985-2000)

	1984-85	1989-90	1999-2000
1. Life Expectancy Male (in terms of years)	56.1	58.1	63.3
Female	57.1	59.7	64.7
2. Infant mortality ratio (per thousand births)	106	90	60
3. Death rate (per thousand)	11.9	10.4	8.2
4. Birth rate (per thousand)	32.6	29.1	23.1
5. Fertility rate (per thousand)	152	132	99
6. Urbanisation (per cent)	24.70	26.85	32.20
7. Per capital GDP (1984-85 prices) (Rs.)	2,616	3,027	4,163
8. *Per capita* consumption of foodgrains (Kg.)	178	193	215
9. *Per capita* consumption expenditure (1984-85 prices) (Rs.)	1,979	2,271	3,124
10. *Per capita* consumption of cloth (Metres)	16.16	17.78	22.36
11. *Per capita* generation of electricity (Kwh)	226	362	578-621
12. Saving-GDP ratio (per cent)	23.3	24.5	25.8
13. Investment-GDP ratio (per cent)	24.5	25.9	26.4
14. Foreign savings-Investment ratio (per cent)	4.9	5.5	2.4
15. Percentage of people below poverty line	37	26	5
16. Labour force (million in the age group 15 plus)	288	327	408
17. Employment (million standard person years)	187	227	318

Source : Seventh Plan Document, Vol. I.

Economic Association demolish the entire edifice of the perspective. Even sympathetic observers like Malcom S. Adiseshia of our planning effort observe : "......We must enter the 21st century without the scandal of the mass of our people living in poverty. That we can achieve not only by adhering faithfully to the development model that we have built over three decades......", but by leaving behind rhetoric which we have so for used as a substitute for action on our 'socialist' programmes. In this context, it should be borne in mind that a discussion on supply constraints, as attempted by Late Prof. Raj Krishna made him shift positions in suggesting measures to break the curse of Hindu rate of economic growth. In analysing the paradoxes of planned development in India, C.T. Kurien observes : "The logic of programme indicates that no major redistribution of income can be sustained with some redistribution of assets......" especially, landed property.

Constraints on the growth of effective demand have been offered as an explanation for inability of manufacturing increasing its sectoral contribution to GDP. Prof. K.N. Raj explained the industrial stagnation of Mid-Sixties by pointing out the failures of programmes for redistribution of income which resulted in restriction of domestic market for manufactured goods to a small stratum of large Indian population. In this context, it is argued that land reforms is not a socialist programme, extraordinarily rapid industrial development in East Asian countries like Japan and South Korea, partly was on account of the impact of land "occupation reforms".

It is argued that among the Seventy per cent Indians, depending on agriculture, only a small proportion of better off households, especially in the green revolution areas have started purchasing manufactured goods both for agricultural and domestic uses. Even the so-called surplus food stocks is a symptom of the under-consumption which affects the vast masses of rural population. It is difficult to resist reference to the observation of S. S. Johl, once chairman, Agricultural Prices Commission that China with food production of 400 million tonnes and Russia, a country have one fifth of India's population with a food production of more than 180 million tonnes are food deficit countries. What miracle then can explain India's food surplus with production ranging around 150 million tonnes. It has to be realised, in this context, that Federation of Indian Chambers of Commerce and Industry (FICCI) had also demanded more rigorous implementation of land reforms to unleash enormous purchasing power of the vast masses of rural India. All the poverty alleviation programmes put together are not a substitute for the much needed redistribution of landed assets. This is the only way to remove demand constraints on the Indian industry, especially the VSI.

The Fiscal Crisis in India

Supply-side economic prescriptions have landed up India in a fiscal crisis. In the name of unearthing black money, direct tax revenue's share in total tax revenue has been brought down from 40 per cent in the early Fifties to about 15 per cent in the late Eighties. This was also done with a view to step up saving rate in Indian economy which was expected to automatically result in economic growth. Reliance on indirect taxation, deficit financing and hike in administered prices to square up the revenue losses, on account of concessions to saving classes, resulted in double digit inflationary pressures which further squeezed the purchasing power of the mass of Indians. On the other hand, savings were not automatically converted into investments, largely on account of demand constraints. Large unutilized capacities in capital goods public sector undertakings resulted in these enterprises proving a drain on national exchequer. These undertakings could also not make surpluses available to sustain public investments.

The increased savings in the economy were mobilised by the government to square its revenue as well as capital deficit. The revenue deficits show that the public borrowings by the government are being increasingly used to finance the unproductive defence on civil administration expenditures. A perceptive observer of this crisis observes :

"Such a fiscal crisis has a self-compounding nature. As

outlays are cut in one direction, recession develops elsewhere which reduces tax revenue and even necessitates subsidies. Certain spheres of production, starved of funds, soon find themselves saddled with obsolete machinery, resulting in high costs which if passed elsewhere, necessitates large subsidies. Cost and time overruns become the rule in State sector projects, bringing down the efficiency of investment enlarging the scale of the fiscal demand. Such instances can be multiplied."

Faced with this problem, the Indian policy makers have started reviewing the economic model followed till date. It is felt that the governments are left with very little funds after meeting the repayment obligations of the domestic and international borrowings. Thus there is a cut on public sector investments on account of which infrastructural and capital goods industries suffer. A good-bye is given to the import-substitution policies because the government can no longer modernise public sector undertakings to supply efficient plant and machinery to private sector. More and more capital goods are being put on OGL. But buying from international markets requires foreign exchange and the government has already exhausted all 'soft loan options'. In fact, with the commencement of repayment of IMF loan instalments, debt-service ratio has already crossed the safe limit of 26 per cent. Domestically, faced with the problem of inadequate demand for wage goods, the private business is increasingly diversifying into consumer durables like automobiles and electronic gadgets which cater to the 'pent up demand' for such items with the upper middle classes comprising of bureaucrats, traders and rich peasants. Most of these products are manufactured or assembled by importing technical knowhow or CKD's or SKD's. This, in turn, increases the burden on foreign exchange requirements for such collaboration arrangements with the multinationals.

Given this demand for foreign exchange, the balance of payment situation is deteriorating in India. The deficit of balance of payments had gone upto Rs. 8,747 crores in 1985-86. In order to remedy the balance of payment situation, a number of concessions have been allowed for taking up investments for export production. Non-resident Indians have been allowed many tax concessions and many of them like Chhabrias who had no production base in the country took over established Indians business firms, with tactic government support. Free trade zones have been created where all kind of multinational business interests have been provided the best infrastructural and tax concessions to produce for the export market. Even multinationals like Pepsi-Cola or Coca-cola have been invited to India with an assurance that they shall export a part of their produce. Numerous schemes and export subsidies have been announced to lure away investments from domestic production to export-oriented production. The decline of traditional industries like Jute and Cotton Textiles even when owned by such established houses like Birlas and Tatas, is partly on account of the fact that these houses are diverting funds from their old business interests to the so called export-oriented or sunrise industries. This is the context in which the much advertised New Economic Policy was announced.

New Economic Policy

In 1985, with the appearance of Seventh Plan Document, certain changes in policy have been initiated in stages after Rajiv Gandhi's ascendancy to power in regard to taxation, industrial licensing, imports, technology and foreign equity capital. The need for rationalising and simplifying the systems of fiscal and administrative regulation and modernising the economy has been stressed. In this context, it has to be observed that the distinctive feature of policy changes taken as whole is the greater scope for unfettered expansion they offer to the private corporate sector and open opportunities for investments by non-Indian private capital of NRI's and multinationals.

The Seventh Plan document while discussing framework of economic policy outlines the need for a judicious mix of indirect or financial controls besides the usual physical controls like licensing. Pursuit of a sound fiscal policy in relation to the private sector is expected to regulate the sector better than licensing and price controls. While outlining long-term fiscal strategy, it is stressed that public sector enterprises should improve their performance so that they are able to generate adequate surpluses to meet the increasing budgetary deficits. While stressing the need to control the public expenditure, it is emphasised that subsidies to poor have imposed a burden on the budget and a time bound programme has also to be worked out to eliminate subsidies to public sector units.

The fiscal policy hinges on measures to ensure increase in savings and growth of the private sector. Household savings are sought to be channelised to capital market by reducing direct taxes and devising schemes of tax exemptions for promoting investments in industrial securities. The capital market is intended to be further deepened by allowing the private business to create new financial instruments, new financial institutions including venture capital firms. It is important to quote the Plan documents about the framework of controls and changes needed :

"......as the economy developed and the industrial structure became more and more diversified and complicated, the licensing mechanism became more difficult to operate......quantitative import controls led to a high wall of protection and the creation of high cost industries. Rigid price controls in many cases led to stagnation of output and perpetuation of shortages. In view of these developments and, more particularly, in view of the enlargement of the resources base and the degree of sophistication attained by the Indian economy, it was considered necessary to reduce the rigour and range of physical controls and place greater reliance on financial controls." (p. 73).

The document makes further plea to lift restrictions on large business and demands that the list of reservations for small scale industries needs to be shortened. The price controls and subsidisation of inputs for agricultural production also comes for a critical comment. Regarding trade policy for international trade, the document makes a case for removing restriction on foreign investments and investments by big business. The document calls for freeing of exports from the adverse impacts of import restrictions and other regulatory measures. Reduction in indirect taxation, emphasis over service exports, export subsidies and duty drawbacks are other measures to reduce trade deficit and remedy the balance of payment situation.

The new policy is prompted by the understanding that restrictions on private sector and infrastructural constraints arising out of inefficient public sector have created conditions of industrial stagnation. In fact, in recent years, consumer goods industry had been growing at the rate of 5.5 per cent and in fact, demand constraints are the real cause of impossibility of further acceleration in the growth rate. As far as capital goods or heavy industry is concerned, imports of capital goods has been liberalised since 1978 and there is a switch in demand away from internal sources, due to difference in price and perceived quality.

According to keen observers of Indian economic scene, the industry, due to protection allowed to their produce have ignored technological upgradation and innovation responsibilities and this is the main reason that India has been forced to open its economy to multinationals. Unfortunately, the public sector which took up production in hi-technology areas and was responsible for supply of key inputs like energy was not able to give the lead in continuous technological upgradation. Of course, our private sector was never very keen about developing indigenous technologies. As a result of this state of affairs, when electronic revolution made the products of electronics industry as important as steel and coal were at one time, our industry had to look to multinationals for modernisation of manufacturing in our industry. Unless, we catch up with the other countries in this crucial areas of technologies, our dependence on multinationals which was eliminated to some extent, by public investments shall be revived.

Prof. K.N. Raj, in a review of New Economic Policy feels that if lowering of taxes is able to generate more tax revenues through a better tax administration, the experiment is worth trying. But the initial eupheria of Long Term Fiscal Policy years has died down. To stimulate further conspicuous consumption, estate duty has been abolished and the expenditure on sales promotion, advertisement and public relations are allowed to be deducted for tax computation purposes. But Prof. Raj feels that the expectation of rapid growth of demand of such products could perhaps give a "strong stimulation to industrial growth......." may prove to be exaggerated because consumer durables had a weightage of 4, compared to 35 out of 100, for the original all industries manufacturing consumer goods, in the organised system. It seems that the change in weighing system in the new index of industrial production was also prompted by the political necessity of giving more weightage to industries like electronics and automobiles which are growing faster. The much advertised growth rates in consumer goods industry are illusory because some industries which started with a very low base are contributing unusually high share of the estimate growth rates. The market for these goods shall get saturated very fast and long range growth in these industries shall be difficult to sustain.

Prof. K.N. Raj feels that the mixed economy model has been sought to be reversed by taking "major steps towards making the economy more explicitly capitalist than so far". But observers ranging from K.N. Raj to Samuel Paul maintain that the case for privatisation of Indian public sector is based on a very complacent assumptions. One of them seems that the private sector in India has resources to take up the activities which were hitherto performed by the public sector. In fact, privatisation campaign means an open invitation to multinationals to take over Indian public sector because native business doesn't have the resources needed for buying the giant undertakings of public sector. Raising of finances by public sector undertakings from the capital market through bonds/debentures is a more sensible suggestion in this regard. Indiscriminate opening up of the economy to multinationals, by liberalised imports of intermediate products, machinery and equipment have far reaching implications. The political system in India will not be able to sustain any regime which goes very far in this direction and hence we see that a halting move towards liberalisation has already been witnessed. In fact, the experiences of Third World Countries clearly show that liberal economies cannot be administered by democratic regimes or the so called 'soft state' as India is.

International Integration

World Bank and International Monetary Fund are proposing export-led growth model for India. But India is stuck in a vicious circle. Exports can expand only if the unit cost of production can be brought down by inducing economies of scale ; economies of scale can take place only if production increases in response to larger demand. Since domestic market is not expanding, scale economies are possible with increase in exports. Thus 'exports wait scale economies and scale economies await exports'. The exports have not increased their share from 5 to 6 per cent of national economy despite the surreptitious and express devaluation of rupee to make our exports competitive.

Except for two years (1972-73 and 1976-77) since Independence, Indian commodity imports have been costlier than exports. The deficit of trade has increased at rate of Rs. 100 crores every year. Starting with a level of Rs. 5,000 crores, in the 50's, these have touched a level of Rs. 9,000 crores per annum in the 80's. Our export promotion measures donot seem to be remedying the situation. Even the surreptitious devaluation of our currency which ranged between 40-55 per cent till the end of 1987 after the express devaluation of 36.5 per cent in June, 1966, has not made Indian exports competitive. 'Invisibles' or the repatriation of incomes by Indians employed abroad has kept the balance of payments situation relatively easy.

Off late, however, even invisibles are not able to keep balance of payment situation easy, they are gradually coming down to about one third of our trade deficit and the current account deficit which was Rs. 2,218 crores in 1980-81 has climbed to Rs. 5,513 crores in 1986-87. Our foreign exchange reserves are depleting slowly but steadily. Trade deficit for 1987-88 was estimated Rs. 6,624 crores which is lower than 1986-87's deficit of Rs. 9,354 crores. But by July-August, 1988, our reserves had come down to Rs. 5,600 crores, some Rs. 2,000 crores lesser than 16 months earlier. Foreign loans or commercial borrowings in international markets is the only way out to remedy the short term balance of payment positions. But loans/commercial borrowings have to be repaid and have disastrous consequences in long run.

The situation with regard to India's international indebtedness is, of course, worsening. In 1980-81, India used only 37 per cent of its Rs. 2,162 crore borrowings for repayment obligations, in 1986-87 of the total loans of around Rs. 3,600 crores, 52 per cent were absorbed for meeting repayment obligations. India had to borrow larger amount of around Rs. 4,500 crores, in order to keep the repayment obligations at less than 50 per cent level in 1987-88. Thus international borrowings are not a long-term remedy for easing the balance of payment situation. The foreign loans which were around Rs. 6,700 crores in mid-70's have climbed upto Rs. 41,402 crores by 1987.

The economists believe that the official version of debt service ratio being 26 per cent is not very accurate and if that is the case we are already caught in the dreaded 'debt trap'. It is feared that the invitation to foreign equity in public sector undertakings, suggested by some economists, may amount to selling of our national assets to meet our international repayment obligations. This type of privatisation may pave way to political upheavals which shall vitiate the business environments in India.

It is hoped, however, that by initiating proper strategic changes to promote sustained technological innovations based on indigenous R & D, India shall be able to meet the challenge of international competitiveness of its exports. Another measure which can help us reduce high costs of production, is massive asset redistribution in rural India to ensure of economies of scale utilizing the vast domestic market. This is the way Japan and South Korea have gone about, on their way to becoming international industrial powers.

Implications of NEP for Industry and Business

Indian industry and business has been afforded a unique opportunity by the contemporary economic environment. It has been called upon to participate in micro-electronics revolution. Not only the present wave of policy initiated modernisation held out the possibility of more productive assets being built into industrial organisations, it has also created strong pressures on non-technical aspects as well. As Socio-Technical systems approach suggests the introduction of a revolutionary technology will force the business to reorganise. The introduction of micro-processor based technology will have fairly wide impact on the functioning of these organisations, especially with respect to the skills required and the structure.

The composition of working force shall alter in favour of a younger and trained work force. The traditional reliance on experiences of a calculating accountsman by the businessman shall shift to the data processing expert, operating his personal computer. The work force engaged in traditional office routines shall be surplus and the entire services sector shall be manned by a fewer, better paid and younger work force. Cheap wage labour shall not be the phenomenon characteristic of the Indian economy in coming days, lesser workmen shall substitute the large numbers, if the wage bill has to be resticted. Schemes like golden hand-shake shall be in vogue restricted and it will be painful but necessary requirement to retire the old, loyal and experienced workers. To absorb the surplus labour force, industry and business have to grow faster or it will be difficult to switch over to the new technologies. The resistance to change encountered in such shift changes in work patterns necessitated by revolutionary transformation of work methods shall be the main challenge before the new managers.

As already pointed out half of the GDP is already coming from the service sector. The new business opportunities lie in this sector. The computerisation in the industry and business accounting, air and rail travel booking, banking, communication, hoteliering, etc., shall be witnessed. If our technocrats keep on getting jobs this unproductive sector, the material wealth producing manufacturing sector may suffer. Better emoluments and perks have to be worked out for S & T personnel because on the one hand, demand is of constantly updating technologies of production and on the other, the technocrats shall find assignments in this sector unattractive. Medicore talent will mean less efficient functioning and obsolescence of technologies.

The steps to activate capital market have started showing signs of change as new instruments for mobilising capital by industry are gaining acceptability. The issues of convertible debentures have been great favourites with the public, at large. About 15 million Indians are to-day keeping themselves abreast on the developments and participating in capital market. However, functioning of stock exchanges leaves much to be desired. Shady deals are not uncommon. When shareholdings get dispersed with the merchant banking operations of large nationalised banks, the promoters' share in equity capital shall decline.

Concessions announced to NRI investments have added another dimension to the corporate scene in India. Some Indian businessmen have recently acquired NRI status to avail the concessions. Some of the NRI's have built business empires abroad but others are content with functioning as frontmen laundering back foreign accounts of Indian politicians and businessmen. These NRI's alongwith a new breed of businessmen have perfected the art of taking over established firms. Low share of promoters in equity makes it easier. The takeover menia started with Swaraj Paul but has quickened its pace so much that it is difficult to keep track of acquisitions, mergers or takeovers in Indian corporate world.

The liberalisation measures exempting businessmen from seeking clearances of Company Law Board, RBI or MRTPC have created a virtual chaos in the private corporate sector of India. "Almost every day, a corporate raider silently creeps on an unsuspecting victim and gradually gobbles it up. It is presumed that undervaluation of stocks of fairly progressive companies is what inspires takeover deals". It new technologies are brought alongwith the foreign exchange to turn around the Indian sick companies, the takeover bids are a welcome sign. If these put an end to the exploitation of minority shareholders, then also these are welcome. But if the bids materialise in well managed companies, with hush-hush support of public financing institutions then the design of substituting physical controls by financial controls is defeated. The unhealthy politician-bureaucrat axis made a mess of our earlier control mechanism and rather than decreasing concentration of economic power it further increased it. The same may be true, if the newly acquired status of Chhabrias and Ambanis is on account of the undue favours shown by the financial institutions or by the Controller of Capital Issues, in allowing particular type of financial instruments to favour these tycoons. The norms of an efficient capitalist economy are very difficult to enforce in a country like India where the share of modern sector is so low in employment as well as national income. We have to wait and watch the impact of current waves of liberalisation and opening up of the economy for a longer period, before passing a premature judgement on it.

The new era for Indian business opens up opportunities of setting up joint venture abroad ; in the sectors, which were hitherto reserved for public sector but also poses threats of global competition not only in the export markets but also in the domestic market. Whether Indian business is ready to face the challenges of the next millenium is an open question. The success or failure of Indian business will also determine the character of Indian polity in times to come.

CASE XII

CHHABRIAS—THE CREATION OF NEW ECONOMIC POLICY

The balance of payments situation in India had assumed

crisis proportions in the early Eighties. Promotion of exports and bringing foreign exchange was the dire need of the hour. With the announcement of new industrial policy welcoming the NRI investments, Chhabrias made an appearance in the Free-trade Zones in 1984. They stepped out to acquire such a clout in the business world within four years that they dared challenge Dhirubhai Ambani in the latest Larsen and Toubro takeover war.

Orson electronics is probably the only Chhabria promoted company. With unlimited amount of cash, made available to them by their trading business in Gulf countries, the Chhabrias have already bagged more than half a dozen prize-catches of Indian companies. They started with small acquisitions like Gordon Wooroffe (turn over Rs. 8 crores) and latter out maneouvred their takeover partners, Goenkas, of Duncan fame.

In 1987, they fought a bitter corporate war to annexe the control of Shaw Wallace from the professional Managing Director-cum-Chairman, S.P. Acharya. They had already invested in Dunlop India with Goenkas but by 1988 they took over complete control over Dunlop India (turnover, Rs. 430 crores). Genelec and Shalimar were the latest acquisitions of these corporate raiders.

Hindujas, who have been much talked of among NRI's for their access to the government have not been able to match the performance of Chhabrias due to premature publicity of their political equations. It is, however, obvious in the case of Chhabrias too, that their takeovers are not without the co-operation of public financing institutions. However, it is their foreign business which has enabled these NRI's in clinching deals with the minority foreign shareholders in the Indian companies. They have bought the stake of the foreign companies in international market.

Chhabrias have emerged as a business group with sales turn-over of Rs. 1,000 crores, *i.e.*, one among the top ten business houses in India, when all their new manufacturing ventures are still to commence production except Orson.

POINTS FOR CONSIDERATION

(1) Isn't NRI investment a temporary measure of overcoming financial crisis when the NRI's only takeover existing business units ?

(2) With hush-hush deals with public financial institutions or negotiated deals overseas, aren't stock markets in India redundant in determining the future of corporate world ?

FURTHER READINGS

1. Adiseshia, Malcom, "The Unfinished Task", *Seminar, 316, The Economy,* 1985.
2. Bose, A.C., "Living Beyond Our Means", *The Times of India Economy,* December, 1988-January, 1989.
3. Government of India, *Seventh Plan Document,* Volume I, New Delhi, Planning Commission, 1985.
4. Krishna, Raj, "The Economic Outlook For India", Roach, J.R., (Ed.), *India, 2000 A.D.—The Next Fifteen* Years, New Delhi, Allied Publishers, 1987.
5. Kurien, C.T., "Paradoxes of Planned Development—The Indian Experience", Roach, J.R. (Ed.), *op. cit.*
6. Mitra Ashok, "On the Brink", *The Times of India Economy,* December, 1988-January, 1989.
7. Patil, S.M., "Four Challenges to Industry and Trade", *Economic Times,* 7th January, 1989.
8. Rai, Kartik, "Four Decades of Post-Independence Economic Development", *The Marxist,* Volume Five, Nos. 2-3, April-September, 1987.
9. Raj, K.N., *New Economic Policy,* Delhi, Oxford University Press, 1986.

Index

A

Accidents, industrial, 114
Acharya, S.P., 250
All India Trade Union Congress (AITUC), 74
Ambani, Dhirubhai, 15-16, 92
    newly acquired status of, 249
Amins, 70
Apeejay fame, 117
ASSOCHAM, 24, 32, 87

B

Backward Castes, 65
Bagchi, Amiya, 21, 24-25
Bajaj group, 97
Bajaj, Jamnalal, 36
Baluta system, 63
Bananzas, 91
Bangurs, 28, 70
Baroda Dynamite Case, 97
Bhartiya Mazdoor Sangh (SMS), 74
BHEL-SIEMENS technological agreement, 55-56
Big Business, emergence of, 32-33
Binny, 25
Bird, Martin, 25
Birla G D., 23, 33, 36, 78-79, 87, 91
    companies of, 28
Birla, J K , 33
Birlas, 15, 24, 32, 70, 87, 137-138, 203
Birth rate, 61
Bonus Act, 1965, 116
Brahmins, 63, 65
British Raj, 21, 24, 163
Buddhists, 63
Bureaucracy, 2
    pattern of, 54
Business
    guardians of, 160-161
    opportunities for, 94-95

Business activities, 3
Business Gaime, rules of, 8
Business management
    fundament rights and, 81-82
Businessmen in politics, 96-98

C

Capital market, Indian, 159-160
Caste and Communalism, 63-64, 66
Caste system
    merits and demerits of, 65
Central-state relations, 84-85
Chaudhary Charan Singh, 92
Chembers of Commerce and Industry, 86-87
Chhabrias, 92, 95
    creation of new economic policy, 250-251
    status of, 249
CITU, 74, 188
Coleman, Bennet, 27
Commercial Banks in Financing, role of, 157-158
Company laws, 103-108
Congress (I), 211
Congress (S), 90

D

Dalal, Sir Ardeshar, 33
Dalits, 64, 73
Dalmia, R.K., 33
Dalmias, 27, 64
    total companies of, 28
Das, Sir Purshotam Das Thakur, 33
Davar, D.N., 161
Death rate, 61
Demographic Characteristics India, 61-62
Dinshaw, F.E., 33

Index

Directive Principles of State Policy, 83-84, 178
Duncan brothers, 27, 94
Dutt, R.C., 194

E

Economic environment, 6-7
Economy policy, new, 241-242
Education
    growth of, 10
    vocationalisation of, 12
Election process, 89
Employment, 67
Energy, sources of, 4, 5
Environmental awareness
    importance of, 4
    need for, 2
Environmental scanning, 13-14
Export-Import policy, 53

F

Family
    joint system of, 68-70, 72, 75
    nuclear, 70
    undivided, 68
Fernades, George, 97
PICCI, 24-25, 32, 87
Financial Institution, 150-156
    terms and conditions, 156-157
Fiscal crisis, 239-240
Fiscal policy, 8, 130-131, 242
Foreign investments, 203-204
Freedom struggle, 89
Fundamental rights, 81-82
    abolition of, 84
    amendment in 83

G

Gandhi, Indira, 91
Gandhi, Mahatama, 33, 36, 87
Gandhi, Rajiv, 92-93, 241
Gandhi, Sanjay, 91
General Agreement on Trade and Tariffs (GATT), 131
Geographical factors, 13
Goenka, B.D., 27
Goenka, Ramnath, 95
Goenkas, 70, 94, 250
    companies of, 28
Gupta, C.B., 90

H

Habid, Irfan, 20

Hindu, 63
    undivided family, 68
Hinduism, 63
Hindujas, 92, 250
Human behaviour, irrational side of, 17

I

Import-Export Policy, 131-133
Independence War, first, 22
Indian economy, 35
    urbanisation of, 20
Indian National Congress, 33, 38, 87-89, 96-97
Indian National Trade Union Congress (INTUC), 78, 188
Industrial Disputes Act, 1947, 113
Industrial Licenses, grant of, 127-128
Industrial Licensing policy, 125-127, 211
    agencies regulation of, 128-129
Industrial Licensing Policy Inquiry Committee, 195-196
Industrial Policy, 122-125
Industrial Policy Resolution, 35
Industrialists, Indian, 36
Industry, modern
    institutions of, 29
    introducing, 19
Integrated systems view, 11
Iron, Mukund, 97

J

Jains, 63
Jaipurias, 70
Jajmani, 63-64
Janata government, 91, 97, 221
Joint Stock Company, 28-29
Joshi, Arun, 23

K

Kamanis, 70
Karma, theory of, 65
Kasturbhai Lalbhai, 33
Kasturbhais, 23
Keynesian prescriptions, 120
Khadi and spinning wheel, 36
Khataus, 23, 70
Kirloskar, 24, 27, 28
Kisan power, rise of, 65
Kochaneck, Stanley, 33

Kothari, Rajni, 65
Krishnamachari, T.T., 97
Kshatriyas, 63,65

L

Labour
  migration of, 73
  mobility and utility of, 65
  retirement benefits, 114
  social division of, 19, 66
  social security, 113-115
  supply of, 66
Labour laws, 112
Lal, Ranchhod, 23
Lancashire industry, 22
Larsen and Toubro, 17

M

Mafatlals, 24, 28
Maharaja of Gwalior, 23
Maharaja Mayurbhanj, 23
Malhotras, 70
Managerial activity, 1
Managing Agency system, 31, 104-105
Manchester industry, 21-22
Mandal Commission, 65
Marxist parties, 94
Memorandum of Understanding, 178-180, 182
Mercantile laws, 109-112
Marwaris, 79
  emergence of, 23
Methai, John, 33
Middle Class, emergence of, 71
Minimum Wages Act, 115
Mirjanis, 92
Mishra, Lalit Narayan, 91
Mitra, Ashok, 86
Modi, K.N., 94, 160
Modis, 70, 160, 161
Monetary policy, 131
Monopolies Inquiry Committee Report, 193-194
Morarjees, 70
Morarkas, 70
Mughal Chieftans, armies of, 20

N

Narasimhan Committee, 51
National movement, 36
Nationality feelings, 11
Nehru, Jawaharlal, 33, 87
Nehruvian Socialism, 97

O

Occupational Structure, 66-77
Open General Licence, 132-133

P

Paris convention, 47
Parliamentary systems, 8
Parsees saw, 22
Partition of India, 35, 73
Patel Committee, 195
Pathak, M.S., 93
Paul, Samuel, 185, 244
Paul Swaraj, 92, 249
Pepsi-Cola, 241
Persian Wheel for Irrigation, 20
Podars, 70
Political and Legal system, 8
Polito-economic system, 10
Price and International Trade Controls, 129-133
Private Corporate Sector, 141
  assets of 20-houses, 202
  during Third and Annual Plans, 193
  financing pattern in, 205-206
  internal stratification of, 200-201
  large and middle companies, 202
  profitability performance of, 207
Public Accountability *Versus* Autonomy, 176-177
Public sector, 140
  contribution of, 167-168
  industrial relations in, 188
  investment in 166, 168-169
Problems of, 173-174
  rationale of, 163-165
  sales in, 170
  types of, 164-165
Public Undertakings, 177
  topten central, 172

Q

Quit India Movement, 26

R

Railways, Indian, 179-80
  tariff structure of, 140
Raj, K.N., 244
Regulatory mechanism, 133-137

Reliance Textile
  recent emergence of, 94
  success story of, 15
Religions sentiments, 82-83
Research and Development
  (R & D), 39-40, 42, 48-49
  expenditure statistics of, 41, 44-45
  policy and legal framework for, 46-47
Rights
  fundamental, 81-83
  property, 83

S

Samant, Datta, 74, 97
Sam Pitroda, guidance of, 48
Sarabhai Ambalal, 33, 36, 70
Shedule caste/Schedule tribe, 64
Science and technological, 38
  organisation for, 39
Science and Technology Entrepreneurship Perks (STEP), 47
Self-employment, 212
Semi-feudal system, 21
Sethi, Prakash Chandra, 91
Sexes, inequality of, 10
Shah, Viren, 97
Shriram, 23, 33, 70
Shroff, A.D., 33
Sikhs, 63
Singh, Viswanath Pratap, 92-93
Singhania, Ramlapat, 33
Singhanias, 28, 70
Small entrepreneurs, problems of, 226-227
Small Industries Development Organisation (SIDO), 146
Small and large factories,
  principal characteristics of, 223-225
Small Scale Industries, 212-213, 215-221, 227
  myth and readity, 230-232
Social systems, 61
Social trends, 10-11
Socio-Cultural Trends, 72
Soda Ash
  expansion of capacity of, 137-138
Star Wars, 1
State, right of, 85
Sudra, 63, 64
Suprasystem, 3, 12

Subsystems of, 13

T

Tata, Dorab, 24
Tata, JDR, 23, 33
Talas, 14, 32, 138, 203
Tax concession, 144
  special feature, 145
Tax, direct, 143
Tax incentive, 141-144
Taxation powers, 8
Technical Collaboration, framework for, 51
Technology, 4-5, 38
  buyer and suppliers of, 50
  natural development of, 21
  organisations, 39
  transfer of, 49-50
Thapar, Lalit Mohan, 93
Thapars, 25
  companies of, 28
Third World Countries, 245
Trade Union Act, 1926, 114-115
Trade Union movement, 12

U

Unemployment, 67
  dimensions of, 68
  problems of, 235
Unileyer subsidiaries, reorganisation of, 208-209
Union Carbide tragedy, 74
Unregistered sector, growth of, 214-215
Urban area, shortage of housing, 63
Urban slums, 64

V

Vaishyas, 63
Varma system, 63
Village and Small Scale Industries, 212-213, 227
  achievement of different sectors of, 217
  contributions of, 215
  financial sources for, 218-221

W

Wadhva, Charan D., 132

Wadia, Nusli, 95
Wages, 82
   payment of, 115
Walchand, 24, 36
   companies of, 28
Women
   role of, 11
   working condition of, 82, 113
Working population, 66-67
World War, 23, 25-26

Y

Yule, Andrew, 23

Z

Zamindari system, 30